Sharing Tokyo
Artifice and the Urban Ecosystem

A publication of the Japan Research Initiative, Harvard University Graduate School of Design

Sharing Tokyo:
Artifice and the Social World

Mohsen Mostafavi
and Kayoko Ota, eds.

Actar Publishers

TABLE OF CONTENTS

TOKYO: BETWEEN LARGE-SCALE DEVELOPMENT AND THE NEIGHBORHOOD

●   MOHSEN MOSTAFAVI

What does it mean to speak of sharing the city? Isn't the city always shared by its inhabitants, by all those who live and work there? One would expect the answer to such a question to be an emphatic *yes*. But invariably this idealism is not matched by the reality of the situation.

The role and participation of citizens in the governance of the city and what it has to offer has always been subject to a host of rules and qualifications. From the very beginning, there have been distinctions in terms of who could, or could not, qualify as "first-class" citizens. In the ancient Greek *polis*, a large portion of the population—aliens, slaves, and women—were not considered citizens at all. While the specific rules may change over time, the city as a physical artifact and as an environment continues to encapsulate the habits, norms, and values of a society, including many of its conditions that might be considered unjust or exclusionary.

This publication investigates the relationship between the city of Tokyo, as a physical construct, and the diversity of its corresponding social realms. The intention is to explore ways in which design can lead to more equitable and inclusionary urban places. More specifically, the book considers the intersection between the physical and the social worlds through a closer analysis of two distinct and dominant models of urban development, namely the recent phenomenon of large-scale mixed-use projects made possible by the increasing dominance of neoliberal policies, and the more traditional concept of small towns or "neighborhoods" of the city that have evolved over a long period of time. The question remains as to how these models can be supplanted, transformed, or modified to benefit a greater proportion of the population. Hence the idea of sharing the city.

The focus of the investigation is the urban core of Tokyo. Around this core is the Tokyo Metropolis, with a population of just under fourteen million. And around this, in turn, are the seven prefectures which make up the greater Tokyo Metropolitan Area, home to a staggering 44.37 million people. This territory includes a vast array of towns and suburbs, each with its own idiosyncratic forms of development, all connected to central Tokyo by a highly efficient rail network, with more than 220 million train journeys made every week. As a result, railway stations have come to play a major role as infrastructural and developmental hubs in the city.

Tokyo was originally a feudal castle town called Edo and was shaped by two geographically and topographically distinct domains, the "high city" and the "low city." The historic capital, Kyoto, by contrast, was planned on the Chinese grid-city model. Edo's governance structure meant the residences of the feudal lords were scattered around the castle on higher grounds, separate from the professional and lower classes who occupied the low city, also known as *shitamachi*, close to the Sumida River. The renaming of the city dates from 1868, when the emperor moved from Kyoto ("imperial capital") to Tokyo ("eastern imperial capital"). Today, traces of the feudal division of the territory can still be seen, for example, in the form of the Yamanote train line, a circular subway route that connects some of the city's affluent neighborhoods, and in the area around the Imperial Palace, built on the site of the old Edo castle.

Both the "high city" and the "low city" evolved through the development of small towns or districts, akin to the European model of the neighborhood. For many of the larger and more prominent areas, such as Shinjuku and Shibuya, their role and prominence has been enhanced by their also being major railway hubs. The stations provide a constant influx of consumers and incentives for redevelopment. In the process, the private companies that own the railways have become responsible for significant clusters of commercial development that certainly supplement, and at times outperform, their core business.

The alternative to these transport-oriented developments, or TODs, is a series of large-scale mixed-use projects realized by a small handful of major real-estate developers, among them Mitsui Fudosan, Mitsubishi Estate, and the family-owned Mori Building. Together, they account for some of the largest and most complex urban projects in the past twenty years. Yet, despite some well-intended aspirations, the financial reality of development rarely makes these projects truly accessible to the ordinary inhabitants of Tokyo beyond their role as consumers for the shops and restaurants that provide the "public" areas of most of the projects.

Mori Building's iconic Roppongi Hills development was master planned by the American firm Kohn Pedersen Fox and completed in 2003. The brainchild of the visionary Minoru Mori, who foresaw the benefits of people living and working in close proximity with no need to commute, it combines retail, hotel, residential, office, and cultural facilities. One of the key innovative features of this project centers around its handling of the complex topography of the undulating terrain, including its use of a "sectional" approach to urban development, a strategy that questions the typical convention of what lies above and below ground on a flat site. The large and uncommon underground retail portion of the complex was designed by Jon Jerde, a pioneer in the planning of shopping malls. At Roppongi Hills, Jerde created an underground realm distinct from the above-ground development and its ever-fluctuating conditions.

The ensemble as designed by a group of foreign and Japanese architects forms an independent, luxurious, and exclusive urban environment on the edge of what used to be a run-down and somewhat seedy part of the city. The project's inward-looking approach is intended to create a buffer zone with the surrounding neighborhood, enabling it to produce the right ambiance for its high-end shops and residences. In some ways, this approach seems to echo the "defensible space theory" of the American architect and city planner Oscar Newman, who in the 1970s argued for the role of architecture and urban design in reducing criminality. But this is the irony of such large-scale developments; the creation of isolated islands of self-sufficiency gives rise, at the same time, to vast territories of privatized public space. While theoretically accessible to all citizens, they only belong to, and are shared by, a relatively small and privileged portion of the population.

Subsequent developments such as Mitsui Fudosan's Tokyo Midtown (completed 2007) achieve a more closely knit connection with the urban fabric by placing the project adjacent to neighboring streets. The development site, a former military garrison, was purchased directly from the government and represents a different strategy from Mori Building's patient accumulation of individual parcels over fifteen years.

The architects of Tokyo Midtown, SOM, were asked by the developer to incorporate Japanese motifs into their designs. The aim was to create a combination of Western and Japanese sensibilities that would appeal to a greater number of middle-class Japanese who might visit the complex. These motifs are predominantly reflected in the exteriors of the retail areas, in the overlapping planes of the *"shoji* screen" elevations, but were also a point of reference for the envelope of the tall office towers designed by SOM.

Despite the desire for Tokyo Midtown to connect with the given infrastructure of the city, the sheer size and scale of such projects, as well as the lack of affordability of their residential units, make them alien destinations for many Tokyoites. In this context, it is worth recognizing the efforts made by the authorities and by Mitsui Fudosan to open parts of the development, such as a small "public park" where 21_21 Design Sight, a design gallery by Tadao Ando, occupies a corner.

The conceptual origins of projects like Roppongi Hills and Tokyo Midtown can be traced back to earlier precedents, such as the Rockefeller Center designed by the American architect Raymond Hood in Midtown Manhattan (1939). Another pertinent example is SOM's own Deutsche Bank Center, formerly Time Warner Center, completed only a few years before Tokyo Midtown. The same architects, David Childs and Mustafa Abadan, were responsible for the master plan and the major buildings at Tokyo Midtown. These precedents account for the reliance of large Japanese developers on US firms who possess the expertise for the delivery of complex mixed-use projects.

The financial assumptions and expectations for these privately owned projects, all realized with the explicit approval and legislative support of governmental authorities, make it almost impossible to include any affordable housing. The concept is contingent on high-end living, the kind that is only possible for today's "first-class" citizens.

In contrast to the large-scale mixed-use projects by developers who control substantial designated areas of the city, and the mega TOD projects of the railway companies, Tokyo is also made up of much smaller traditional neighborhoods, such as Shimokitazawa or Yanesen, among many others. The scale of buildings and the diversity of uses in these neighborhoods often recall an older Tokyo. Their urban morphology continues the same pattern of smaller streets and secondary alleys which historically defined the city, regulated by a specific unit of urban development called the *cho* (equivalent to ca. 10,000 square meters or 2.5 acres). It also responds to the specific geography of old Edo, with its many hills and canals.

The spatial characteristics of these small neighborhoods offer proximity and intimacy and can lead to greater social and visual interaction and cohesion for those who live or work there. Japanese building regulations, which are partly based on the relation between the width of the street and the size of the building, act as a form of protection for some of the older neighborhoods, where the narrow streets act as a disincentive for development. Some developers, however, have been able to combine two or more parcels and construct larger buildings than has historically been the norm. For this reason, residents keen to preserve the identity of their neighborhood are generally resistant to large-scale developments, preferring instead to support community-based programs and projects. A case in point is the popular neighborhood of Yanesen, created when local activists redefined three adjacent neighborhoods—Yanaka, Nezu, and Sendagi—as a single entity to raise public awareness of the need for preservation, a notion that was new to Japanese society in the 1980s.

As an alternative strategy to commercial mixed-use developments, others have promoted the possibilities for a cultural district near Yanesen. The logic of this proposal is made manifest by the presence of various universities near Ueno Park. The notion of a cultural district in the northeastern part of Tokyo recalls an earlier project for a university city devised with the help of Eika Takayama and Kenzo Tange, among others. Reminiscent of Oxford or Cambridge and based around the activities of the University of Tokyo and other educational and cultural institutions, the project was never realized. But there are no systematic alternatives to the projects of big developers. Most neighborhood projects are either attempts at preserving the history of a district, or generic buildings that take little account of their impact on the surrounding areas.

How might the dualism between large-scale developments and the preservation of neighborhoods be challenged so as to provide forward-looking environments that can benefit, and be shared by, a greater diversity of Tokyo's inhabitants? Are there ways in which the private and public sectors can collaborate on projects that do not require the massive financial capital associated with the mega-projects but which, at the same time, transcend the limitations of small historic neighborhoods by providing new opportunities for all sectors of society—including the young and the elderly?

Already there are signs that a new generation of Japanese architects is willing to take the risk to experiment with a range of modest, innovative projects that contribute to their neighborhood. These projects, for housing or small local businesses and enterprises, are being realized in places such as Shimokitazawa (Tokyo), while many of the important architects of the earlier generation are continuing to focus their energies on projects in other countries or on the Japanese countryside, away from the metropolis. What can we learn from the experiments of the architects who still find Tokyo a fertile ground for speculation?

One of the reference points of the French philosopher Henri Lefebvre's concept of the "right to the city" is the formulation of the notion of spatial inequality. This notion has been primarily discussed in relation to access to resources such as hospitals and schools; in poorer economies, this applies to the even more fundamental needs such as drinking water. But how might such a concept apply to Tokyo, a global city that already provides most basic resources for its citizens?

What seems clear is that the increasing privatization of the city caused by large-scale development regulates and controls patterns of use in ways that are generally uncommon in the smaller neighborhoods of the city. How can we conceive of new ways of constructing the city that can overcome the tendency towards spatial inequality?

In response, this publication offers alternative ideas and strategies that are based on neither the small-scale model of the neighborhood nor the large-scale development. In addition to the contributions of contemporary scholars, architects, and urbanists, it also includes design research conducted at the Harvard University Graduate School of Design. Our aim has been to use the conventions of our discipline, such as drawings and models, to help decipher the evolution of Tokyo's urban morphology and to imagine its potential futures. At the same time, we hope that the lessons and the discoveries linked to Tokyo's future will be of relevance in other contexts as well.

The consideration of the future of the city, whether in Japan or elsewhere, is always a collaborative project that benefits from the contribution and engagement of a diversity of players and participants. Similarly, the research and thinking documented in this book has been a collaborative endeavor based on the conviction that the city, as a socially constructed artifice, must be shared by all.

TOKYO: URBANISM IN PHOTOGRAPHY

● KENTA HASEGAWA

❶ THE POST-GROWTH CONDITION

Are there limits to how much a city can grow, continuing to expand its territory and its population? Over the next decades, Tokyo will face the consequences of Japan's declining birth rate and aging society, with more elderly citizens living longer lives post-retirement than ever before. The combination of a shrinking population and the current limits on immigration have produced a conundrum for the politicians whose social agenda is contingent on a growth model of the economy.

The impact of a reduced labor force is often first felt outside the major urban areas, which still benefit from the migration of people seeking greater opportunities. But sooner or later, this buffer will erode, and cities like Tokyo will need to find new ways of coping with the effects of slow or no growth.

How might the city, as well as urbanists and designers, plan for such an outcome? Many thinkers have not only anticipated a no-growth model of economic planning but have actively promoted the benefits of prosperity and happiness without growth.

The French economist and social scientist Serge Latouche is associated with the concept of "décroissance," or de-growth, a phenomenon that embraces a more caring and ecologically sensitive approach toward the use of resources while also emphasizing the value of conviviality and sharing. However, this type of approach requires a recalibration of normative desires and expectations. For the city to survive, it will need to play its role in promoting ecologically sustainable models of urban living based on a more sharing, less consumerist model of society. Tokyo's neighborhoods provide an important testing ground for the realization of such ideas. How might their scale enable greater interaction and possibilities for the rebuilding of sociability and community in the context of Japan's post-growth condition? What are its challenges?

TOKYO: PORTRAIT OF A CITY IN FLUX

● JAPAN RESEARCH INITIATIVE TEAM

Tokyo, the world's largest metropolis, is at the forefront of important changes that will soon impact other cities around the globe. Japan is aging rapidly, and its population continues to concentrate in a handful of large cities. Empty houses, once a rural phenomenon, are now common even in the center of Tokyo. With immigration low, politicians have emphasized automation as a solution to labor shortages. But despite the demographic decline, urban redevelopment churns on, leveling aging neighborhoods to produce new high-rises. Tokyo is a bellwether city at a moment of inflection.

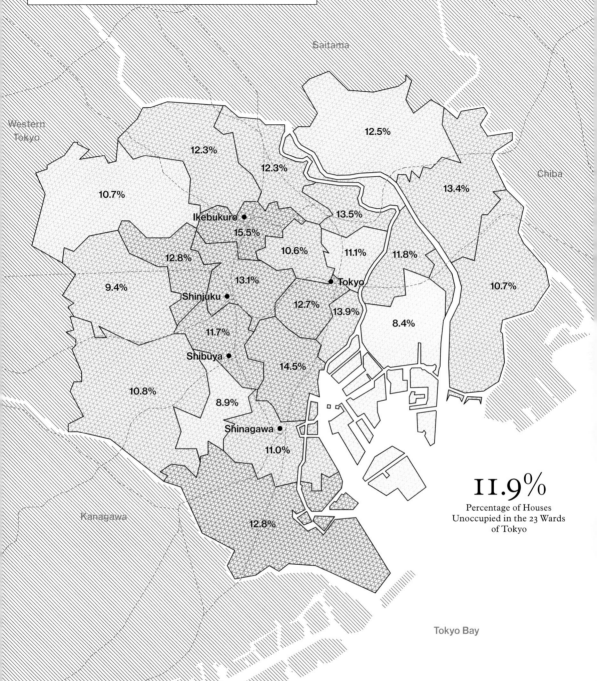

Percentage of Houses Unoccupied in the 23 Wards of Tokyo[1]

Saitama

Western Tokyo

Chiba

12.3%

12.3%

12.5%

13.4%

10.7%

Ikebukuro ●
15.5%

13.5%

12.8%

10.6%

11.1%

11.8%

9.4%

13.1%

Shinjuku ●

Tokyo ●

10.7%

12.7%

13.9%

8.4%

11.7%

Shibuya ●

14.5%

10.8%

8.9%

Shinagawa ●

11.0%

Kanagawa

12.8%

11.9%
Percentage of Houses
Unoccupied in the 23 Wards
of Tokyo

Tokyo Bay

More than one in every ten houses in Tokyo is empty. Nationally, the figure is nearly one in seven.

Japan is one of the most rapidly aging societies in the world.

Population of Japan[2]

% of Pop   5%   Male   0%   Female   5%

1950

By 2050, nearly 40% of the population will be over 65.

Population of Japan[2]

Age

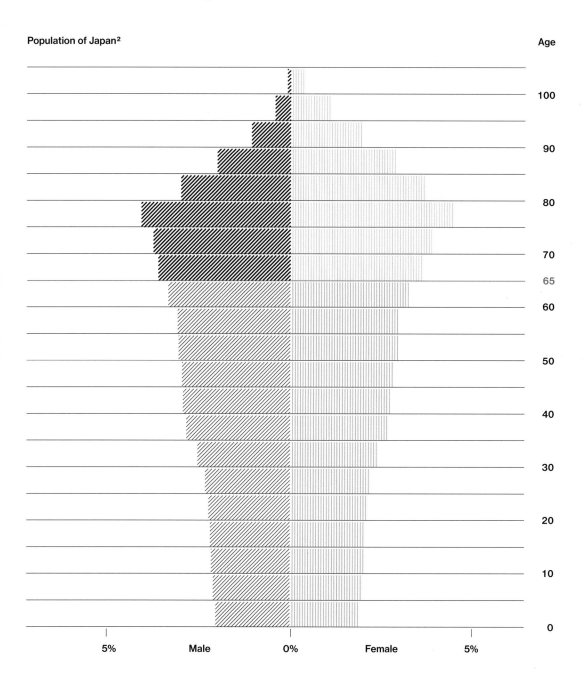

5%   Male   0%   Female   5%

2000

Nearly 35% of people in Japan live alone, one of the highest rates in the world.

Percentage of One-Person Households[3]

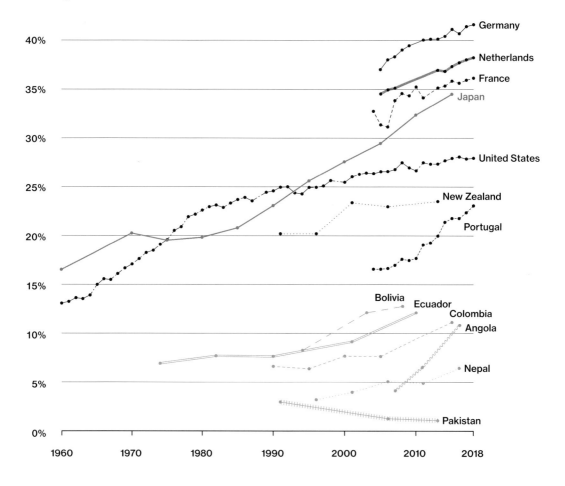

The number of privately owned public spaces has soared in recent decades.

This trend was encouraged by regulations that reward the production of privately owned public spaces with density bonuses and the Urban Renaissance law of 2002 that incentivized development in designated zones of the city.

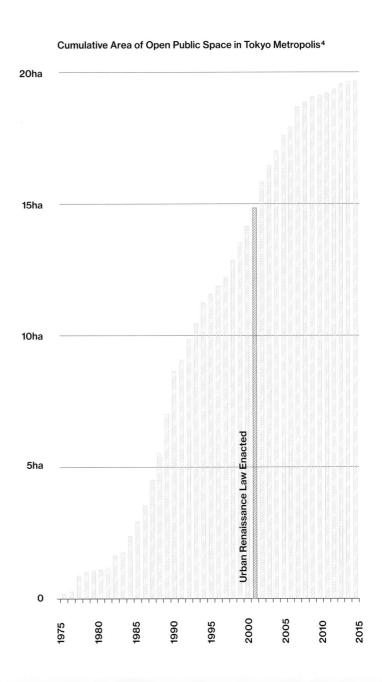

Cumulative Area of Open Public Space in Tokyo Metropolis[4]

The Japanese people continue to consolidate in a handful of large cities as the population of most of the country shrinks rapidly.

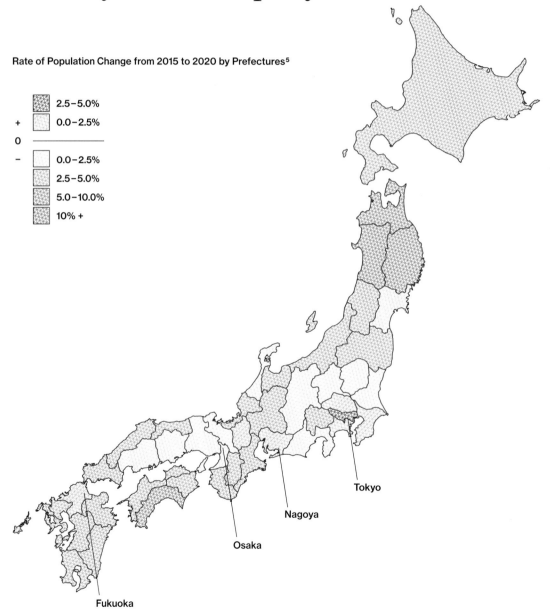

Rate of Population Change from 2015 to 2020 by Prefectures[5]

+

2.5–5.0%

0.0–2.5%

0

–

0.0–2.5%

2.5–5.0%

5.0–10.0%

10% +

Tokyo

Nagoya

Osaka

Fukuoka

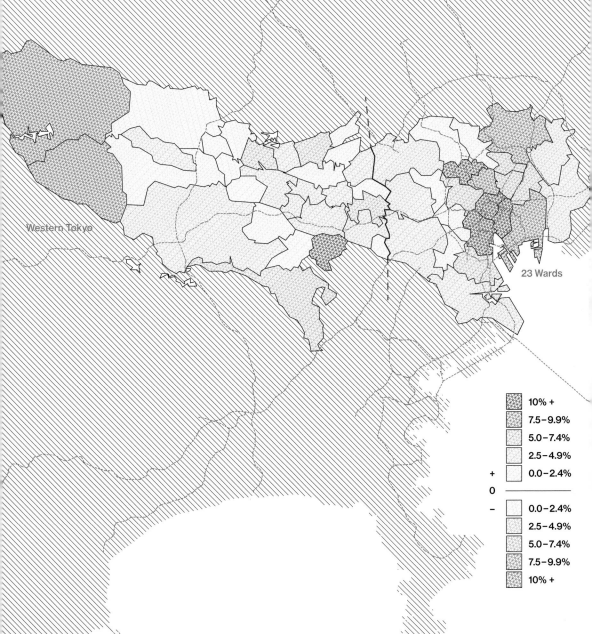

Growth Rate of the Municipalities of Tokyo Metropolis, 2005–2010[6]

Western Tokyo

23 Wards

+	10% +
	7.5–9.9%
	5.0–7.4%
	2.5–4.9%
	0.0–2.4%
0	
–	0.0–2.4%
	2.5–4.9%
	5.0–7.4%
	7.5–9.9%
	10% +

In Tokyo, growth is highest in
central districts, while outlying areas
lose population.

Forty-four million people live in greater Tokyo.[7]

It has the largest population of any world city, as well as the largest metropolitan economy.

Of all households in Tokyo, 50.2% are single-person households.[8]

Stockholm has the highest rate of singles among world cities at 60%, followed by London at around 57%.[9]

Over 20% are over the age of 65.[10]

The figure is 15% in New York City[11] and only 10% in London[12] proper.

Only 11.4% are children under 14.[13]

Nationally, the figure is 12.8%: among the lowest in the world.[14]

Only 3.2% are foreign born.[15]

In Dubai the number is 83%.[16] In London and New York it's 37%.[17]

Tokyoites take 44 million rail trips a day.[18]

The five busiest rail stations in the world are in Tokyo. Forty-five of the 50 busiest in the world are in Japan.[19]

Only 12% of them commute by car.[20]

This is the second lowest among world cities after Hong Kong.[21]

Tokyo's population may peak in 2025.[22]

Cities in countries like Spain, Switzerland, and Sweden could follow soon after.

1   Statistics Bureau of Japan. *Housing and Land Survey: Basic data on housing and households.* Tokyo: Ministry of Internal Affairs and Communications, 2018

2   United Nations, Department of Economic and Social Affairs, Population Division. *World Population Prospects 2019, Volume II: Demographic Profiles.* New York: United Nations, 2019

3   "Percentage of one-person households, 1960 to 2018," Our World in Data, 2019, https://ourworldindata.org/grapher/one-person-households

4   Urban Management Subcommittee for A New Era, Ministry of Land, Infrastructure, Transport and Tourism. Changes in the number of large-scale development projects and the area of open public space in these projects in Tokyo, 1976–2013 in "On Urban Facilities and Infrastructure" compiled from Bureau of Urban Development, Tokyo Metropolitan Government, "Urban Planning Projects." Tokyo: Ministry of Land, Infrastructure, Transport and Tourism, 2014

5   Statistics Bureau of Japan. *Rate of Population Change from 2015 to 2020 by Prefectures and by Municipalities (Population Census of Japan).* Tokyo: Ministry of Internal Affairs and Communications, 2020

6   Statistics Bureau of Japan. *Growth rate map of municipalities of Tokyo Metropolis, Japan, 2005–2010 (Population Census of Japan).* Tokyo: Ministry of Internal Affairs and Communications, 2010

7   Ministry of Land, Infrastructure, Transport and Tourism. "*Reiwa-4-nen-ban shutoken hakusho*" [Metropolitan Area White Paper, 2021]. Tokyo: Ministry of Land, Infrastructure, Transport and Tourism, 2022. https://www.mlit.go.jp/toshi/daisei/content/001485146.pdf

8   Statistics Bureau of Japan. *2020 Population Census.* Tokyo: Ministry of Internal Affairs and Communications, 2022

9   K. D. M. Snell, "The rise of living alone and loneliness in history," Social History vol.42, no.1 (2017): 2–28

10 Statistics Division, Bureau of General Affairs, Tokyo Metropolitan Government. *Population of Tokyo (estimates): Demographic Composition by Age.* Tokyo: Tokyo Metropolitan Government, 2022

11 United States Census Bureau. *US Census Quick Facts: New York City, New York.* Washington D.C.: U.S. Department of Commerce, 2022. https://www.census.gov/quickfacts/newyorkcitynewyork

12 Trust for London. *London's Poverty Profile: Population by age-groups.* London: Trust for London, 2021. https://www.trustforlondon.org.uk/data/population-age-groups/

13 Statistics Division, Bureau of General Affairs, Tokyo Metropolitan Government. *Population of Tokyo (estimates): Demographic Composition by Age.* Tokyo: Tokyo Metropolitan Government, 2022

14 The World Bank. *Population ages 0–14 (% of total population): Japan* (World Bank staff estimates based on age/sex distributions of United Nations Population Division's World Population Prospects, 2019). Washington D.C.: The World Bank Group, 2022. https://data.worldbank.org/indicator/SP.POP.0014.TO.ZS?view=map

15 James Beardsmore, "Cosmopolitanism, the global middle class and education: the case of universities in London," *Globalisation, Societies, and Education* vol. ahead-of-print (2021): 1–16

16 Ibid.

17 Ibid.

18 Ministry of Land, Infrastructure, Transport and Tourism. *Daitoshi kotsu sensasu dai 12-kai* [The Twelfth Metropolitan Traffic Census]. Tokyo: Ministry of Land, Infrastructure, Transport and Tourism, 2017: 91

19 Master Blaster, "The 51 busiest train stations in the world– All but 6 located in Japan," Japan Today, 2013. https://japantoday.com/category/features/travel/the-51-busiest-train-stations-in-the-world-all-but-6-located-in-japan

20 Land Transport Authority of Singapore. Passenger Transport Mode Shares in World Cities. Singapore: Government of Singapore, 2011

21 Hong Kong Transportation Department, *Travel Characteristics Survey 2011 Final Report.* Hong Kong: The Government of the Hong Kong Special Administrative Region, 2014. https://www.td.gov.hk/filemanager/en/content_4652/tcs2011_eng.pdf

22 Statistics Division, Bureau of General Affairs, Tokyo Metropolitan Government. *2060-nen made no Tokyo no jinkou suikei* [Estimates of Tokyo's Population through 2060]. Tokyo: Tokyo Metropolitan Government, 2015

HOW TO SHARE TOKYO: THE URBANISM OVERVIEW

SHIN AIBA

1   New high-rise buildings in Shibuya (foreground) comprising one of the major large-scale development projects underway in Tokyo, photographed in 2019. Photo courtesy of the Tokyo Metropolitan Government

It is often said that a city has multiple origins. One of them is certainly a market, as we can glean from the fact that the *kanji* character 市 for "market" also means "city." Markets came into being so people could exchange food they had harvested or game they had hunted. Thus cities were originally aggregations of tools to help us live and work. However, those tools rapidly grew, and grew apart from the individuals who had made them in the first place. People could still use a small city as a tool in itself—a means of meeting other people, finding work, or obtaining goods. They understood how the city worked, and how they could use it to procure the resources they needed for their life or livelihood. But as cities grew larger, they became too unwieldy to serve as tools, and people began to feel as if the city was using them as a tool instead.

Tokyo, with a population exceeding ten million, is obviously a city well beyond anyone's grasp, whether one tries to walk around it, explore it by car, fly over it in a helicopter, or simply view it on Google Earth. How are we to utilize this megalopolis as a tool with which to build our own lives and work? And how are we to share Tokyo's urban space with one another?

We can divide the people who inhabit and share a city into two types. On the one hand are those who take initiative in building their lives and careers, actively employing the city as a means to that end. On the other hand are those who passively rely on the support of the city without any clear-cut aspirations to use it for their own ends. Examples of people who take an active stance toward the city are developers, social entrepreneurs, civic activists, and the people who launch a new business—a bakery, say—on a neighborhood shopping street. At the other extreme are those who can be described as having a passive relationship with the city—people who sit absently for hours on end in a food court, people who seem unable to extricate themselves from poverty, people absorbed in playing games on their smartphones all day long. We tend to think that increasing the number of citizens actively engaging with the city would make it an even more wonderful place. However, the city also has an obligation to support the passive citizens who make up the majority of its population. In other words, a balance must be maintained between spatial development spurred by active intentions and spatial development that supports a city's passive inhabitants.

Until the 1990s, Japan's population was young, its economy was healthy and growing, and its cities grew concomitantly as well. During this period urban developers gave little thought to the passive sector of the population whose presence lay hidden in the shadows of growth. But as the baby boomers who sustained Japan's economic growth began to age, and the country's population begins to decline, the cities are becoming balkanized into separate enclaves for the elderly, for the young, for redevelopment and growth, for nondevelopment, for the active sector of the population, and for the passive sector.

Tokyo has undergone a myriad of changes since its birth 450 years ago, and all of them have been associated with the city's growth. Since the turn of the century, however, a more dramatic transformation has been taking place with the disappearance of the conditions upon which that growth was predicated. Today we must address the new changes that accompany the maturation, or contraction, of the city.

Tempering Neoliberal-Style Urban Planning

To begin with, let us examine the methodology by which Tokyo's urban spaces are created. This can be described, in a nutshell, as the neoliberal approach to urban planning. Tokyo's population decline was first predicted some two decades ago, at a time when urban spaces were already in plentiful supply. Urban planning methodology consequently shifted from the systematic provision of new spaces for new populations to the matching of existing spaces to people who needed them. Thus "matching" replaced "planning."

The distinction between these two approaches may be clearer if we refer to them as "government-led planning" and "market-led matching." The government was adept at using tax revenues to create spaces and redistribute them, whereas the market is adept at rapid exchanges of space via the medium of money. In the case of housing, the government-planning approach reached its zenith with the massive sixties-era residential project Tama New Town, while the market-matching approach has spawned more recent developments packed with detached houses built by various homebuilding concerns.

The conflict between government and market, between planning and matching, has existed throughout the history of modern urban planning. In Japan, privatization began to accelerate in the 1980s as policymakers followed the lead of the UK and the US. After Japan's economic bubble burst in 1991, efforts to revive markets included, around the year 2000, a revamping of urban planning laws that sparked a dramatic shift from government-initiated planning to market-driven matching. Though it was mere chance that the switch to matching coincided with the start of Japan's population decline, it came to be viewed as inevitable in light of that decline—in other words, there now seemed to be no choice but to adopt a policy of matching people who needed space to spaces that already existed.[1]

The shift did not occur overnight, but over a period of two decades. When the government changed course some 20 years ago, it interviewed members of the "active" sector of the population, asking them if they had aspirations to use the city to build their lives and careers, and if so, what they expected of the government.[2] The majority of interviewees were Tokyo developers, and the government acceded to their wishes by relaxing numerous regulations, notably those restricting the ratio of building volume to lot.

The result was a redevelopment boom in Tokyo. And, indeed, if you gaze over the city today from a peripheral vantage point, the massive building projects created by those same developers are what will most likely capture your eye (FIG. 1).

These developers did not, however, maintain an oligopolistic grip on urban development for long. As the neoliberal approach made rapid inroads, its modes of development diversified. Small and midsize developers offered customized schemes that the big firms could not handle, while community designers held workshops and incorporated the interests of diverse citizens. Neoliberalism permeated the methods adopted by the market and the citizenry alike.

Needless to say, numerous problems have cropped up under this approach. If we apply the label "free" to the development of cities for the purpose of enabling individuals, or groups of individuals, to pursue better lives or careers, we must also acknowledge that such "freedom" does not extend to everyone. People can behave "freely" if they share the same behavioral norms, but those norms are not always universally accepted. Be that as it may, the past three decades have seen virtually no examples of liberalized nations reverting to a socialist system—testimony to the fact that, once having gained "freedom," people are loath to relinquish it. Therefore, if problems ensue under a "free" system, we have no choice but to seek solutions by tempering the neoliberal model of urban planning.

The Macro Structure

Just because we prize "freedom" does not mean we have the kind of freedom associated with painting on a blank canvas. An urban space has a particular shape that determines the parameters of our freedom. What, then, is the shape of Tokyo's urban space?

Urban space in Tokyo has a macro structure and a micro structure, and both of them limit the forms "freedom" can take. First let us look at the macro structure that defines the shape of development in the city. This structure is composed of concentric and radial vectors of expansion, and a topography divided into plateaus and lowlands (FIG. 2).

1   Japan's population decline is by no means uniform throughout the country. Although the primary factor is the demise of the baby-boom generation, the pattern varies from region to region, depending on the demographics of each city and on the urban migration patterns of younger generations. In response to these complex factors, government planning relies on projections of a city's optimum population in the future (usually a figure higher than the present), while matching via the market is based on actual demand. Although it is still too early to tell which approach will yield a solution in the short run, the unabated construction—despite the inevitability of population decline—of high-rise housing in central Tokyo is in some sense a realization of the government's vision of the "compact city" for the low-population era, insofar as such housing is the cumulative product of rational, one-on-one "matches." Japan's "compact city" policy aims to offer a designated area as a destination for people planning to rebuild or replace their houses, something that homeowners typically do in a 30- to 40-year generational cycle. If a compact city is our goal, then "tower mansions" are making it a reality willy-nilly. As for what will happen to those high-rise residential complexes 50 years from now, that's another question.

2   Shigetaro Yamamoto, "Urban Revitalization Takes Off: Implementation of the Act on Special Measures Concerning Urban Reconstruction," Transcript of the 82nd Regular Lecture of the Land Institute of Japan, 2002, accessed December 2021, https://www.lij.jp/html/jli/jli_2002/2002summer_p053.pdf.

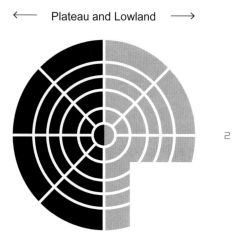

←—— Plateau and Lowland ——→

Concentric Expansion Radiant System

2

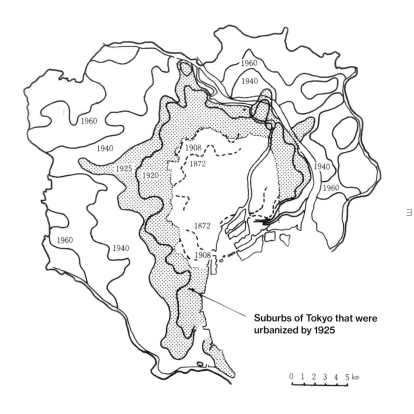

Suburbs of Tokyo that were
urbanized by 1925

0 1 2 3 4 5 km

3

2 | The shape of Tokyo: the topography
divided into plateaus and lowlands has
expanded with concentric and radial
vectors. © Shin Aiba

3 | The conurbation of Tokyo in continuous
growth from 1872 to 1960. Source:
Yorifusa Ishida, *One Hundred Years of
Modern Urban Planning in Japan* (Tokyo:
Jichitai Kenkyusha, 1987)

Tokyo expands in a pattern of concentric circles (FIG. 3). At the center is the Imperial Palace; the city has grown outward from this nucleus. People who migrate to Tokyo have traditionally first built up their resources and then acquired a place for their life or work on the outer rim of the city. If Tokyo were surrounded by steep mountains, it would have spread unevenly around such obstacles. But aside from one quadrant that faces Tokyo Bay, it has expanded more or less evenly and concentrically in the other three directions.

Sustaining this expansion is a network of railways that extend radially from the city center. Tokyo's railways were developed before the construction of trunk roads for automobile traffic, so the city grew out along the train lines in a pioneering example of transit-oriented development (TOD). Workers in secondary- and tertiary-industry jobs in Tokyo built their houses along these lines, which enabled them to commute downtown. The radial format of the rail network is what made it possible for the city to grow evenly in every direction.

An equally significant aspect of Tokyo's macro structure is its topographic duality of plateau and lowland. The western half of Tokyo's circle lies on the Musashino Plateau, which was formed over one hundred thousand years ago. Erosion by numerous rivers and streams has given the plateau a complex microtopography. The eastern half of Tokyo, on the other hand, is a low-lying area formed over ten thousand years ago. Much of it was once underwater, and it is vulnerable to earthquakes and flooding. This is the area that sustained the worst damage from the Great Kanto Earthquake of 1923, for example.

Tokyo's two-tiered topography is reflected in the disparities of the urban society that exists atop it. According to the *Social Atlas of Tokyo*, a publication based on research conducted since the 1980s by a study group of urban sociologists led by Susumu Kurasawa and Tatsuto Arakawa, the city's lowland population is primarily blue-collar, while that of the plateau is largely white-collar (FIG. 4). This segregation has its origin in an urban planning scheme that zoned the city by socioeconomic class 450 years ago.[3] Tradesmen and artisans, collectively known as *chonin*, or "townspeople," were assigned to live and work in the lowland district. According to the most recent edition of the *Social Atlas*, the same distinction persists today, demonstrating that Tokyo has grown up with the class differences that were embedded at its birth still intact.

An Aggregation of Privately Owned Units

Tokyo's micro structure, on the other hand, is simple but robust: the division of its land into many small, privately-owned plots.

---

3   During the Edo period (1603–1867), the samurai, artisan, merchant, and farmer classes were assigned to live in different districts of the city.

1975

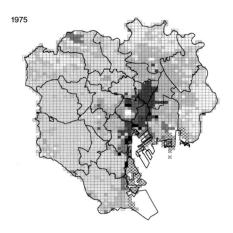

- ■ Typical downtown district
- ■ Traditional wholesale trading district
- ▨ Old residential district turning into downtown
- ▨ Old residential district turning into office district
- ▨ Downtown district in proccess of change
- ▨ Old residential district turning into shopping district
- ■ Large wholesale and distribution business district
- ☐ Established residential district turning into commercial district
- ☐ Established residential district with white-collar residents
- ▨ New residential development with hybrid residents
- ▨ Established residential district with blue-collar residents
- ☐ New residential development with blue-collar house renters
- ▨ New residential development with blue-collar house renters
- ▨ Government and office district
- ■ Area of low population density A
- ■ Area of low population density B
- ■ Area of low population density C
- ☐ Area of low population density D
- ▨ Area of low population density E
- ☐ Area of low population density F
- ☒ Not included

1990

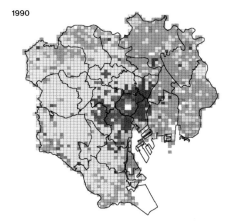

- ■ Downtown district A
- ☐ Downtown district B
- ■ Office and condominium district
- ☐ White-collar district
- ▨ White-collar district with reproductivity
- ▨ White-collar district with a high aging rate
- ■ Blue-collar district
- ▨ Blue-collar district with reproductivity
- ▨ Blue-collar district occupied with detached houses
- ■ High-density apartment (danchi) district A
- ■ High-density apartment (danchi) district B
- ■ High-density apartment (danchi) district C
- ■ High-density apartment (danchi) district D
- ▨ Large-scale facility district A
- ▨ Large-scale facility district B
- ▨ Large-scale facility district C

2010

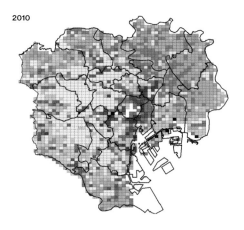

- ■ Downtown district
- ■ Downtown district with a high aging rate
- ■ Downtown district with a high rate of single male households
- ☐ White-collar district
- ▨ White-collar district with reproductivity
- ▨ White-collar district with a high rate of female residents
- ▨ White-collar district with a high rate of aged female residents
- ■ White-collar district with micro business offices
- ☐ Blue-collar district
- ▨ Blue-collar district with a high aging rate
- ☐ Blue-collar district with rented houses
- ■ Blue-collar district with reproductivity
- ■ High-density apartment (danchi) district for renters
- ☐ High-density apartment (danchi) district for owners
- ■ Large-scale facility district

4

4   Tatsuto Asakawa, Social Atlas of Tokyo in 1975, 1990, and 2010. Source: [maps of 1975 and 1990] Susumu Kurasawa and Tatsuto Asakawa, eds., *New Edition: Social Atlas of Tokyo Metropolitan Area 1975-1990* (Tokyo: University of Tokyo Press, 2004); [map of 2010] Kenji Hashimoto and Tatsuto Asakawa, eds., *Inequality and Urban Space: Social Atlas of Tokyo Metropolitan Area 1990-2010* (Tokyo: Kajima shuppankai, 2020)

As Tokyo expanded, its land was repeatedly divided up and transferred via the market into the hands of the people who continually flowed into the city.[4] Land owned by a single farming household might be subdivided into several dozen lots and sold, or multiple houses might be erected on the former grounds of a large mansion. Behind this trend was a postwar policy of promoting of owner-occupied dwellings, based on the notion that every family should own its home. Tokyo was built up by countless owners of small plots of land.

Land ownership is a powerful right in Japan; even the government or a developer will have difficulty persuading a private landowner to do its bidding. As Tokyo grew, it took on, over the years, the character of a conglomeration of countless tiny units of land, each under the control of a different, independently minded owner. Landowners make decisions about their land on the occasion of certain milestones in life—marriage, childbirth, finding a steady job, retirement. This means that the urban space in the aggregate does not change except as a sum of changes in the units that comprise it. Changes may readily occur in any given unit at the owner's whim, but there is no dramatic overall transformation. I think of Tokyo's urban space as many flexible parts that form an unyielding whole.

This micro structure makes itself apparent across Tokyo's visible cityscape. In Shanghai, a single neighborhood might suddenly metamorphose into a forest of high-rise condominiums, but this does not happen in Tokyo. Careful scrutiny of the expanse of the city will show that its high-rise developments are surrounded by expanses of low-rise buildings (FIG. 5).

However, a change is coming to Tokyo's urban space that is not yet conspicuous but will inevitably advance with the population's decline, particularly as the baby-boom generation begins to die off. This is the contraction of the city that will occur as more and more houses or lots become vacant, as if little holes were opening up here and there in every neighborhood. Since Tokyo expanded outward when its population was growing, we tend to think of its future contraction as the reverse of that, a kind of collapse inward. In fact, however, contraction will take the form of countless tiny holes perforating the fabric of the city. This phenomenon, too, is a consequence of Tokyo's micro structure. We cannot alter that structure, so we will have to figure out how to work with it.

A City of Assemblage

The shape of Tokyo will continue to change within the constraints imposed by its macro and micro structures. At the same time, the balance of influence between these two structures will gradually shift, with the micro structure

4   The system for land sales in Tokyo, which establishes ownership rights for each plot and permits their transfer between individuals, has its origins in an eighth-century contract known as the *koken*, or deed of sale. This system was formalized in the seventeenth century and has undergirded the city's expansion since the beginning of the era of modernization in the nineteenth century.

5

5 | A typical view of the urban fabric of Tokyo where high-rise developments are surrounded by expanses of low-rise buildings. Photo © iStock.com/anzeletti

eventually dominating. As the population dwindles, fewer people will move outward in search of land to own, and the city's concentric/radial configuration will no longer serve a purpose. Meanwhile, as it becomes increasingly feasible to procure goods, work, education, medical care, and welfare services without leaving one's home, the radial transportation network will also lose its preeminent role in citydwellers' lives.

In short, it will no longer matter whether one lives or works downtown or in the suburbs, near a train station or along a major thoroughfare. Instead, countless small plots of land will be put to use as each owner sees fit, unrestricted by the dictates of any macro structure. The new task of urban planners is to recognize the rhythms of these minuscule changes and steer them in directions beneficial to the population at large. If many people wish to live in the same place, then it is certainly possible to spend money to alter that space in a specific direction, as large-scale developments do today. Such places will be few and far between, however. More important is to create spaces of value that until now were considered the exclusive purview of large projects—public plazas, disaster evacuation areas, shopping malls full of global chain stores— by utilizing the many tiny, balkanized lots that will be available, employing methods suited to the unique characteristics of each location.

Here the word "assemblage" comes in handy to describe such spaces. By contrast, "community," as the term is used by urban planners in Japan, connotes a package of requirements for making a space livable; hence it signifies "what is lacking" in a place.[5] "Assemblage," on the other hand, signifies "what happens to be" in a place, and is therefore useful for contemplating how existing things can be arranged or combined together. In many parts of Tokyo we now see efforts to convert old storefronts into community centers, or vacant lots into parks or plazas, with the aim of fostering new ties among the people who happen to meet there. This method of freely assembling urban spaces by creating loose, temporary, improvised relationships among the people who happen to be there resembles the way ants improvise to make their nests.

What if the ants were free to enter not just vacant lots and houses, but high-rise buildings in redevelopment projects? What if we also applied the assemblage process to the "free" spaces created by neoliberal urban planning, assigning them new value as things to be shared? As I wrote earlier, if problems emerge in the neoliberal urban planning process, our only hope is to solve them by tempering that process. Perhaps urban planning assemblage-style is the next step we should take to refine that neoliberal model.

---

5   This is only how the word is used in the context of Japanese urban planning. Another term for the same concept, *kinrin juku*, is usually translated as "neighborhood" or "neighborhood unit." *Kinrin juku* came into use in the late 1950s among Japanese urban planners when evaluating the environment of existing urban spaces, but later became associated with the design of "new towns" like Senri and Tama. Meanwhile, older urban spaces came to be described as *machi* ("town" or "neighborhood"), causing some ambiguity in the usage of these terms. Today "community" (borrowed verbatim from the English) is often used in a sense that includes the physical environment.

23 Wards composing the mo st
urbani zed pa rt of Tok yo

mo u ntains

urban sp rawl

City Center

Yaman ote
(High ci ty)

Shi tamachi
(Low ci ty)

Tama N ew Town

Tamakyu ryo Hills c overed with n ew
towns and planned urban a reas

High-densi ty Wooden
Housing Di strict

6

6 | The main categories of characters in the
Tokyo Metropolis. Map drawn by the author

The Shape of Tokyo (FIG. 6)

A city that expands concentrically can be likened to an aggregation of rings of varying radii, like the rings of a tree. But while tree rings record the passage of time in a regular progression from the center outward, urban spaces undergo a process of metabolism, so the city center is not necessarily a repository of old buildings. We can view Tokyo as consisting of four concentric layers, starting with the center.

The City Center

Downtown Tokyo is in the lowland area of the city. It has been destroyed by fire twice in the past century: once in the Great Kanto Earthquake of 1923, and once again in the US air raids of 1945. The land readjustment projects undertaken during the postwar recovery period imposed an orderly grid of streets on this district, which is now packed with small and midsized buildings. From around 1960, the proliferation of office buildings and commercial establishments began to squeeze residents out of the city center, triggering a migration of people to outlying districts in search of housing and creating the "donut phenomenon" of a hollowed-out center. In the late 1990s, however, a plunge in land prices reversed that flow. The years since 2000 have seen a trend toward redevelopment of downtown commercial and industrial sites for housing, sparking a rebound of the population over the past two decades. Though the high-rise condominiums colloquially known as "tower mansions" may be the most conspicuous sign of this trend (FIG. 7), they are surrounded by developments of smaller apartment houses of varying sizes.

The High-Density Wooden Housing District

The city center is surrounded by neighborhoods densely packed with wooden houses. A mix of small residences, businesses, and industries, this ring-shaped district was created by the exodus of people in all directions from the city center after the Great Kanto Earthquake of 1923. Because the area was built up before the advent of systematic urban planning, it is a complex, labyrinthine urban space. Though this part of Tokyo is notorious for its vulnerability to fires and other disasters, it is not lacking in other respects and hence does not constitute a slum. Rents tend to be low, however, so many artists choose to reside there.

The Sprawl District

The Building Standards Act of 1951 and the City Planning Act of 1968 facilitated attempts to regulate Tokyo's rapid expansion through urban planning. These laws included a stipulation that building sites must provide access to public roads; the establishment of zoning laws for development; and the setting

7

High-rise condominiums in the bay area,
Tokyo, 2012. Photo courtesy of the Tokyo
Metropolitan Government

of technical standards for developments over a certain size. The new regulations were not based on lofty ideals, but rather on realistic expectations that any conscientious developer could meet with only a little effort. Though this had virtually no effect on "the high-density wooden housing district," where little if any development took place, it did lead to a more or less orderly expansion of the city *outside* that district. Development of this new area proceeded in patchwork fashion due to the diverse interests of farm owners, producing a mix of small plots of farmland and citified spaces—a uniquely Japanese form of urban sprawl. The City Planning Act of 1968 established zones to accelerate the urbanization process, but it was simultaneously government policy to respect the wishes of farmers who wanted to continue farming. Hence even today, small farm plots cling tenaciously to life here and there throughout Tokyo.

The Planned Development District

In the early 1970s, private developers began to flex their muscles, buying up large plots of land and building massive housing projects complete with their own roads and parks. Unused farmland and hilly areas outside the "sprawl district" were transformed into planned communities. Meanwhile, government entities competed with the private developers to build their own sprawling "new towns," projects that were largely occupied by postwar baby-boomers. Today, however, the boomers' grown children are gravitating to the high-rise condominiums of downtown Tokyo, raising concerns that the "new towns" will rapidly hollow out as the boomer generation dies off.

POSTWAR JAPANESE DWELLINGS: HINTS FOR THE FUTURE

● KOZO KADOWAKI

1 A Tokyo suburb during the postwar construction boom (Kyodo, Setagaya Ward, Tokyo, February 1954). The neighborhood is a mix of detached houses and apartment blocks. Photo courtesy of Kazuo Takamizawa

To this day, Tokyo retains an urban layout dating back to the Edo period (1603–1867). This configuration survived virtually intact even when the buildings that crowded atop it in the post-Edo years were utterly destroyed in the air raids of World War II. That vacuum was filled immediately after the war in a construction rush spurred by the critical need to address a housing shortage of some two million dwellings nationwide.

The strategy deployed by the Japanese government to mass-produce this housing was a curious mix of idealism and realism. In that sense, the housing stock that resulted was a reflection of conditions in Japan at the time, and it makes up a significant part of the Tokyo cityscape to this day.

By the standards of today's wealthy metropolis, the housing that defined postwar Tokyo was lacking in a variety of ways. Nonetheless, it is my view that a reassessment of this housing stock from a contemporary perspective offers meaningful hints on the creation of housing in Tokyo from this point on. Here I would like to explain how we might devise a strategy for the housing of the future by analyzing the characteristics of postwar dwellings and putting housing stock that is largely treated today as a negative legacy to constructive use.

The Ideal of Apartment Living
vs. the Reality of Detached Housing

The housing that was mass-produced after the war consisted mainly of two types, apartments and detached residences (FIG. 1). In the past Japan had row houses known as *nagaya*, but no multi-story multi-unit housing with dwellings stacked atop one another. In the postwar years, however, apartment living became the norm for many Japanese because that was the format made available by the Japan Housing Corporation, local governments, and other public entities throughout the country.

The provision of apartments by the public sector came about because the common wisdom in Japan at the time was that steel-reinforced concrete apartment houses were the ideal form for urban housing. With its resistance to fire and earthquakes, ferroconcrete was hailed as an "everlasting" building material that would permit the efficient redistribution of Japan's limited environmental and spatial resources. Thus the modern apartment building was considered eminently suitable as an architectural format for urban life.

If the apartment house was the ideal housing format, the detached house in many respects represented the reality of postwar conditions. Nearly all stand-alone dwellings in Japan were made of wood, a material intimately associated with the building methods and technology of traditional Japanese architecture. After the war, however, wooden structures were viewed as relics of a bygone era. The incineration of so many cities in the war's firebombing traumatized the nation and gave wooden construction a bad name. Despite

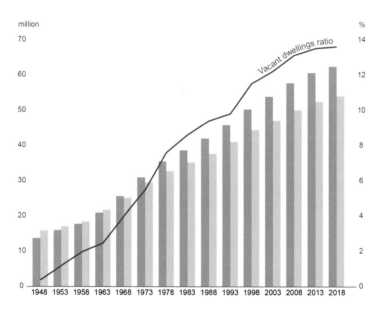

■ Total number of dwellings
■ Total number of households

million   %

70   14

                                                    Vacant dwellings ratio

60   12

50   10

40   8

30   6

20   4

10   2

0   0
   1948 1953 1958 1963 1968 1973 1978 1983 1988 1993 1998 2003 2008 2013 2018

2   Changes in the number of dwellings and
         households, and the percentage of vacant
         dwellings in Japan from 1948 to 2018.
         Source: Housing and Land Surveys,
         Statistics Bureau of Japan

this, a vast number of wooden houses sprang up in the early postwar period, thanks to a production base supported by a still robust labor force skilled in the building of such structures. For several years after the war, Japan's acute housing shortage dictated the provisional use of wooden construction.

What is more, the postwar demand for housing was so great that public projects alone could not address it. In response, the government backed the provision of home loans to encourage ordinary citizens to build residences on their own. These loans could be viewed as a way of getting young homeowners to invest in housing construction by mortgaging their future, as well as a means of promoting economic recovery via self-help. Offering young householders a practical way to secure funds accelerated the construction of detached housing.

The Aftermath of the Ideal Dwelling

As we have seen, some sharp contrasts defined the relationship between detached housing and apartment housing in postwar Japan. The latter was an entirely new, idealized form of citizen housing, a semipermanent component of the cityscape that was funded by public capital and had no direct link, technically or compositionally, to premodern Japanese housing. Detached housing, on the other hand, was meant to be temporary, a stopgap solution to the pressing needs of the postwar period. It was also a means of recovery undertaken by citizens with their own resources, and it made full use of the construction methods and production base inherited from the prewar days. In other words, postwar detached housing represented a compromised acceptance of the status quo.

The coexistence of publicly funded, publicly owned apartment housing and privately funded, privately owned detached housing was also a reflection of the fact that Japanese politics of the day were not dominated exclusively by capitalist interests; communist thought also held considerable sway. Just as market economics became preeminent in the world at large after the end of the Cold War, however, housing in Japan today is purely market-driven.

By the 1970s Japan was no longer facing a housing shortage (FIG. 2), and the construction of public apartment projects abruptly fell off. Around the same time there was a surge in Tokyo land prices as well as stock prices. This triggered a boom in condominium construction—in other words, the prevailing trend shifted to the private construction and ownership of apartments. This "condo boom" accelerated during the economic bubble of the 1980s, and even after the bubble burst in the early 1990s, speculators continued to invest in condominiums. The subsequent long-term stagnation of the economy spurred deregulatory moves typified by a relaxation in the 2000s, as part of a policy of urban revitalization, of restrictions on the ratio of building to lot size in Tokyo. The upshot was that apartment houses were increasingly viewed

3

High-rise condominiums on the waterfront
of Tokyo, where they began to dominate
the skyline in the 2000s (Tsukuda, Chuo
Ward, Tokyo, 2020). Photo courtesy of the
Tokyo Metropolitan Government

as investments, and downtown Tokyo began its transformation into a forest of high-rise condominiums (FIG. 3).

During this period, as individual apartments came under separate ownership, the law was changed to permit the conversion of apartment owner-ship into securities that could be bought and sold in small lots. Thus apart-ment houses, which began as shared property under public ownership in the postwar era, are today more like containers legally divided among multiple owners—a far cry from their ostensible purpose as a means of enabling people to gather and live in a limited space.

Shared Housing: A Seed of Possibility Sprouts from Exhausted Soil

While multi-unit housing has metamorphosed from something shared to something owned in bits and pieces, detached housing, built primarily in the suburbs for sale to actual occupants, has reached a state of exhaustion with the aging and depopulation of Japanese society. From this parched soil, how-ever, we now see the emergence of an unprecedented development that points to a new direction in urban living.

Contributing to the new trend is a change in Tokyo's suburban residen-tial areas brought about by the spread of the Internet, which has enabled businesses to attract customers via social media word-of-mouth and establish themselves in neighborhoods less accessible by public transportation. It is now commonplace for a new type of resident to run a small business out of a corner of an older, refurbished house. Detached homes built during the era of rapid economic growth typically have three or four bedrooms; with the average household in Tokyo Prefecture currently down to less than two people, home size and family size are frequently mismatched these days. In this way, small businesses in residential areas are a means of utilizing space that has been freed up by the decline in family size (FIG. 4).

Tokyo is a metropolis sustained by an extensive network of railways. The farther from a train station a business is located, the more it must depend on word-of-mouth advertising. This in turn is conducive to the proliferation of small neighborhood enterprises with distinctive characters. The wooden housing stock available in places some distance from the city center further serves as an incubator for new, experimental types of businesses.

Deep in the innermost reaches of some residential neighborhoods, one can find houses in which the residents have opened up a section to activities that occupy a gray area between for-profit and non-profit. Take the example of a house with a deck and garden that are always open to the public and func-tion as a common space that is sometimes used for events such as flea markets and concerts (FIG. 5). Increasingly, people are finding value not so much in

4

5

4   A detached house where surplus rooms have been converted into a bakery (Chofu City, Tokyo, September 2014). Photo © Kei Ono

5   A detached house where the deck and yard have become an "open garden" for common use; flea markets and other events are held here on an ad-hoc basis (Chofu City, Tokyo, September 2014). Photo © Kei Ono

ownership per se as in the utilization of houses in residential areas that have been showing signs of exhaustion as more and more houses become vacant or begin to deteriorate. This productive use of spatial resources is a positive development outside the purview of the market system.

Because of its independence from market forces, this "house opening" phenomenon is catching on not only in Tokyo, but also in the outlying suburbs and regional cities where surplus housing stock and economic stagnation are highly conspicuous. The plethora of wooden houses also offers a potential solution to the dearth of housing for the economically and socially disadvantaged, for whom publicly owned apartments once served as a residential safety net.

The Resilience of Fragile Structures

The proliferation of efforts to make surplus space in wooden detached homes accessible to the surrounding community is not unrelated to the physical fragility of these structures. Wooden buildings have less rigidly defined spatial boundaries than those made with reinforced concrete, a characteristic that facilitates the creation of flexible spaces for shared use.

Having lost their original residents over the years, Japan's detached houses now seem like ghostly vestiges of an era when families were larger than they are today. However, their continuing presence in neighborhoods where housing space exceeds residents' needs has made possible the flexible sharing of human habitats among members of a generation less fixated on ownership of their living or work spaces. Scarce resources tend to be hoarded; when resources are plentiful, they present opportunities for sharing with others. As Japan's population declines and its suburban residential areas begin to hollow out, we see an unmistakable trend toward the sharing of spatial resources.

Amid the novel circumstances we now face—an aging society coupled with aging housing stock—the broad acceptance of habitat sharing may foster a change in the way "dwelling" is perceived in Japan, extending the concept beyond the physical boundaries of the house per se. This would mark a departure from the trend toward divided ownership of housing in the decades since World War II; it could also lead to a revival of the sense of community that has been lost in the apartment blocks that were once touted as the ideal form of housing.

In the center of Tokyo, housing has become entangled in the market economy, which treats it as a commodity to be parceled out to multiple investors. But as Japan's metropolitan centers inevitably contract in the years to come, I believe that the future of housing lies in new formats that emerge not in the downtowns, but on the periphery of cities. The first signs of this new kind of community are already beginning to appear in fragile wooden structures that were built after the war as temporary housing.

THE URBAN PLANNING OF TAKAMASA YOSHIZAKA: SUBLATION OF THE LARGE AND THE SMALL

● SHUN YOSHIE

Takamasa Yoshizaka (1917–1980) was a designer of forms on every scale, from architecture to entire cities and from furniture to small gadgets. He is also known as a mountaineer who traversed equatorial Africa and climbed Mt. Kilimanjaro and as the author of a prodigious number of written works. Moreover, he was a concept maker who coined such original terms as "lukeiology, the study of tangibleness and forms" and "discontinuous unity."

Yoshizaka was constantly asking questions, but before they could be resolved with neat answers, he would move on to a new question—a tendency that led one critic to remark that he seemed to fear any state of completion.[1] This has made it difficult to appreciate the totality of his endeavors, a lack of understanding that has led to many of the structures he designed being torn down in recent years. But as I will explain here, Yoshizaka's thought—which constantly migrated between architectural and urban planning, between worm's-eye and bird's-eye views—poses significant questions that are now more pertinent than ever.

Urban Planning and Urban Engineering

Yoshizaka is known as one of the three Japanese architects, following Kunio Maekawa and Junzo Sakakura, who apprenticed with Le Corbusier. After World War II he designed a great number of buildings, but he also established an urban planning lab at Waseda University, where he taught. This was in 1966, when most city planners in Japan concerned themselves with large-scale public works; the Yoshizaka lab was one of the first urban planning studios to have its roots in architecture. Unlike planning up to that point, which revolved around civil engineering infrastructure and zoning restrictions, Yoshizaka argued for "thinking in pictures." What sort of landscape would emerge, what buildings would rise, how would streets and plantings be laid out? His mind encompassed every scale, from the entire Japanese archipelago down to the textures of a city under the touch of its inhabitants.

The sixties represented the dawn of urban design in Japan. At the forefront were several universities that opened new departments or labs in the field: urban engineering at the University of Tokyo, urban planning at Waseda University, and social engineering at the Tokyo Institute of Technology. The University of Tokyo's urban engineering department, led by Kenzo Tange, established the engineering of urban space as its own field independent of the departments of architecture and civil engineering. Many of its graduates went on to work for the national or local governments, or in the construction and transportation industries.

1   Architect Hiroshi Naito, who studied with Yoshizaka, has told the author more than once that "Maturity means you're approaching death." This remark gives one, I think, some hint of what Yoshizaka's "fear of completion" may signify.

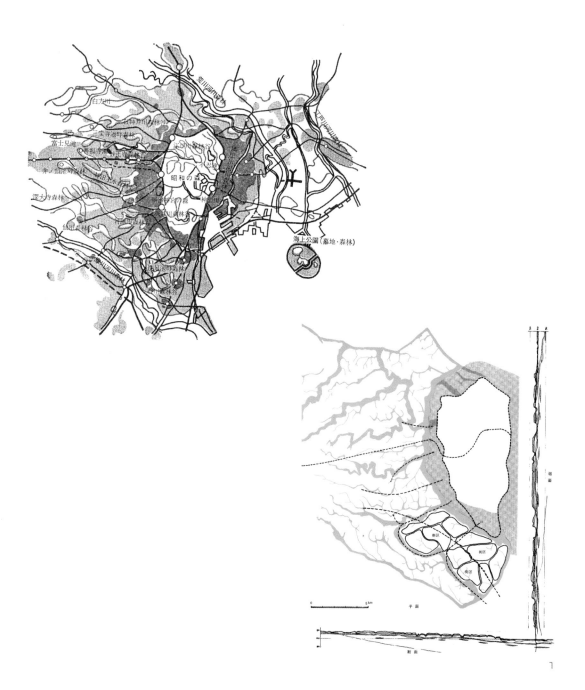

1   Takamasa Yoshizaka, Plan for Tokyo, 1974. At left is his Fissure Plan; at right is a plan highlighting his proposed "islands" and "fissures" that take advantage of Tokyo's topography, with sections corresponding to the plan. Sources: (left) *Toshi Jutaku* [Urban Housing], August 1975: 65; (right) Study Group for Japan in the 21st Century at Waseda University, "Designing Japan's Future: II. From Pyramid to Network," 1971: 27

Yoshizaka's lab for urban planning at Waseda, on the other hand, based its approach on his belief in visualizing everything—from individual lifestyles to the entire city—as a picture. Because it was an elective graduate-school master's course for those who had studied for four years in the university's architecture department, it was skewed heavily toward architectural design, and most of its graduates went on to open their own studios. Notable examples include Toshi (Urban) Design Associates, Ecological City Organizer (ECO), Atelier Zo, Atelier 74, Fishery Communities Planning Co., and the Capital Region Comprehensive Planning Institute. These were among the first urban design offices in Japan to handle everything from architectural design to urban planning.

In contrast to the approach of Tange's group at the University of Tokyo, Yoshizaka prioritized the relationship between the individual and the city. While Japan's economy boomed, he expressed misgivings about the explosive growth of the nation's cities as they became linked by Shinkansen high-speed railroads under the government's Plan for Remodeling the Japanese Archipelago announced in 1972 by Prime Minister Kakuei Tanaka. As the cities expanded, Yoshizaka warned, the existence of human beings would be increasingly ignored. And if the cities grew too big, they were likely to die out, like the dinosaurs.[2]

Plan for Tokyo 1974: Islands and Fissures

Unlike Kenzo Tange's Plan for Tokyo 1960, which proposed facilitating the limitless expansion of the metropolis by filling in Tokyo Bay, or the ideas of the like-minded Metabolist movement, Yoshizaka's own Plan for Tokyo 1974 proposed that the entire area within the Yamanote Line, which makes a loop around the center of Tokyo, be restored to nature. This park, which he named Showa Forest, would be accessible via all the railways that radiate like spokes from the Yamanote Line. He further proposed a Fissure Plan aligned with Tokyo's microtopography (FIG. 1). He described the significance of these ideas this way: "My plan for Tokyo in the 21st century aims for the recovery of a sense of presence and place [for city-dwellers] by restoring the natural topography and opening human-scale fissures in it." The Fissure Plan called for the resuscitation of Tokyo's natural terrain, which had been rendered invisible—buried beneath the city's relentless growth (its population had exceeded ten million by this time)—by unearthing the riverbeds and creating ecological districts amenable to citizen participation. These districts were planned in two stages: first, for a population of 200,000 to 300,000 people (a larger district)

2   Yoshizaka sounded his warning about the dangers of bloated cities in many of his books. See, for example, the introduction to his Plan for Sendai submitted to that city by the Waseda University Yoshizaka Lab + Sendai Developers Commission (*The Ideal Form of Sendai, the City of Trees: A Proposal for Its Future*, 1973, 14).

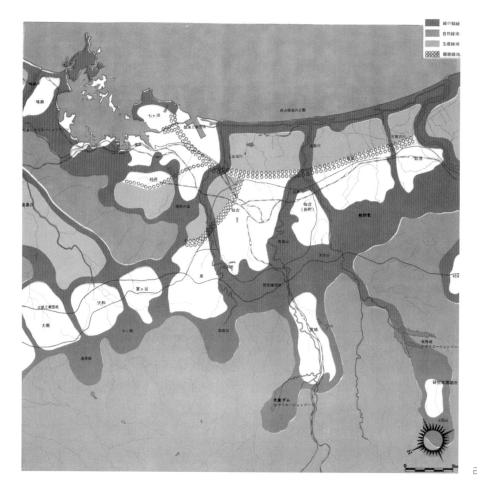

2 | Yoshizaka's most extensive plan for
Sendai. The "green frames" segment the
city, while the area along the coast is
returned to nature as an agricultural land.
This productive green space overlaps
with the area that was hit by the tsunami
after the Great East Japan Earthquake.
Takamasa Yoshizaka, *Green Frames*, 1973.
Source: Waseda University Yoshizaka Lab,
*The Ideal Form of Sendai, the City of
Trees: A Proposal for Its Future* (Sendai:
Sendai Developers Commission), 1973, 26

and then subsequently for a population scale of 30,000 people (a more site-specific district).

Alongside these grand-scale proposals, the Yoshizaka lab produced more detailed plans based on meticulous surveys of specific sites. The objective was to create "islands" and "fissures" in Tokyo's increasingly chaotic cityscape. As part of a project commissioned by the Tokyo Metropolitan Government's Bureau of Urban Development, the lab carried out case studies of three selected districts with three distinct objectives: Takinogawa (Kita Ward), to develop a low-rise, high-density, resident-friendly neighborhood; Wakagi (Itabashi Ward), to foster living in a greenery-rich environment; and Doshida (Nerima Ward), to encourage households to engage in farming. The overarching theme was how to break the megalopolis up into appropriate units and provide residents with familiar public spaces to enhance their sense of belonging to a hometown. Based on extensive questionnaires and field surveys, the Yoshizaka lab generated multilayered maps illustrating these neighborhood "islands," and proposed plans for road-based "street units" and community-based "turfs."

Yoshizaka thus tackled this project not only by developing proposals for the shape of Tokyo in the twenty-first century that reflected an overarching philosophy without addressing a specific means of implementation, but also by conducting studies of specific neighborhoods and sites based on research into methods and legal issues pertaining to implementation. These two approaches occurred in parallel and did not always dovetail. Developing simultaneous big-picture and small-picture proposals was, indeed, characteristic of Yoshizaka. When he established his lab at Waseda, he decided to maintain a division of labor with his existing studio, Atelier U: the studio would handle design, while the lab would engage in urban planning. Atelier U accordingly developed the grand urban designs he proposed, while the university lab was in charge of carrying out the surveys and more specific proposals.

Plan for Sendai: Discontinuous Unity

Yoshizaka first attracted attention for his urban planning work with his 1973 Plan for Sendai. At the time, Sendai, the capital of Miyagi Prefecture in the northeastern Tohoku region, had a densely inhabited central district with a population of 300,000, placing it midway between a large and a small city, and had been earmarked for construction of a Shinkansen bullet train station. Based on his thorough study of Sendai, Yoshizaka produced a plan for a city that would coexist with the natural environment, dividing it into sea, plain, river, and mountain districts (FIG. 2) and proposing the creation of "green frames" and "green hands." The green frames were defined as fissures of greenery intended to block unbridled urban sprawl. From the air, they resembled the tentacles of amoebas, connected to one another but breaking Sendai up into multiple neighborhoods (FIG. 3). The "green hand" was a design incorporating five existing radial roads—the "fingers"—that would be lined with trees; Yoshizaka had in mind the creation of a city symbol that was not a major building or monument. He also proposed making a "productive green zone" out of the coastal district of the city—an area, it should be noted, that was later devastated by the tsunami following the Great East Japan Earthquake of 2011.

Sendai was a politicized environment in which conservative and reformist forces were vying for control, a situation that made it extremely difficult to decide what direction a city plan should take. However, the city established a committee for which the chamber of commerce would serve as a neutral liaison office and commissioned the Yoshizaka lab to carry out surveys and make proposals. Their intermediary was Yoshihiko Sasaki, who taught rural planning at Tohoku University. Sasaki and Yoshizaka had been fellow students of Wajiro Kon,[3] Yoshizaka's other great mentor besides Le Corbusier.

Sasaki asked Yoshizaka to "express the greater part of your plan in pictures." Accordingly, the lab packaged its presentation as a square booklet filled with colorful photographs, drawings, and diagrams illustrating its fieldwork and proposals. The booklet presented multiple alternate images of Sendai by varying the center of a fish-eye map of the city (FIG. 4). As Yoshizaka put it, "However remote a place may be, it's the center of the world to the people living there." A fish-eye map, which shows the center in the greatest detail (with the degree of precision decreasing the farther one goes from the center) was Yoshizaka's answer to the question of how to "overcome and sublate the large and the small"—in other words, how to address the gap between individual human existence and urban planning. Yoshizaka's concept of "discontinuous unity," unlike the "group form" that Fumihiko Maki posited in opposition to Tange's "megaform," deals not only with form, but with the question of how to negotiate between the scale of human existence and that of the city.

Third-Order Urban Planning

When Tange's city plans now look like anachronistic relics of Japan's era of rapid economic growth, why do Yoshizaka's plans still seem so relevant? The reason is that Yoshizaka distanced himself from the trends of the time period, consistently adhering to a long-term perspective that embraced the livelihoods, indeed the very existence, of human beings (FIG. 5). I refer to this approach as "third-order urban planning." The conflict between modernists

3   Wajiro Kon (1888–1973) was an architectural scholar and ethnographer. He made meticulous sketches of the recovery and modernization process in Tokyo following the Great Kanto Earthquake of 1923, coining the term "modernology" for such research. Later he developed another concept, "lifology," from his studies of rural villages. Yoshizaka accompanied Kon on these village surveys, and that influence can be seen in his own graduate thesis.

and romanticists—between urban development on a massive scale and those who espouse the revitalization of rural villages and other older forms of community—is a motif that has repeated itself around the globe, a classic example being the clash between Robert Moses and Jane Jacobs. In response, Yoshizaka championed a third way that entailed going back to the basics.

Yoshizaka's unflagging pursuit of this third way invited misunderstanding by his contemporaries, who treated him as an architect of undefined principles, an accusation that has contributed to his reputation as something of a cipher. Yet his third-order approach to urban planning is needed more than ever today as we confront the crippling limitations of modern society's addiction to binary, either-or thinking, whether the dichotomy is artificial vs. natural, commercial vs. public interest, group vs. individual, city vs. village, old vs. new, private vs. public, or quiet residential area vs. bustling shopping district. Yoshizaka's concern—how to devise a third way that ties up the loose ends when these dichotomies unravel—is a challenge that my contemporaries and I, the generation of Yoshizaka's grandchildren, have chosen to take up.

Reconsidering Yoshizaka's Plan for Tokyo

Yoshizaka was active in the earliest days of urban design in Japan, a time when cities around the country had begun drawing up their own master plans. Their approaches were multifarious, and urban planners at the universities who collaborated with them often took the opportunity to pursue bold new visions. Today, however, urban planning has become a highly compartmentalized process, and efforts to develop future-oriented visions for local communities are increasingly rare. It is a sign of the times that no comprehensive urban or architectural vision was introduced in the planning for the Tokyo Olympics of 2021.

In that light, I would like to conclude by proposing an update, adapted for present-day Tokyo, of the Plan for Tokyo introduced by Yoshizaka half a century ago. Yoshizaka's question—how to restore a sense of existence on the human scale amid our megacities—is one we must address now, and I think we can begin by adopting, unaltered, Yoshizaka's emphasis on the presence of nature in the city. To this I would like to add the following four proposals:

I   Reverse the center of Tokyo, but with a caveat. The area enclosed by the Yamanote Line is a network of mature commercial districts that continue to function as valuable assets of the city. Therefore I do not advocate turning the entire area into a park, as Yoshizaka proposed. Instead of destroying those neighborhoods, I suggest turning them into a pedestrian space, with automobile traffic diverted to ring roads around the periphery. Unlike travel by car, travel on foot sensitizes

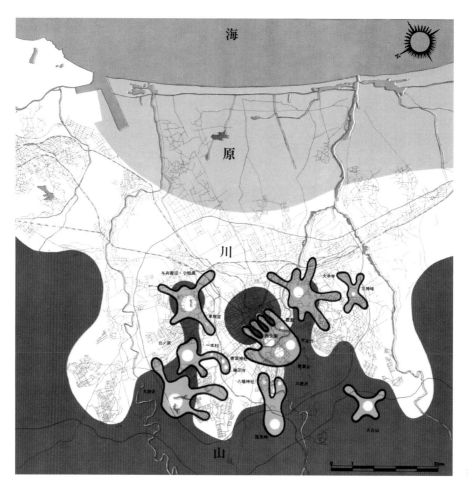

海

原

川

山

3

3   A close-up view of the central part of Sendai in Yoshizaka's urban planning proposal. He divided the city into four parts: sea, plain, river, and mountain. Nature is planned in amoeba-like forms; the blue represents the sea; the pale green is the plain; the white area (river) depicts the residential areas, and the darker green the mountain. The "green hands" that overlap the red of the city core indicate natural areas such as parks and green belts. Takamasa Yoshizaka, *Sendai of the Sea, Rivers, and Plain*, 1973. Source: Yoshizaka Lab, *The Ideal Form of Sendai*, 28

4   Takamasa Yoshizaka, Fish-eye map of Sendai, 1973. Source: Yoshizaka Lab, *The Ideal Form of Sendai*, 63

5   Takamasa Yoshizaka, *From Pyramid to Network: The Future of the Japanese Islands*, 1973. Source: Yoshizaka Lab, *The Ideal Form of Sendai*, 24. During the post-war boom years, Japan's population, as well as its communication and administrative hubs, became concentrated in the "Tokaido Megalopolis" along the country's south-eastern seaboard. Yoshizaka believed that the Japanese archipelago had to be "turned upside down"—i.e., that the population should spread evenly across the islands and form "regional zones" to balance out the overwhelmingly dominant "capital zone" around Tokyo. Yoshizaka positioned this image at the beginning of his Plan for Sendai, declaring that "Sendai must not be merely a service counter, a branch outlet or branch culture for Tokyo and the Tokaido megalopolis." Instead, he envisioned an autonomous Tohoku Zone that would not be Tokyo-dependent. Source: Yoshizaka Lab, *The Ideal Form of Sendai*, 24

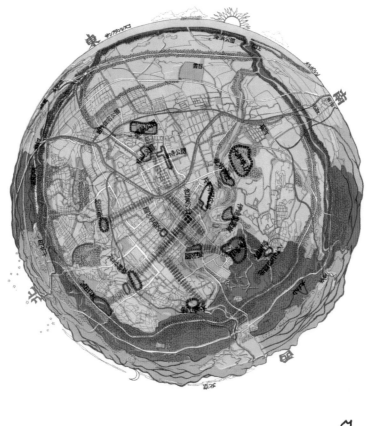

4

5

people to the topography of a place. In a city center reborn as a pedestrian space, people will discover their own human-scale spaces as well as the original names given to these small neighborhoods.

2   Create two kinds of commercial/entertainment districts: those providing anonymity and those providing conspicuity. Tokyo already possesses several entertainment mega-districts, like Shinjuku, Shibuya, and Ikebukuro, that are located along the peripheral Yamanote Line. There is no need to break them up into smaller units; indeed, many people are drawn to such districts precisely for the anonymity they afford. They also give people who may have been in the minority in a small town the opportunity to meet others of like circumstances without feeling vulnerable to the prying eyes of strangers. Therefore, I propose creating two different types of entertainment district in separate locations: large districts for anonymity and small ones for conspicuity. The latter would be on a scale that facilitates encounters among acquaintances; Yoshizaka envisioned them as having a capacity of around 100,000 people. While the large "anonymous" districts would remain along the Yamanote Line on the edge of the city center, the small "conspicuous" districts would be located farther away on the outskirts of the metropolis, which would thus be structured like a set of concentric rings.

3   Reconnect the neighborhoods to the sea. Since the end of World War II, relentless land reclamation has moved Tokyo Bay farther and farther from the city's neighborhoods, and the new waterfront is lined with high-rise condominiums. In some respects, the result—in which older neighborhoods are totally cut off from the water—resembles the future city envisioned by Tange. I propose restoring the waterfront to its natural state, prohibiting the construction of high-rises there, and extending the ambience of the seashore all the way back to the original coastline. This would reunite the waterfront—not the current one of tourist attractions built on landfill, but a place that once nurtured human livelihoods, culture, and industry—with the bay, thereby making it part of neighborhood life again.

4   Finally, revive the rivers as catchment areas of knowledge and intellectual activity. Tokyo is home to countless rivers that flow into the bay, in the process dividing the metropolis into the alternating river valleys and highlands that define its topography. Tokyo's river valleys have long hosted numerous universities and professional schools. I propose that the universities open their urban campuses to the surrounding neighborhoods and establish satellite campuses farther upstream outside

of town, thus creating a network of knowledge that extends along the rivers. This would provide open spaces for informal exchanges of knowledge beyond the confines of the campuses.

Besides the issues addressed above, there are other critical problems we must confront, such as the availability of housing and the growing gap between rich and poor. For the purposes of this essay, however, I will simply conclude by noting that since the advent of the twenty-first century, Japan has seen its population go into steady decline, its fiscal health suffer, and its population grow older—and that these trends have also hampered efforts to develop a large-scale vision for the country. Yet it is precisely this age of uncertainty we live in that calls for an approach like that of Yoshizaka, whose planning theory crossed disciplines and transcended different scales of space in order to find a way forward.

❷ THE NEW
URBAN ENCLAVES

How is Tokyo, as a contemporary city, developed? Who plans and owns the large new mixed-used urban enclaves? How do they function differently from the surrounding areas of the city in terms of accessibility, conviviality, and sense of community?

The history of Tokyo is intertwined with that of private real-estate companies. Two of the country's largest firms with significant holdings in Tokyo, Mitsubishi Estate and Mitsui Fudosan, were founded in 1890 and 1914 respectively. Mitsubishi was responsible for "London Town" and "New York Town," Japan's earliest examples of Western-influenced urban development projects, both built in the Marunouchi district of Tokyo.

Together, these companies have played and continue to play a major role in shaping the city. Generally, each repeatedly employs a certain development model. For example, the concept of nature in the city, reflected in the use of the word "Hills," has been a constant for Mori Building's visionary leader Minoru Mori, whose company began with smaller-scale work like the Ark Hills project before embarking on the more ambitious Roppongi Hills development.

The Japanese government's neoliberal economic policies have played a major role in enabling large real-estate developers to undertake ever-larger and more ambitious projects. If Minoru Mori had to wait for fifteen years before his company could assemble all the necessary land parcels before embarking on the construction of Roppongi Hills, the equally charismatic leader of Mitsui Fudosan, Hiromichi Iwasa, was able to acquire the site for the company's iconic Tokyo Midtown project, a former military garrison, all at once—albeit with a hefty price tag. Despite their financial success, both projects represent the complexities and risks involved in such endeavors.

Should the development and construction of massive parts of contemporary Tokyo remain the sole prerogative of private companies? How could this type of large urban design project be made less dependent on consumerist assumptions, and more inclusionary in terms of the provision of common resources?

TOKYO MIDTOWN:
A DEVELOPMENTAL PERSPECTIVE

● CONVERSATION I WITH YOSHIHIKO SONE

1

1 | Aerial view of the entire complex of Tokyo
Midtown, 2007, master planned by SOM.
Photo © Shinkenchiku-sha, courtesy of SOM

●   MOHSEN MOSTAFAVI: Sone-san, you have been overseeing large-scale development projects in Japan and overseas at Mitsui Fudosan over the last 20 or 30 years, Tokyo Midtown in Roppongi (FIG. 1) being a recent and prominent one. I assume the project was a manifestation of your best efforts for such a large-scale mixed-use development project. We're interested in learning what kind of vision, ideas, and attempts were crystallized in the outcome. Let me first ask you to trace back the process of the project.

I understand that the land for Tokyo Midtown was exceptionally large and expensive and that Mitsui Fudosan had to be brave and adventurous when choosing to acquire it. The company must have had very strong feelings or aspirations in terms of what you could do with this site. So, what were the internal discussions for after the acquisition? Was it something like, "Okay, we have this expensive site and we have these interesting ideas. How do we prepare?"

●   YOSHIHIKO SONE: Well, I got on board this project after the acquisition of the land, but as far as I can tell, our president and CEO at the time, Hiromichi Iwasa, was very insightful and wanted to make this development become a super-project since the land parcel was much larger than what we had dealt with in the past. The grand picture we had at the outset was to accommodate various types of uses—residential, commercial, hotels, convention and conference facilities (although they came in later), and a museum, an art gallery, and a medical center—and have them work in synergy. Diversity: a city within a city.

But in order to have a realistic vision, we also needed to understand what was legally possible. One critical factor was the shadow restrictions over this land, which could not be eased because it would influence the neighboring area to the north of the site where there were a lot of residential buildings. Nikken Sekkei, who were committed to the tasks up to the acquisition, helped us cope with this issue. There was a risk that we might not be able to use the FAR to the maximum allowance.

●   So, before the acquisition, Mitsui Fudosan was preparing what would be possible on the land because you needed to know what you would do as part of the bidding. And Nikken Sekkei was hired to provide information about volume, among other things, so that Mitsui Fudosan could calculate what the returns would be in terms of a potential FAR (floor-to-area ratio) of the size and the diversity of functions. Correct?

●   That's correct. Through this preparatory process, we came up with the strategy of taking advantage of the binding conditions and making "diversity on the green" the concept. One condition was obviously the shadow restrictions. It became clear that we were going to have a sub-stantial amount of unbuilt area. Even if we built buildings in that area, we'd only get very little floor plate.

The other condition was that there was Hinokicho Park, which belongs to the Minato Ward, to the northwest of the site. We proposed that we redevelop the park, which used to be very gloomy, with people sleeping there at night (not favored by the neighborhood), as a continuation of our land.

This meant that we'd leave northern portion of our land open, make it a lush green space with the abundant existing trees, and tie it to Hinokicho Park. At this point, the concept of "diversity on the green" emerged. As a result, we came up with the plan to build one super-tower surrounded with lower buildings facing the main street side, while keeping nearly half of the site as green space on the residential side.

A Single Tower Formation

● But at some point you did think about more than one tall tower or not? Wasn't it possible to think about two towers?

● No. Always one tower. At one point we called it the Mont Saint Michel scheme—a fortress of buildings around a tower.

● It was always Mont Saint Michel?

● Yes, more or less. We reached the conclusion that this was a strategy that would maximize the potential of the land and keep the gigantic tower away from the neighbors, which would make the development integrate with the existing urban context in a comfortable way. I say "more or less" because it's different from Mont Saint Michel in terms of openness to the neighborhood.

● And so then the acquisition happened and you chose SOM (Skidmore, Owings & Merrill) to design it.

● Correct, but not just to design it, but also to be the master architect. First, we wanted to make sure that all the designers that come on board are the best in the world, and I think we did that. Second, in order to make the townscape intriguing, we wanted different architects to design different buildings. Finally, we wanted the master architect to design the main tower while coordinating the other architects, designers, and consultants. We thought this would differentiate it from Roppongi Hills, which we regarded as a great precedent and which was even larger in scale.

The process of selecting the master architect started off with a long list of about 30 architects, mostly from the US and Europe. It was when the Time Warner complex at Columbus Circle was just completed or nearly completed, and David Childs was in charge of that. We thought Time Warner was an extraordinary development, one similar in many aspects to what we were aiming for.

As mentioned, at the very beginning, considering the size of the complex, we thought that the tower and the two buildings in front were going to be designed by different architects. But the scheme of SOM's competition RFP was really strong; they recommended that the tower and the two buildings in front interact with one another, which was an essential aspect of the master plan. This would create a foreground leading from the main street to the main tower, like at Rockefeller Center. We came to think that it made sense for all three towers to be designed by SOM. Mustafa Abadan, who led the design team for the entire development, did a great job.

From the design point of view, of all the different programs, retail was the most important because that's where the complex meets invites the public to enter. At the very beginning we even wondered whether we should hire a commercially oriented architect as the master architect. But judging from SOM's proposal, experience, and vision for the project, we became confident that they were capable of integrating retail design in this kind of large-scale complex.

● Mustafa Abadan, whom we interviewed for this book, also mentioned that he thought the fact that they'd done Time Warner was important and made it more likely for them to be selected. So on the one hand, you had SOM's Time Warner project, and on the other hand you had KPF's Roppongi Hills, where they'd done something comparable. In terms of the relationship to the street, Tokyo Midtown seems more accessible or more open to the street than Roppongi Hills. Apparently, you tried to open the development up to the city by making it more porous.

● That's true, yes. There were two issues. One, as you mentioned, was to open up the project as if we were spreading out our arms to the street as a welcoming gesture. And the other was to make the plan, which is very complicated due to the multiple programs, as straight-forward as possible. Both issues were about making the complex more accessible.

Mixing of Programs

●   Speaking of diversity, is there a science involved in the mixture of the program, what you wanted between retail, residential, and the small hotel?

●   Well, first, we wanted to create as much retail as possible, even more than what we ended up with, since it's the element that attracts people to the complex and creates a vibrant venue and revives the district. There was a restriction, though, of how much retail we could accommodate in the complex, because more vehicles would add to the existing congestion. Similarly to the shadow restriction exercise, we tried every strategy in order to maximize the retail space floor area.

●   Which is what percentage?

●   Approximately 10%. That was what we could get.
       The second, obviously, was to maximize the office area, because that'll be the financial basis of the whole project and it would allow us to include cultural facilities that are not as profitable. But the bonus FAR that was to be granted in compensation for public facilities or spaces was already designated for other non-office-space programs, so we could not allocate any more FAR for offices than the standard regulation limit.
       Our office marketing strategy was unique. We decided to convince not just one but multiple major large-scale companies to bring their headquarters to this complex. To achieve this goal, we provided many features that office buildings normally cannot offer, essentially offering the companies the benefits of occupying their own building without taking the risk of owning it. For example, the reception area of each of the headquarters of the five major tenants opens directly off the common lobby.
       Our third program goal included residential and hotel areas. We wanted the complex to be inhabited not just in the daytime, but for 24 hours a day. Again, our marketing strategy was unique. We offered three different kinds of residences: SoHos [ed.: Small office Home office, or a small office that can also serve as a residence] for Roppongi-oriented professionals, high-end serviced apartments for expat residents, and others for upper-class residents. It was also important to include a top-class hotel in the development, located at the top of the tower. Then there were the cultural, medical, and convention facilities that added to the diversity.
       There's one factor on the business side I should also mention. We could only afford to invest 40% of the project costs, so we had to ask

other investors, like insurance companies and financial institutions, to fund 60%. But since decisions had to be made quickly throughout the project, we needed to create a project structure that would enable us to make decisions without consulting our investors. From our numerous experiences, we knew that everybody involved would want to have their say, and the endless communication would not only delay decisions but also blunt our creative process. So we set up a system whereby we asked our investors to not participate in the project development, but rather be kept abreast of every aspect of the process via status reports. This meant that we were accountable for every aspect of our decision-making.

●   Right. So, retail is 10% of all the programs. When you were developing the brief from the client perspective, did you have a rough allocation of percentages for different functions, from retail to residences to offices to culture programs?

●   Yes, the program ended up being 58% offices, 19% residential, 10% commercial, 8% hotel, and 4% cultural.

○   KAYOKO OTA: Regarding retail, the lineup of shops in Tokyo Midtown is more accessible price-wise than those in other large-scale developments such as Marunouchi or Roppongi Hills, where you see top-brand lines. What was the strategy in terms of target customers?

●   Indeed, the project team aimed for the affordable and down-to-earth yet sophisticated and edgy kind of shops. I think our sales people did a good job.

Architecture

●   Now I'd like to ask you about the architecture. On the one hand there is, as you know, the philosophy of SOM and the kind of thing that they do. On the other hand, there is Mitsui Fudosan's own company tradition for architecture. I'm wondering whether you had some specific ideas in mind for the architecture, and how the exchange evolved between the client and the architect.

●   As I mentioned, we had the concept of "diversity on the green" from the very beginning. There was no particularly Japanese quality to that from the outset, but SOM strongly recommended in their RFP that this project have a more Japanese slant. So, in addition to our original concept, another concept was brought in. Subsequently, the exchanges

2

The suite of high-rise buildings designed by SOM, Tokyo Midtown. Photo © iStock.com/ gyro

between us and SOM were ongoing throughout the design period. But I would say the SOM's influence as master architect brought a significant difference to the project.

● Their influence is present in the volumetrics and the relationship of the elements and the participants, as well as in the specific qualities of the architecture and the materials. SOM, as a design firm, spent a lot of time working on the facade, especially with the towers. Historically, you could say that when they're modern towers, they are designed as cladding or as some form of combination between structure and cladding. But in the case of Tokyo Midtown, a lot of attention was given to what I call "filigree." There are a lot of horizontal lines on the surface of the glass that create a certain affect, a certain quality (FIG. 2).

So, it's not only about the volume but also about the textures, almost like a textile. And the eaves opened up. I'm wondering what you thought about that. Was there a lot of support for them working on the facades to that level of detail, with so much attention to surfaces?

● Yes, they did a great job on that, and it went beyond our expectations. Also, it made sense that they took advantage of the shadow restrictions. In order to maximize floor plates within the restricted shadows that we cast, the corners of the building had to be cut off. SOM cleverly designed the facades as if there were layers of weightless lattice claddings rather than a solid chunk of volume cut off (FIG. 3). The building began to look slender and lighter and not overwhelming, offsetting one of our big concerns about its tremendous volume. This was integrated into woven patterns that reference Japanese textiles. As the building goes higher up, the windows open up, and then it blends into the sky.

There are different strategies for each of the four facades. The design takes into consideration minimizing the solar gain in the offices in the directions they face: the most horizontal fins are on the south side, there are more vertical fins on the east and the west sides, and there is more glazing on the north side, while all four share a woven pattern.

If it hadn't been for SOM's great efforts and insight, we might not have invested so much into the tower, since our original intention was to develop the base of the building more richly while keeping the higher section simple. There were discussions within the team along the line of, "Who cares about the upper tower? After completion everybody will be looking at the base, the retail area, and the landscape."

● Which is not true, because Tokyo Midtown is visible from very far away.

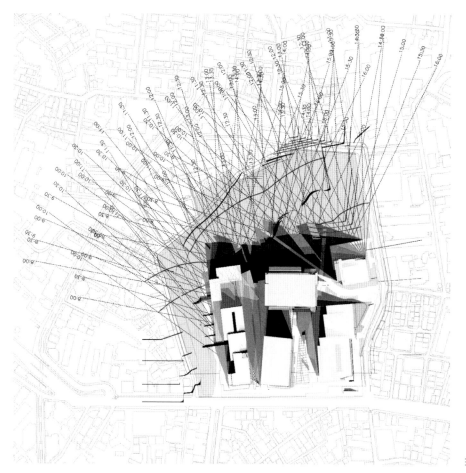

3

●   Yes, I'm glad that we kept the proposed design, because it stands up elegantly even from kilometers away.

●   So you were happy with them involving elements of Japanese culture. I know that you traveled with Communication Arts, the retail architects, to different parts of Japan to look at precedents or inspirations for the project.

●   Ever since SOM introduced Japanese elements into the design, we wanted to use the aesthetics of Zen for the retail area. The project's focus shifted from townscaping to architecture, and the galleria (atrium) design developed. The retail design settled into what we have now, which I think is a good contemporary interpretation of traditional Japanese design.

Diversity

●   You mentioned the word "townscape." How is the word used within Mitsui Fudosan? I'm asking because when you use "townscape," I assume that the idea is to produce an image that communicates with the user. Which brings us to another issue about the audience for Mitsui Fudosan.
    Whether it's Tokyo Midtown or Roppongi Hills, the users of the project generally have to be quite wealthy, perhaps apart from those people who are using the retail facilities. I'm wondering whether you see it as a possibility that large-scale developers in Japan could, in future, afford to or might be interested in creating developments that combine different sectors of society or people with different incomes. Is that something that you think is possible in Japan? You also mentioned the phrase "diversity on the green," but what about actually having a genuine diversity of inhabitants? Would such a thing be possible financially with these kinds of projects?

●   To be honest, very unlikely. That is because Mitsui Fudosan like other developers is a private enterprise that has stakeholders who expect it to maximize revenues.
    I know that New York City, for example, has a regulation that designates a certain proportion of residential development to affordable housing. I think it's a very good system. Firefighters can afford housing in Manhattan. I worked for Mitsui Fudosan in New York for a short period of time to help out with the projects 55 Hudson Yard and 50 Hudson Yard (the latter is currently under construction). At that time, they were also developing residential buildings in which a portion of the apartments were allocated to affordable housing as per requirements,

but the project still looked great. If we were asked to incorporate such a program in a level playing field, we would be more than happy to do so. But this is not currently the case in Japan. Essentially, we need to maximize the revenue for our company as well as for our stakeholders.

●   It's also unlikely that the municipal government would do that, right? Because they probably feel the pressure from large-scale development companies.

●   I don't see why the New York City system can't happen in Japan or Tokyo; if such a system were set up in Japan, Mitsui Fudosan would probably be willing to accommodate it.

●   That's great to hear.

○   Did the government of Tokyo have any say or control over this develop-ment project, especially in terms of accessibility to the site in relation to the residential neighborhood or the public park on the site?

●   They didn't get too involved in the planning or in how to design the site. Obviously, they were most concerned with how Hinokicho Park would be incorporated into the development. Since our concept was to be very open, and we tried to preserve the rich greenery and as many existing trees as possible, nobody was against the idea of opening up the complex to the public or the idea of placing as much retail along the street as possible.

○   The Tokyo Midtown development was one of the Urban Renaissance projects propelled by the local and the national governments.[1] Did the designation affect the project in any way, for example, in terms of planning or execution?

●   Indeed, the project was designated as a special zone for development by the national government. The greatest difference that the des-ignation made was that official approvals were expedited. That's one of the reasons that this project took only five and a half years from start to completion, including the two and a half before start-ing construction.

---

[1]   "Urban Renaissance" is an economic booster program sponsored by the Japanese government that grants FAR bonuses and other incentives to private investors.

Learning for the Future

● As our final topic, I'd like to ask you about the takeaways that have since been applied to other projects. What were the key lessons learned here?

● I would say, for one, a firm conviction about the scale of impact that a mixed-use development of this size has on a city. Another is the experience of collaborating with architects and designers who work globally in order to achieve this. It was a learning process for us to execute such a development.

● But in the new projects that Mitsui Fudosan executed after Tokyo Midtown, there is more retail, as in Coredo Muromachi in Nihonbashi, no? Proportionally, it's primarily a retail project, and the idea of the street seems really all shopping, whereas Tokyo Midtown does seem to be like a miniature city with a park, housing, and retail. So on the one hand, you could say the Nihonbashi project fits more into the streetscape because it's all shops and retail. On the other hand, is it not that the company achieved what it wanted, which was more retail? Is the company pushing for more large-scale retail development overall because that produces more income, or is that an unfair assessment?

● I think that both types are in line with what Mitsui Fudosan is aiming for, and the difference comes from the existing urban contexts. Generally speaking, we get lower returns from retail. Producing offices would be the most straightforward way to maximize revenues. But we think that would not enhance the neighborhood in the long term. We need to create an attractive townscape, not just by design but also by content, so that visitors will flow into the area. With this approach, at the end of the day those neighbors who typically oppose new construction will welcome our development and want to be next door to it. In the end, the value of our building and the whole neighborhood will go up, which will create the virtuous spiral of improving the business environment. If we just produced offices, that would never happen.

● So what is the percentage of offices in Nihonbashi compared to Tokyo Midtown?

● 70% in Nihonbashi, versus 60% in Tokyo Midtown. The retail ratio of Tokyo Midtown was lower due to restrictions, and that project allocated a substantial portion to residential, accommodation, and cultural facilities as a way of achieving diversity.

●   So it's more visible.

●   Right.

●   What are you looking forward to doing in terms of future projects? If it were up to you, what kind of projects would you like to see? Is there a different kind of development that you would like to do?

●   I would be very much interested in getting involved in green buildings, more energy-efficient buildings. With Tokyo Midtown, we made a significant step in this direction. I was involved in the energy aspect of the project, and Tokyo Midtown is one of the most energy-efficient projects of Mitsui Fudosan's. So to answer your question, I would be interested in pushing sustainability as far as possible, without sacrificing the competitiveness of the project or its positive effect on the townscape. It will be an interesting challenge.

●   So, sustainable development. Would that be buildings as well as the whole infrastructure of development—how it's built, the subway system, the kinds of materials, all of these things?

●   Well, we are unable to go into infrastructure. It's a different field, a different sector.

●   Yes, in reality, I understand. But based on what you're saying, it seems that it would be a good thing for large-scale developers and the city to collaborate on the future of certain areas or neighborhoods so that the whole question of the relationship between infrastructure and development is something that's part and parcel of a more cohesive, integrated form of thinking. Don't you agree?
      When we were studying the history of Tokyo, we saw how much the city did during the 1964 Olympics. It was phenomenal how much was achieved during a very short period of time. So, I assume that if there's a will, the government has the know-how and the expertise to make things happen. Somehow, that could happen with the inspiration of large-scale development companies as well. Who knows?

●   Well, it would be great if that happens, yes.

●   It might be a nice thing.

○   Currently, large-scale developments are under way in many parts of central Tokyo. At the same time, a new awareness of social inclusiveness is emerging in the society. Do you think there is a new awareness on the side of the developer for making the sense of inclusiveness visible, or an intention to conceive of development in a more inclusive manner, so that not only shoppers and office workers but also the neighbors and the public at large can share in the benefits of the new developments?

●   In every aspect of its projects, Mitsui Fudosan is trying to push forward the notion of social inclusiveness. For example, most of the time our large-scale development projects start with a town management program that we call "area management." This aims to revitalize the whole neighborhood in collaboration with neighbors, as we think it's important to have our projects help the entire society around it mature and the quality of life improve. That's one way of making our work "inclusive." After all, I think our long-standing principle of making our built environment "improve by aging," reversing the common notion that buildings "degrade by aging," is at the basis of these efforts.

TOKYO MIDTOWN: THE DRIVER FOR URBANISM

● CONVERSATION II WITH MUSTAFA K. ABADAN

1

1   SOM, Time Warner Center (later renamed
Deutsche Bank Center), New York City,
2004. Photo © James Ewing | OTTO,
Courtesy of SOM

●   MOHSEN MOSTAFAVI: SOM has a history of designing large-scale developments in metropolitan areas, for which David Childs has played an important role in precedent setting. And you, Mustafa, have created a large, diverse body of work across different scales at SOM. It would be exciting to understand what approach or body of knowledge David brought to the Tokyo Midtown project, and how you two collaborated on it. First, did you know why SOM was invited to the project competition?

●   MUSTAFA K. ABADAN: Throughout my career at SOM, David Childs was an invaluable mentor and guide. Over time our work together evolved from my working for him to working with him, and then ultimately to our working side by side. The Tokyo Midtown project came into being just around the time of transition of when David and I became colleagues and collaborators.

    One of the primary reasons we were invited to this competition was the positive reputation of the Time Warner Center (FIG. 1) [currently Deutsche Bank Center] in New York. Among the challenges of the TWC were about seven different programs in the building, all stacked on top of each other, which made it extremely complicated to resolve each for maximum efficiency and functionality.

    We learned many lessons from the Time Warner Center that we thought were quite applicable to the Tokyo Midtown project. For example, during the process of the competition we advised the prospective client, Mitsui Fudosan, that it would perhaps be better to be more selective about how many uses one stacked in a single building. The site was large enough to allow that to happen, and indeed ultimately that is how the project finally developed.

●   Was your involvement with Tokyo Midtown your first project there?

●   Yes, the Tokyo Midtown competition was my first serious involvement in a project in Japan. Although previously I had a small role in a project in Tokyo, I did not have a chance to travel to Japan at that time to appreciate the cultural and aesthetic beauty of the country.

●   Do you remember your first impression when you learned what Mitsui Fudosan wanted to do in terms of the program? Was there something different about it as a large-scale mixed-use development?

●   My first reaction was: "What an amazing opportunity... to reintegrate a site that had been carved out of the city fabric for decades in one of the most dynamic cities of the world."[1]

●   I heard that Mitsui Fudosan had also hired Dentsu, the advertising and public relations company, to do some program brief development. I'm curious to know if there was anything in terms of what the client wanted that was different than other precedents that you had in mind.

●   I wasn't aware of Dentsu's involvement, but what Mitsui Fudosan tried to do on the site, programmatically, was create a level of richness both from a commercial and cultural perspective, as well as focus on the inclusion of as many 24/7 activities as possible on the site, so that the new development didn't feel disconnected from the rest of Roppongi and Akasaka.

    Roppongi is a very lively neighborhood. A day there starts in the morning and goes all the way into the wee hours of the night. Part of the programming that Mitsui Fudosan suggested was the creation of many different venues that would fill out that broad time frame. For instance, at a later stage of the project, they began to realize how much value "Jazz at Lincoln Center" brought to the Time Warner Center, and so a small performance venue was added at the very end of the retail galleria, overlooking the park.

    The program evolved throughout the project, so it was never completely fixed, and we continued to develop it to create the rich experience that was desired.

●   So what do you think were the key differences between Tokyo Midtown, Time Warner, and, on the other hand, Roppongi Hills, which was a slightly earlier project [designed by KPF, another American design firm]? In Roppongi Hills, you had a Japanese precedent; in Time Warner, you had worked on a US version. Were there any key differences, either from your perspective or from the client's perspective, saying, "We want this to be different than this project or that project"?

●   When we began to do our research and study of Tokyo, we noticed that many of the newer developments that were being done in Tokyo at that time tended to be these isolated urban islands. A lot of the redevelopment sites were being assembled by the developers and almost all felt disengaged in some way or another from the city life.

    There were many reasons for that. There were sectional issues that were creating some of this disconnect, such as at Roppongi Hills, where the ground plane was predominantly left to the vehicles, and as a result the public space was elevated. That created a natural disconnect between the street life and the buildings themselves.

    Another aspect that was apparent, particularly in the Roppongi Hills project, was that the buildings were conceived as individual elements and not necessarily thought of as a collective that could work together. One building was designed by one architect with their own aesthetic; another building was designed by another architect with their own aesthetic. And the Mori company, I'm sure, made sure that there was some functional cohesion, but aesthetically it was hard to see a harmonious collection of buildings.

So, when it came to Tokyo Midtown, we had the opportunity as a master architect to extend our thinking across the whole site, and we established what we called the "aesthetic DNA" that allowed the seven architects, including Jun Aoki, Kengo Kuma, Sakakura, Tadao Ando, Nikken Sekkei, and Communication Arts, who did the retail, to share a common design approach. This allowed each design architect to bring their own ideas to the project, yet we were able to create a level of unity and cohesion lacking in other similar projects.

Rock garden strategy

● Let's move on to the design of the master plan. I'm wondering whether the client informed you as to why you won the competition. What do you think was the main difference between your project and what Pelli, your competitor for the project, did?

● No, we were never formally informed why we won the competition. But as far as I can assume, I think the differentiator was our idea of metaphorically linking the massing of the development to the concept of objects in a Zen garden. The fundamental idea of the three objects or rocks harmoniously arranged in space resonated with the competition jury.

● That's an interesting observation. The client, Mitsui Fudosan, is a very big developer dealing with numbers and making things work financially. In the end, however, they liked how you linked their project to Japanese cultural philosophy and the history of the Japanese garden. I also noticed that in the book about Tokyo Midtown the idea of the rocks is strongly presented as a concept reference.

● Yes, that was what made sense to us. This was the largest open site in Tokyo that was going to be transformed. If you're going to transform a site like that, you need to have some level of understanding of and

I   The site of the Tokyo Midtown project had been a military enclave in the middle of Tokyo, off limits to the general public, since the Second World War.

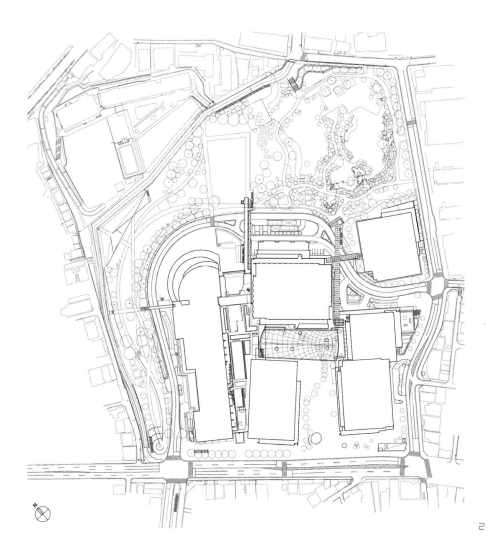

2 | SOM (master planner and architect), Tokyo
Midtown, 2007. Roof plan of the entire
complex. Drawing © SOM

respect for the place. In Japan, they've been able to do incredibly powerful things in the smallest of spaces. So why not attempt to do something powerful like that on this precious site? It was probably one of
the few times during my career when a metaphor like that really
made sense.

●   Maybe we can talk briefly about the shifts that were occurring in your
own master plans. In terms of the urban design concept, is the shift from
a slightly looser fit to this more orthogonal composition something that the
client asked for? That is, the change in the grouping or the way the projects were
clustered. I'm just trying to understand, on reflection, how you analyzed the
changes that happened and what you ended up with as a final set of structures.

●   It was much more about compliance with the client's requirements
and modifying the scheme accordingly. But even though we made the
scheme a lot more rational and thus somewhat orthogonal, we didn't
put it on a pure grid as we would have done in New York City. We let
the buildings be slightly skewed; again, this was in reference to the
organic way that the city of Tokyo developed over time. Due to topography or rural development patterns, in many neighborhoods of Tokyo
generally most buildings are set askew with regard to one another and
never truly aligned. We tried to retain that feeling even in the semi-
orthogonal version of our final plan (FIG. 2).

●   I see. Do you not think that there's a tendency now toward large-scale
developments that follow the alignment of existing streets, and that this
notion of an entity, a kind of cluster, is maybe harder to do as a total ensemble?
And the latest approach is to melt the development into the existing street
fabric rather than to think about the integrated totality?

●   I think that's more a result of the challenges of assembling sites, meaning that developers can assemble sites at a more reasonable scale
because these redevelopment projects in Tokyo basically happen through
a semi-voluntary version of imminent domain. In essence, the local
municipal government strongly encourages developers and small landowners to assemble strategic sites within the city. This allows for
a greater level of density, which is more appropriate for newly developing business districts.
   So, I think your observation is right that in the sense that these
larger groupings of buildings are less prevalent right now, which probably has something to do with the cyclical nature of investments in
large-scale developments. But also my guess would be that it's because

of the lack of existence of large sites and the difficulty of assembling sites with multiple owners.

Prioritizing the street-ness

●   I'd like to talk about the high-rise building and the interaction between it and the other spaces: the offices, retail areas, and the hotel. What was the nature of the high-rise building's relationship with the retail spaces, and what were some of the things you were asked to do in order to make the buildings competitive as a high-rise?

For example, when KPF built the Roppongi Hills high-rise, they collaborated with Jerdi on the retail spaces. What you would say are the differences between how KPF worked with Jerdi, the way that Jerdi designed the retail spaces, and the offices-to-retail relationship that SOM tried to establish?

●   Unlike in other developments, the retail within Tokyo Midtown is not the biggest driver of the master plan. The retail is there to enhance the experience and attract people there during the day and evenings. But having said that, the way that the retail is organized does have a linear aspect to it, which is unusual.

Most retail spaces try to create either a bipolar connectivity, or, in other words, a dumbbell kind of organization; that is, when you look at the flow of people through the spaces in the galleria, one will see large anchor stores as destinations at either end. In the case of Tokyo Midtown, however, the visitor enters from the street and meanders through the galleria until arriving at the park. It's conceived much more like a traditional, meandering commercial street in old Tokyo.

That's how I think this project was distinct from what KPF and Jerdi would have done, which would have been to create a more typical, mall-like shopping environment. This was trying to be less formal and much more of a contemporary interpretation of an authentic Japanese main street.

●   So, both SOM and the client wanted the project to be more accessible and more open to the street. The street plays a very large role in your project, opening it up and making it much more accessible. For example, there seems to be a direct link between the streets and the garden with the building elements in between.

●   Active street life is the essence of our cities, that is what makes them so desirable. Therefore, in these large-scale urban interventions,

engagement with the public at every touch point with the public realm
is critical in creating attractive environments. At Tokyo Midtown,
not only did we try to have a positive impact to the streets surrounding
the site, but we also very consciously tried to bring the pedestrian
activity deep into the site both through public plazas and parks as well
as through the porosity of the buildings themselves.

●   And by the time you were doing the final iteration of the master plan,
presumably you already had EDAW [landscape architects] and the other
participants involved?

●   Yes. From the very beginning of the project we engaged all the consultants. EDAW was quite helpful in mitigating the scale and bringing
a degree of human scale to the open space. While the buildings are big
and tall, the public realm needed to feel intimate. The retail consultants Communication Arts brought their knowledge of how to organize
retail environments for Japanese customers to the project. We were in
constant dialogue, building upon each other's expertise and ideas to
integrate all these inputs.
     In other parts of the world, we could have most likely designed
monumental bases to the office towers. But here, Mitsui Fudosan
wanted the scale to be much more fine-grained and human-centric.
As one can see now, the shop fronts, building entrances, and canopies
were all designed with that scale in mind.

●   That's great.

Merging and distancing

●   When you look at the open space on the site, you notice that the building elements are placed along the street edge, with the park and a garden
behind them.

●   You asked me earlier about my first impression of this project and
whether there was something different about it than other large-scale
mixed-use developments. What I thought was intriguing about this
project was that it was not just about a collection of buildings; it was
equally focused on creating cultural resonance, a sense of place,
and public interaction. Integrating all those private and public elements was a fantastic design opportunity.

●   Was it clear from the beginning that a significant portion of the site would be the park?

●   Yes, the park was preordained by the city government. To be precise, there was a municipal park in one of the corners of the site that had to be retained for public use. It was part of the negotiation with the city, the Akasaka neighborhood, and the developer. The negotiations had been carried out by Nikken Sekkei for at least a year and a half before the competition even started. We worked with our own landscape consultants to integrate the open space within the project site and the municipal park, which also works as a buffer to the residential neighborhood, into a one holistic open space.

The built structures within the park are mostly located in one corner of the site, closer to the more commercial activities in Roppongi, so as not to interfere with the accessibility of the adjacent residential neighborhoods.

●   Was that deliberate in terms of the pressures of adjacent neighborhoods? Was there, for example, any conversation in which you realized that the park would be the buffer on one side as opposed to the other?

●   There were sensitivities involved in creating a proper buffer so that the residential character of those areas would not be disturbed by the development, while at the same time, the project at large could still add some positive attributes to the neighborhood. So, part of the park space that's today Tokyo Midtown is truly public, and the other part is technically private. However, they're designed in such a way that there's a seamless integration between the two, and it's difficult to determine the exact boundary. That's how the neighborhood, all in all, benefited not only by being able to revitalize the existing park, but also by having it extended into the Tokyo Midtown site.

Diversity

●   Perhaps this is a little bit unfair to ask you, but the developments like Tokyo Midtown and Roppongi Hills are very exclusive developments. They're really intended for one particular sector of society. At the level of public space and the garden, one of the things that's very important about Tokyo Midtown is that it's open to the public and it's inviting, and it enables people to essentially move through most parts of the project even though it's a privatized public space.

But I'm wondering whether you think it would be possible to conceive of versions of urban development which might include, for example, residential components that would be potentially more affordable and would not only be intended for a very small sector of society? In terms of our research, it's interesting to see if there is a way that one can conceive of the future of the city for a more inclusive society or for a more inclusive Tokyo. What are your thoughts about the question of urban design?

●   You mean diversity…

●   Yes, diversity, essentially, so that people can basically live next to each other.

●   You're touching upon a very important point. There's clearly a desire for our cities to be diverse and not be separated economically or culturally. But I think this can only really be implemented when it comes through a public policy. In New York City now, there are requirements for inclusive housing. And there are arguments about whether it should be ten, fifteen, or twenty percent of affordable housing that's integrated into any kind of large-scale development. That's an attempt to begin to create a little bit of what you're describing. But ten or fifteen percent of affordable housing incorporated into a complex where only billionaires live may also not be the ideal solution—it has the potential of creating different issues of coexistence that may or may not result in desirable outcomes.

     But I think public policy is something that we need to think about as we develop our cities. There's a lot of need, as well as a desire, to have public policies that begin to address some level of built-in diversity and desired coexistence. It may not necessarily happen on every site, but maybe a level of diversity will be built into a neighborhood scale, and that can come through zoning and other regulatory mandates. We, as a society, need to share responsibility in shaping the future of our cities and strive for a more just and diverse makeup of our urban environments. But if left up to the development community, it's likely not going to happen by itself, because when finances are the primary drivers, we all know where that leads. For better or worse, these luxury residential units are the most profitable part of these mixed-use projects.

●   That's great. I also wonder what your thoughts are about the future of firms like SOM and high-rise building; obviously that's where your expertise lies, and people appreciate its iconicity.

I'm curious whether you think, architecturally, there are other ways that you could go. For example, you worked with David on the much smaller-scale Checkpoint Charlie project in Berlin.

● Yes, in Berlin at Check Point Charlie we worked at scale of six- and seven-story buildings, where we created a collection of buildings that were commercial, cultural, and residential, all within a singular complex. That mixed-use approach wasn't common in Germany at the time. While it unfortunately didn't get built then, it served to introduce a new approach to other projects in Germany, as seen in projects at Potsdamer Platz, for instance.

● Which year did the Berlin project take place?

● 1991.

● In Berlin, the idea of the urban block was the focus: buildings that were six and seven stories tall with courtyards, and so on. Typologically, is there some other way that SOM could think about developing large-scale urban projects that are not towers?

● Clearly not everything has to be high-rise. But often it comes down to the economics that drive these projects to be large-scale and tall in order to make them financially viable. I think the nature of scale in development is dependent on the availability of affordable sites and finding the right developers.

● Maybe this is not a fair thing to ask, but what are the lessons of Tokyo Midtown in terms of the future of mixed-use development? I noticed that Mitsui Fudosan hasn't done anything similar to this, partly, I assume, because this was a very unique site.

● In terms of lessons learned, one can say that the successes of these large-scale interventions in cities depends on their ability to engage and enhance the urban environments. For instance, Rockefeller Center in New York is a great example of a harmonious balance between large-scale development and a series of wonderfully rich public spaces, cultural venues, and commercial uses. Similarly, Time Warner Center, with its public grand atrium and cultural institutions, shopping arcades, hotel, and residential towers has completely revitalized a once undervalued corner of Central Park. Each of these examples has built upon the positive outcomes of previous examples. So, in that sense, Tokyo

Midtown naturally followed that pattern; however, the sheer scale of the site and the urban guidelines that were established with stakeholders provided an opportunity like no other. The finished project has been recognized in Asia as one of the most successful integrations of public and private interests, drawing a record number of visitors each year.

Looking into the future, these types of large-scale mixed-use developments built with clear public benefits in mind continue to have great potential to enhance our urban environments, as long as they consciously turn outward as much as they turn inward.

3

Tokyo Midtown viewed from the main street. Photo © iStock.com/y-studio

EVALUATING DEVELOPMENT PROJECTS IN THE LONG TERM

● JOUJI KURUMADO

Who actually creates a city? By understanding the driving forces behind the making of cities today, we can predict our own city's trajectory and ask whether it is a direction that reflects the will of its residents.

In a business mega-district like central Tokyo, nearly all the development projects are corporate undertakings. This produces a distinctly different set of circumstances from the suburbs, which consist largely of housing built by individuals. The objective of a corporation is not the contentment offered by a private residence, but the pursuit of economic profit.

It is apparent that urban development projects in Japan share a certain standard configuration. Most of them consist of a multi-story office tower with shops, eateries, and other commercial establishments filling the bottom floors. This is true outside of Japan as well. The purpose of this configuration is to maximize selling prices and minimize costs—in other words, such projects are a form of economic activity. Of course, the quality of an urban space is judged not in terms of individual development projects, but in terms of their aggregate real estate value. However, the ultimate purpose of each project is corporate profit, the pursuit of which is a self-propelling mechanism that moves forward unchallenged.

Is it such a good thing to entrust urban development to economic activity of this sort? Is there not a disconnect between the city as we should envision it and the type of city that emerges as a result of such economic activity? If there is, how might we resolve this contradiction?

Development Confined to a Site

The projects that constitute the greater part of redevelopment in central Tokyo—primarily office buildings with retail shops and other commercial functions added on—are carefully designed with an eye to maximizing profits as soon as they are completed. Those profits derive from tenant rents and the interest from securitizing the development as an asset. To increase rental income, buildings are designed with a minimal core to accommodate large, regularly shaped, column-free universal office spaces with flexible layouts; they also attract tenants by adding restaurants and other urban facility enhancements.

Because the designers of a project can have free rein only within the boundaries of the building site, priority is given to maximum utilization of the site, which generally entails wiping away every last vestige of the lot's previous relationship to the surrounding urban context. Moreover, the building's facade is designed to assert its presence, and therefore must stand out by interrupting the continuity of the cityscape rather than harmonizing with it.

Even under Japan's urban reorganization system (*sogo sekkei seido*), which permits increased building volume in exchange for the provision of

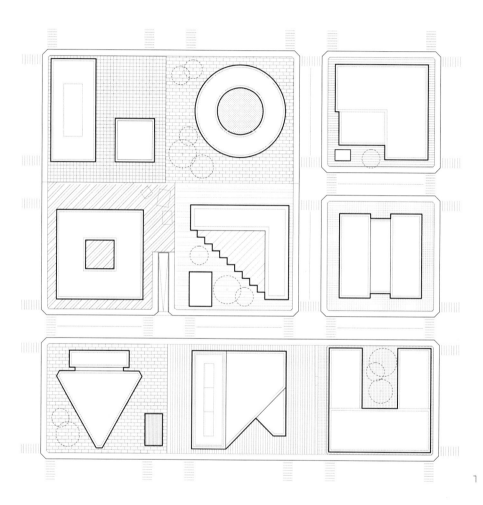

1 The typical open-space situation
in large-scale development.
© Japan Research Initiative

public space or other urban facilities, the usual approach taken by a mixed-use (office and commercial) development project is to set aside public open space in accordance with the rules of the system, expand the building volume as much as allowed, and maximize the rate of return on a tower that occupies that entire volume. The public open space, too, is typically connected with the urban context only by means of the road fronting the site, as stipulated by the rules. Even if the project next door has a large open space, or a park or river or promenade lies only a block away, one rarely (if ever) sees evidence of attempts to link up with them. And even when neighboring redevelopment sites adhere to the same urban reorganization system, the sites' respective open spaces will not necessarily be connected by a pedestrian walk, for example, unless they were all planned at the same time (FIG. 1).

In short, one sees few examples of collaborative efforts to enhance a neighborhood's overall appeal by adding value that will exceed whatever sacrifices are required. That is because each project is concerned exclusively with optimizing its own rate of return, so there is no incentive for neighboring projects to cooperate in any way.

The Urban Profit Mechanism

There is a structural aspect to the conditions that define these urban mixed-use development projects, one that derives from their economic framework. Developers must be able to explain to their investors that the organization of a project is designed to ensure maximum return on their investment. Since the investors are usually not trained architects, such explanations rarely go into details on the project's layout, site conditions, or urban context, focusing instead on the abstract concepts of investment value, development strategy, and return.

Within this abstract investment/return context, arguments for additional outlays to foster a more attractive environment in the area around the site—because it may yield an indeterminate amount of added value in the future—will fall on deaf ears, unless that investment promises a measurable monetary return. The notion is all the less appealing if it entails a reduction in cost performance or building volume. Without knowing when or how neighboring sites may be developed or rebuilt, there is always a risk that factoring them into a project will merely create problems down the line. For example, one might incorporate access to a nearby park only to have a new building erected next door that cuts off that access. In most cases, anyway, an adjacent site is not an ally but a rival in the real estate market.

In the process of converting a concrete architectural plan into a vehicle for profit in a capitalist economy, details that ought to be the purview of architectural design fall by the wayside. The only results recognized by the market are those that generate the maximum return achievable by developing a site to the maximum extent permitted. In this way urban space is transformed into many thin slices of land, with each plot telling a pinched, inwardly focused story set exclusively within its own boundaries. The larger context of which each site is a part is sliced and diced in similar fashion. Most crucially, this process of dissection eradicates the unique qualities and possibilities that give a city its charm.

No doubt those involved in project development of this sort are carrying out their duties in good faith. Many of them may actually attempt to resist the attendant process of decimating a community's appeal. However, the economic system that drives the society we live in—one that seeks profits in the short term relative to the actual lifespan of a city or a building—does not necessarily contribute to the creation of the comfortable, attractive city we ostensibly envision.

The economic value of a project is an abstraction derived from a calculation made in the instant that profit generated by the project, primarily from tenant rent, can be determined. If the project incorporates an approach that increases the value of the city at large, on the other hand, it will take some time before this approach finds reflection in the project's asset value. That is because it may take decades to reach that point. The hoped-for scenario goes like this: a project is created that interacts with attractive elements—a river, a park, a historic site, a view—of its urban context. Other projects follow suit, enhancing the area's overall appeal, drawing more tenants who favor this approach and, in turn, other businesses associated with them. As talented human resources flock to the neighborhood, the vitality of the entire area increases. Therefore, even if a project aims to augment its tenant income with a rise in asset value, its development plan cannot incorporate collaborative strategies with neighboring projects unless the design is understood to offer a return only in the long term.

Suppose, for example, that a developer wants to build a network of pleasant, tree-lined pedestrian walks independent of the district's vehicular road network. Since such a plan necessarily involves other neighboring projects or buildings, all those developers will have to agree to cooperate, of their own volition, out of a shared interest in augmenting the appeal of the area—even if that goal entails some degree of sacrifice on the part of each project.

Is there some method by which we can create a city that a diversity of people will enjoy living in by making its neighborhoods, or the entire city, more attractive to a degree that vastly exceeds the sacrifice required of the developers of individual buildings? Imbuing a neighborhood with its own unique charm should lead to immense benefits by increasing the asset value or competitiveness of the entire area—benefits that will revert back to each project. Conversely, the adoption of this strategy by a few cities around the world could negatively impact the relative appeal of other cities.

Creating Value on a Local Scale

Cities are turning into industrial products. This is of course true to the extent that the buildings that comprise cities are made of highly industrialized parts, much like an automobile. However, these buildings also resemble industrial products in the sense that they are built to perform to the same specifications regardless of what part of the world one might place them in. The standard configuration is what we call universal space: an expanse characterized by uniform lighting and air conditioning, large windows, minimal columns, and no individuality. Most large-scale developments in the world's major cities consist of these universal spaces.

Until recently, a building was thought of as a unique entity, deeply imbued with the character of its location due to the fact that it was not mobile. In this respect buildings stood in contrast to more typical industrial products. Yet the people who use buildings are mobile, as is the capital that flows in and out of every corner of our borderless world. Corporations move, as do their staff if the company is not locally based. The current spread of telework reinforces this trend, since businesses need no longer choose a specific physical location. All in all, there seem to be fewer and fewer reasons to concentrate workplaces in the high-priced cities of developed countries. The upshot is that large-scale developments today have no use for uniqueness in their buildings; all they require are spaces that will provide the same performance and quality regardless of where they are built. In a word, buildings are being commodified—they are becoming industrial products.

In the case of redevelopment in Tokyo in particular, showcasing a building's uniqueness incurs the risk of a "peer pressure" backlash from neighboring projects. Instead, the trend is toward ensuring compatibility through uniformity, just as having the same operating system on everyone's computer permits the sharing of all kinds of applications. Universal spaces further heighten indifference toward a building's context precisely because their objective is a uniform, fully controlled environment. The result is a proliferation of spaces in every city that float, balloon-like, above the greater urban context.

If you line up a number of development projects, each composed of universal spaces that accentuate spatial uniformity in the interest of maximizing the rate of return within the bounds of their site alone, you will get a row of motley yet fundamentally look-alike buildings. Though each one may have certain distinctive elements, the general effect is a sort of noise that drowns out any individuality in the overall cityscape. If, on the other hand, each building is designed to visibly resonate with its neighbors, even through the use of relatively minor elements, it can have the effect of enhancing the distinctive character and hence the appeal of the area at large.

Daizawa, a typical Tokyo residential area in Setagaya Ward, includes a neighborhood that boasts unusually high rents at a level rarely seen that far from the city center. These rents are sustainable simply because 300-*tsubo* (approximately 990 square meters) lots, several times the lot size in surrounding districts, are maintained by local agreement. Elsewhere in Tokyo, the popular Hillside Terrace mixed-use complex in Daikanyama draws passersby at least in part because they can stroll from building to building through a sequence of pilotis and outdoor walkways parallel to the main road. Other developments in the neighborhood have followed the same low-rise, pedestrian-friendly approach, enhancing the "Daikanyama-esque" ambience that has made the district a new go-to destination.

Traces of a city's history, venues for seasonal events, places that figure in well-known stories...these are things found nowhere else, the elements that make a neighborhood unique and give its residents a sense of belonging. Belonging begets attachment, which begets a desire to preserve and promote the special attributes of one's neighborhood. What do people ultimately seek out in their rapidly commodifying cities, if not spaces where they can relax and share in the pleasure of some quality that sets the place apart from the rest of the city? If that is so, such pleasures are at risk if the commodification process continues to fill cities with stereotypical, indistinguishable developments.

When a city loses its distinctive character, it loses its appeal, just as a human personality devoid of any unique characteristics would. The charm of uniqueness is what is lost in development projects that only prioritize the rate of return on sites and towers composed of universal spaces. Such places may well find it increasingly difficult to attract intellectually skilled workers. And in the long term, that can precipitate a decline in a city's competitiveness on the global market—an economic loss that could prove fatal.

The Lifetime Profit of Urban Development

Real estate development generates two types of profit. One is from rent, the other from the property's value as an asset. In addition to rental income, the property may yield massive profits—or losses—over the long term based on the valuation of the entire district, or city, or even country. If a given development project attracts top-flight corporations or workers, other successful businesses seeking synergy will set up shop there, and the business ecosystem of the entire city will thrive. Economic success may then draw global notice, raising the asset value of properties in the city and generating huge profits for everyone.

For investors abroad who are wondering which cities around the world are good candidates for investment in development projects, the future potential of a city vis-à-vis the global market is a major criterion. Conditions are much like those of the stock market, where investors anticipate income not only from annual dividends but also from rising share prices as the value of a corporation grows. Despite the fact that significant increases in corporate business typically take several years, the stock market reacts nimbly to a company's periodic financial statements, rising and falling according to the latest projections of its future value.

A substantial rise in the value of a city inevitably takes longer than that of a corporation. However, if we could analyze a number of indexes, as we do for stocks, we should be able to forecast the fortunes of a city with some degree of certainty. A long-term increase in the estimated value of a city's real estate will without question reflect the growth of its long-term competitiveness. What, then, would such indexes be? In other words, what must we do to improve the value of a city over the long term?

If we could identify these indexes, it would be a step toward nurturing a healthy competition among cities to become places that are truly easy to live and work in. A city that pursues such qualities as character, comfort, friendliness, and sustainability will surely survive in the market of "future potential." If so, what is required of individual development projects for a city to achieve its potential?

As I have already noted, investors are not likely to put their money on the line when the chances of growth in an area's value look ambiguous. To overcome this hurdle and contribute to the creation of a truly attractive city with a critical mass of development projects that are competitive and turn a profit in the long term, each project must engage with the surrounding neighborhood in a collaborative effort to make it a comfortable, charming place to be. This necessitates a plan for increasing profits not only from tenant rent, but also from a project's asset value relative to the global market. Our goal must therefore be the maximization of the long-term, "lifetime" profit represented by the sum total of an area's asset value from its development projects.

To this end, I propose that we attempt to improve the value of cities over the long term by identifying specific indexes to be shared among developers as criteria for each new project's value. If this effort translates into a rise in value on a citywide scale, we can anticipate that investors worldwide will take an interest in more desirable urban designs, and that economic activity will trend toward competition to develop cities that are more comfortable to live in.

MODELS OF AGGREGATION
●   JAPAN RESEARCH INITIATIVE TEAM

In 2003, the prominent development firm Mori Building opened Roppongi Hills, a vast mixed-use complex in central Tokyo. Anchored by the 54-story Mori Tower, the complex includes a kaleidoscopic array of programs: hotel, shopping mall, art museum, observation deck, apartments, and office space for major foreign corporations like Apple and Goldman Sachs. The site was formerly occupied by a complex network of streets and alleyways, lined by more than 400 buildings that Mori Building meticulously acquired over 15 years. This form of wholesale urban transformation is increasingly common in Tokyo today.

Roppongi Hills exemplifies the growing polarization between developer-owned urban enclaves and the heterogeneous urban fabric that surrounds them. Spurred by deregulation and incentives, large-scale redevelopment projects have become the most visible change to the city in recent decades. Similar forces are in action around the globe in projects like Hudson Yards in New York City and Marina Bay Sands in Singapore.

In Tokyo, large-scale urban design initiatives have been the purview of a small cast of characters. In the aftermath of World War II, the government created the Nishi-Shinjuku office district in the western part of the city. In the years since, the private sector has taken the lead. The efforts of each major developer are distinct in character and often concentrated in a particular part of the city. Mitsubishi Estate owns land in one of the oldest areas, where it has preserved and built within the historic street pattern. Tokyu Corporation and other large railway operators own and manage land near their stations to complement their ridership income. Mitsui Fudosan has developed landmark complexes on special sites around the city. Mori Building may at first appear as a more extreme vision of Mitsui's complex-based approach, but it has grander ambitions. More than any other private developer in Tokyo, Mori Building has a comprehensive vision for the city—a future of interconnected towers scattered in a verdant landscape. Some find the images of this new Tokyo appealing, others frightening.

These projects are bolstered by a strong economic and regulatory rationale, but they are also the object of growing public interrogation. As Tokyo's growth slows and Japan's population declines, is this amount of new construction necessary? With the effects of climate change intensifying, can the material costs of demolition and construction be justified? What kind of life is fostered by these new environments? What forms of business, culture, and community do they support? And do these large, purpose-built complexes offer the same flexibility as older forms of urban agglomeration in which individual elements can be reused, renovated, or redeveloped piecemeal?

The drawings that follow analyze the difference in approach between the major Tokyo developers and demonstrate the evolution and impact of megaprojects on the city and its residents' way of life. They examine not only individual buildings but the public spaces and urban connections they frame. The drawings suggest how we might critique, improve, and advance these models of urban development, and how we might search for alternatives.

Public to Private: Expansion of the Sub-Center

The development of the Nishi-Shinjuku office district was initiated by the
Tokyo Metropolitan Government starting in the 1960s. The new office district,
located near the terminus of several important commuter rail lines, marked
the westward shift of the city's financial center of gravity. The district occupies
the site of the former Yodobashi water treatment plant. The pattern of isolated
towers and plazas established there has been advanced by nearby private developments in the intervening years, enveloping much of the surrounding fabric.

Footprint of original
Nishi-Shinjuku district
development

1955

N

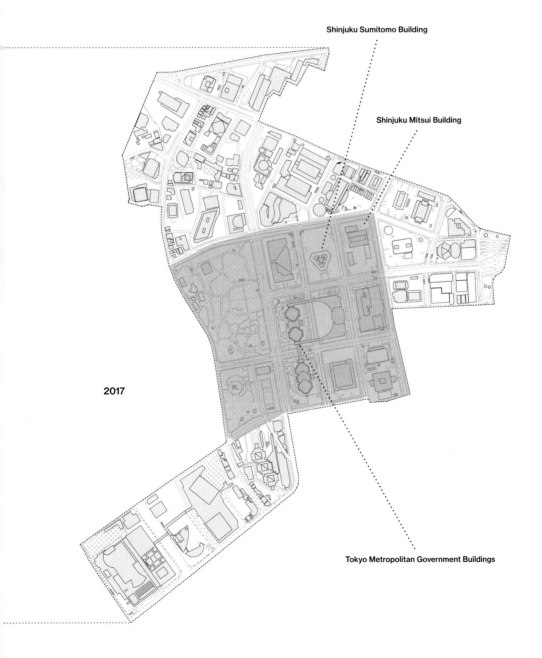

Shinjuku Sumitomo Building

Shinjuku Mitsui Building

2017

Tokyo Metropolitan Government Buildings

Nishi-Shinjuku Office District

Though most commuters travel to Shinjuku by train, the design of the district is governed by cars. Its two-level street system and famous sunken West Exit Plaza (a center of postwar counterculture and public demonstrations), once symbols of national progress, are now anachronisms.

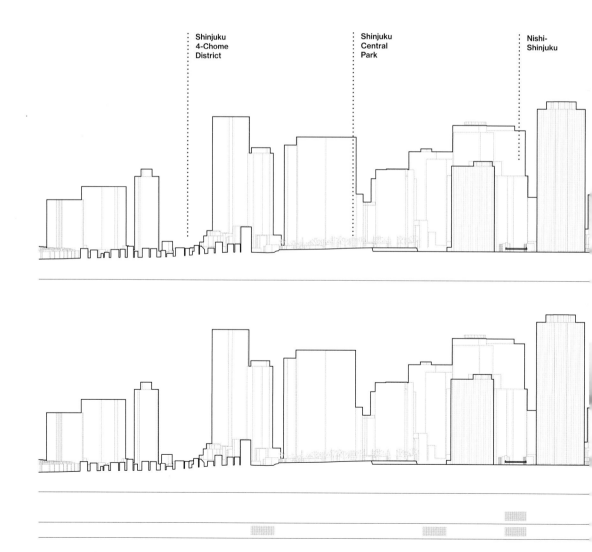

Shinjuku
4-Chome
District

Shinjuku
Central
Park

Nishi-
Shinjuku

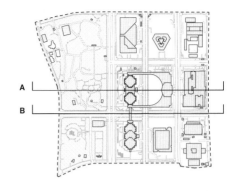

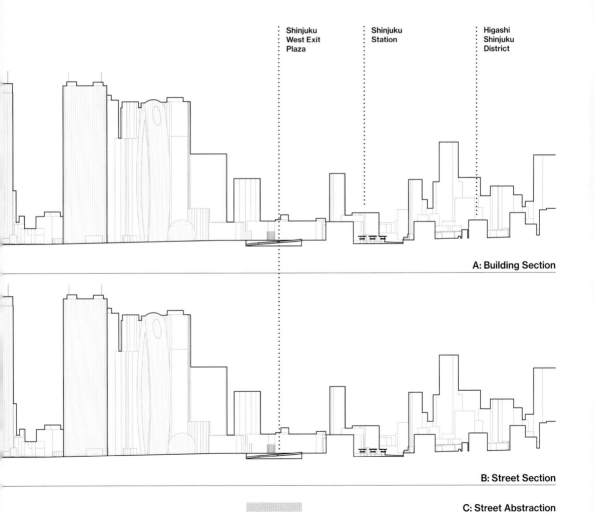

Shinjuku
West Exit
Plaza

Shinjuku
Station

Higashi
Shinjuku
District

A: Building Section

B: Street Section

C: Street Abstraction

Variations on a Theme: Towers in Nishi-Shinjuku

At first glance, the environment around Shinjuku station seems to be polarized between the heterogeneous fabric of the east side and the single-tower blocks of the west. Closer examination reveals important distinctions in how each tower meets the ground. Some, like the Shinjuku Sumitomo Building, are isolated objects in a plaza. Others, like the Shinjuku Mitsui Building, have complex podiums that negotiate the district's woven, two-level street system.

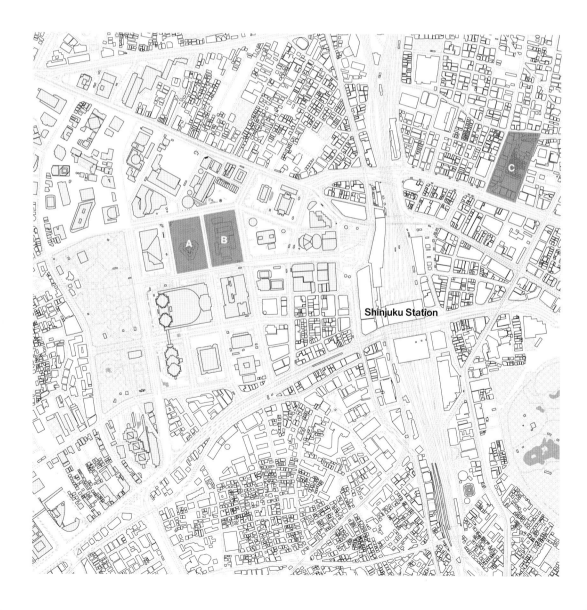

Tower and Plaza

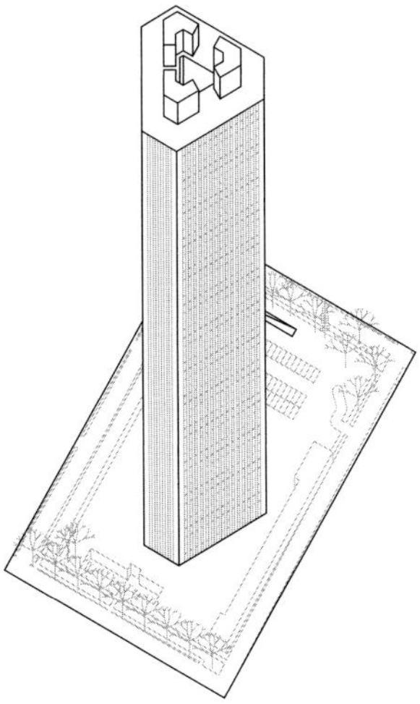

Fragmented Podium

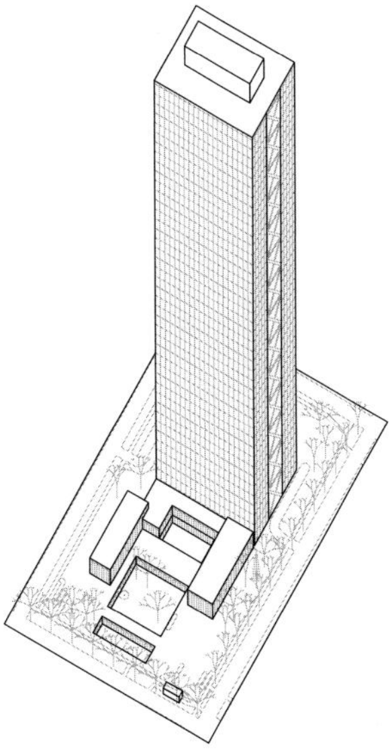

Mixed Fabric

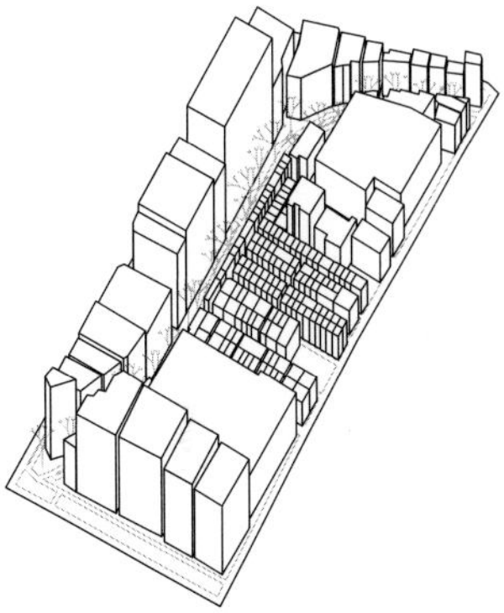

A: Shinjuku Sumitomo Building

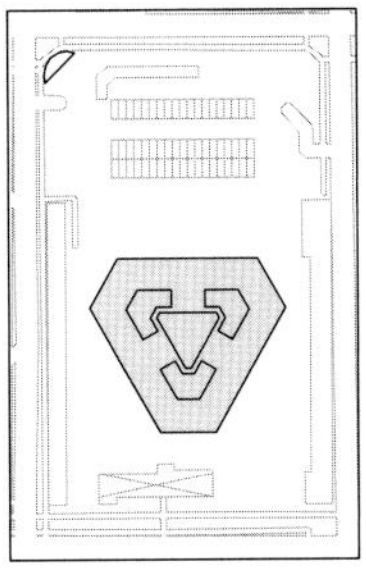

B: Shinjuku Mitsui Building

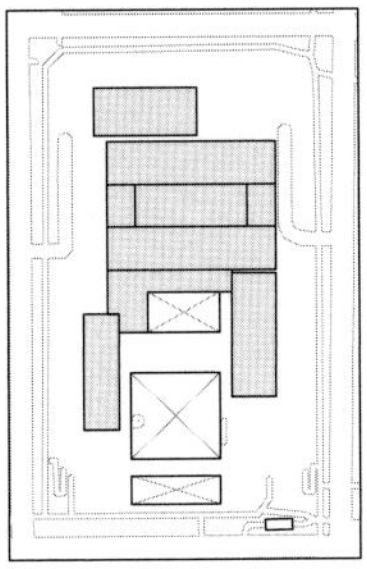

C: Golden Gai

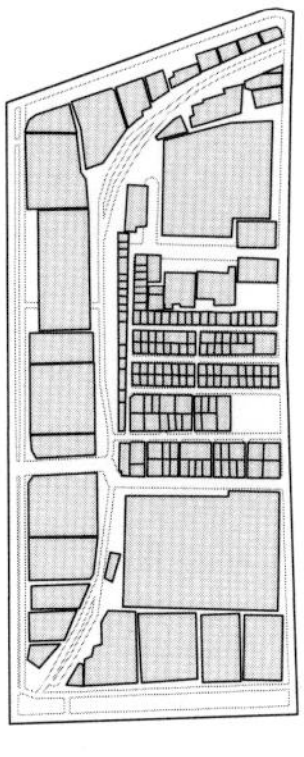

Fragmented Podium: Public Space at the Shinjuku Mitsui Building

The terraced podium of the Shinjuku Mitsui Building is perhaps the most successful urban space in Nishi-Shinjuku. Though many of the plazas in the area are generously scaled, most are only grand entryways for the office tower that they serve. The base of the Mitsui Building is fragmented into small volumes, increasing the interface between the interior commercial spaces and the network of small plazas and courtyards outside. The outdoor spaces are densely planted and have both fixed seating and movable chairs and tables. The main plaza, known as 55 Hiroba, is a regular gathering space for workers in this district and the site of occasional evening events.

A view over 55 Hiroba. Photo © Don O'Keefe

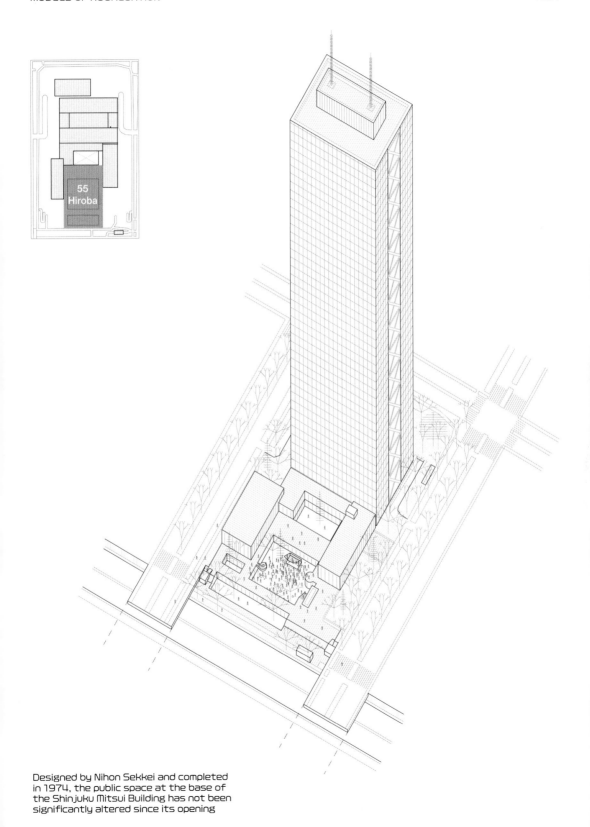

55
Hiroba

Designed by Nihon Sekkei and completed
in 1974, the public space at the base of
the Shinjuku Mitsui Building has not been
significantly altered since its opening

From Plaza to Podium

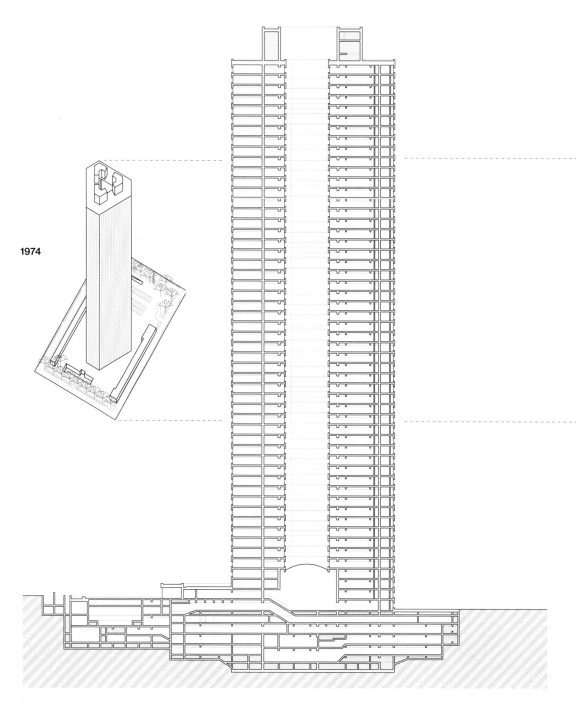

1974

1974: Open-Air Plaza

The Shinjuku Sumitomo Building opened directly next door to the Mitsui Building, which was completed earlier in the same year. At its base was a comparatively severe open-air plaza and surface parking

A   Kita-dori street
B   Triangle Plaza
C   Chuo-dori street

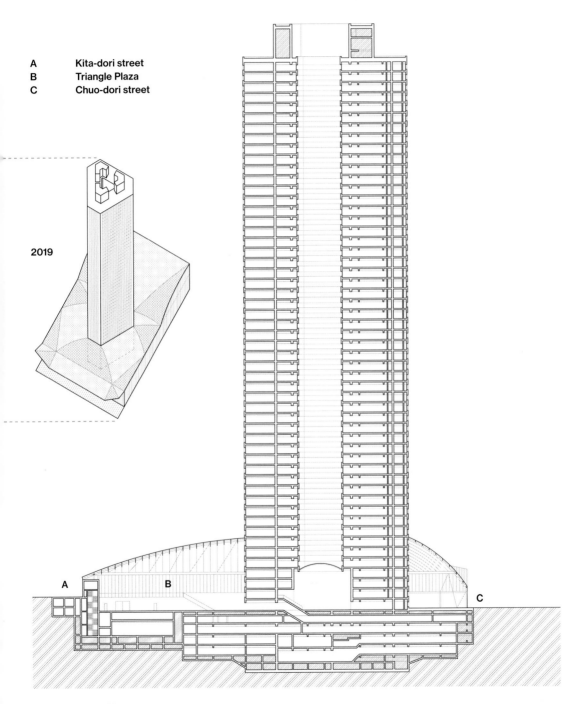

2019

2019: Triangle Plaza

In 2019, after years of disuse, the exterior plaza was enclosed with a glass canopy and renamed Triangle Plaza. The new space contains an indoor restaurant court and event space with a massive electronic display

Revising the Public Realm

With many of its public spaces underused, could the plaza-to-podium con-version pioneered by the Shinjuku Sumitomo Building presage a wider trans-formation of Nishi-Shinjuku? If so, its buildings will increasingly resemble the linked tower-and-podium model of development now popular globally. Enclosing the plazas may make them more useful (and lucrative), but will it also make them less public? Until now, Nishi-Shinjuku has been defined by its open, if sterile, corporate landscape.

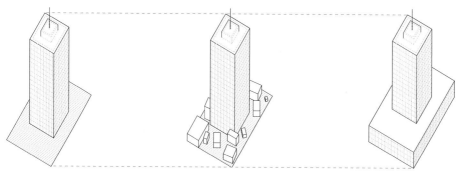

Tower and Plaza   Occupied Plaza   Enclosed Podium

Interior of Shinjuku Sumitomo Building Triangle Plaza. Photo © Don O'Keefe

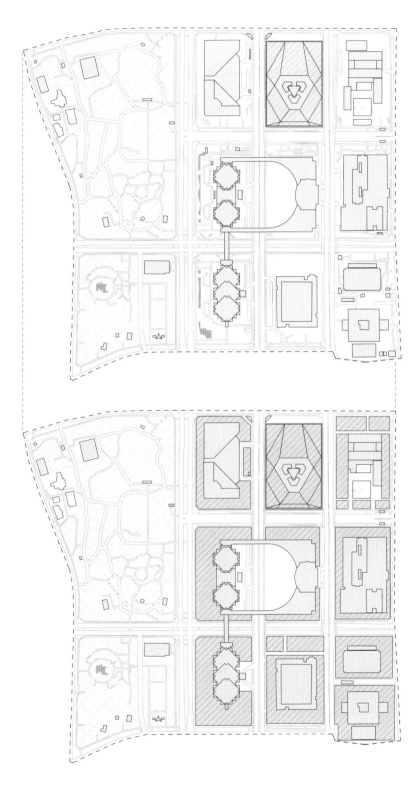

2019

2040?

Nishi-Shinjuku Central Park
Developer: Tokyo Metropolitan Government

Fully public and without direct connection to surrounding towers, Nishi-Shinjuku Central Park is the most open and civic of the spaces profiled here. The park is used casually at all hours and hosts a large weekend flea market.

Flea market at Nishi-Shinjuku Central Park. Photo courtesy of Guilhem Vellut

Naka-dori/Marunouchi Street Park
Developer: Mitsubishi Estate

Naka-dori is an important thoroughfare and pedestrian amenity in the
Marunouchi business district. During the COVID-19 pandemic, Marunouchi
Street Park developed as a temporary outdoor gathering space. It intermit-
tently occupies a closed-down portion of Naka-dori with new furniture
and kiosks, complementing the existing paving, lighting, public art, and tree
canopy. This experiment in tactical urbanism suggests new directions for
Tokyo's post-pandemic public space initiatives.

Marunouchi Street Park taking over the Naka-dori thoroughfare. Photo © Nozomu Ishikawa,
courtesy of Sotonoba

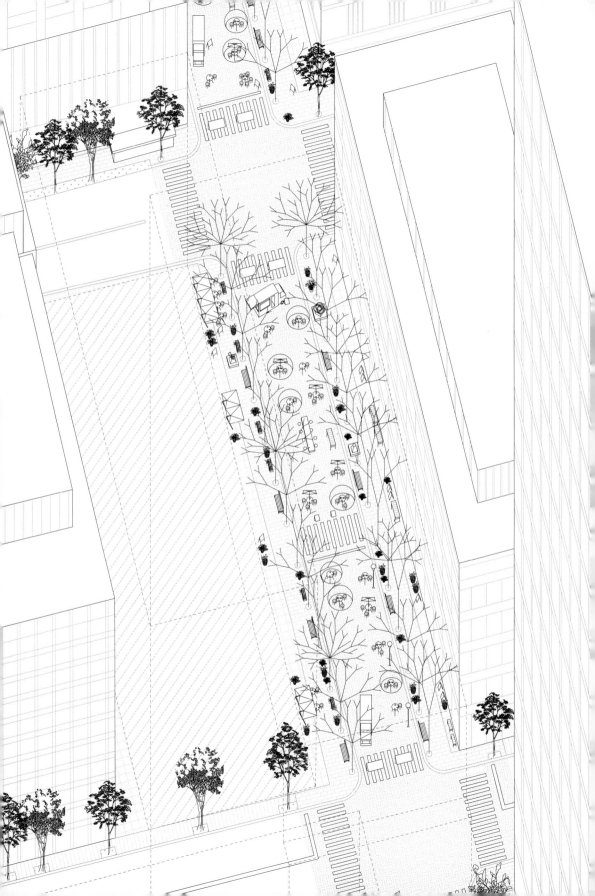

Roppongi Hills
Developer: Mori Building

Landscape and architecture are blended in the podium of Roppongi Hills,
following a pattern typical of Mori Building. Complex layers of shopping
and open space terrace upward from the original ground level and reach over
a large nearby roadway to link with other structures.

Shopping complex at Roppongi Hills. Photo © d. FUKA from Yokohama, Japan, CC BY-SA 2.0

Mori Building Strategic Area

Ark Hills was the first development by Mori Building to articulate founder
Taikichiro Mori's vision of integrating mixed-use towers with a recreational
landscape. Many of the company's recent projects have been sited nearby
in an effort to comprehensively transform this central sector of the city, which
it calls its "strategic area."

Roppongi Hills
1990

Ark Hills
1986

Toranomon Hills
2022

Toranomon-
Azabudai Project
2023

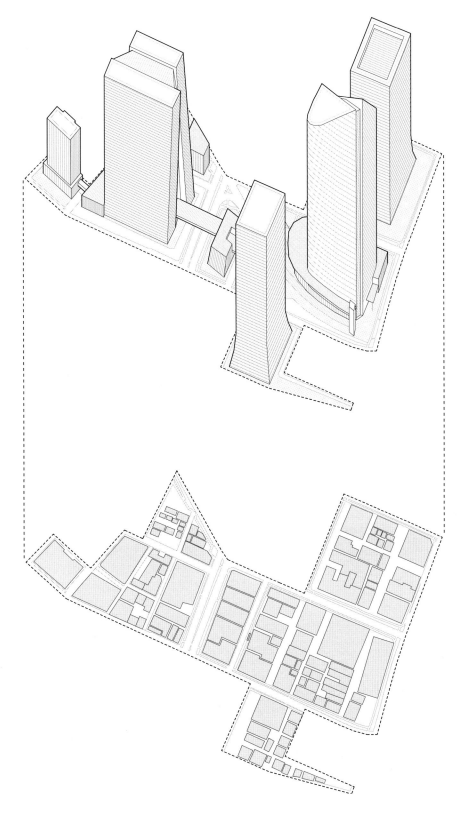

Tokyo Midtown/Hinokicho Park
Developer: Mitsui Fudosan

The architecture of Tokyo Midtown is clustered in the corner of the site nearest Roppongi station, leaving a crescent of landscape around it. Part of this space predates the complex and is administered publicly as Hinokicho Park. Landscape and architecture are divided by a loop road that services a parking deck.

Pedestrian bridge in the garden of Tokyo Midtown. Photo © Kenta Hasegawa

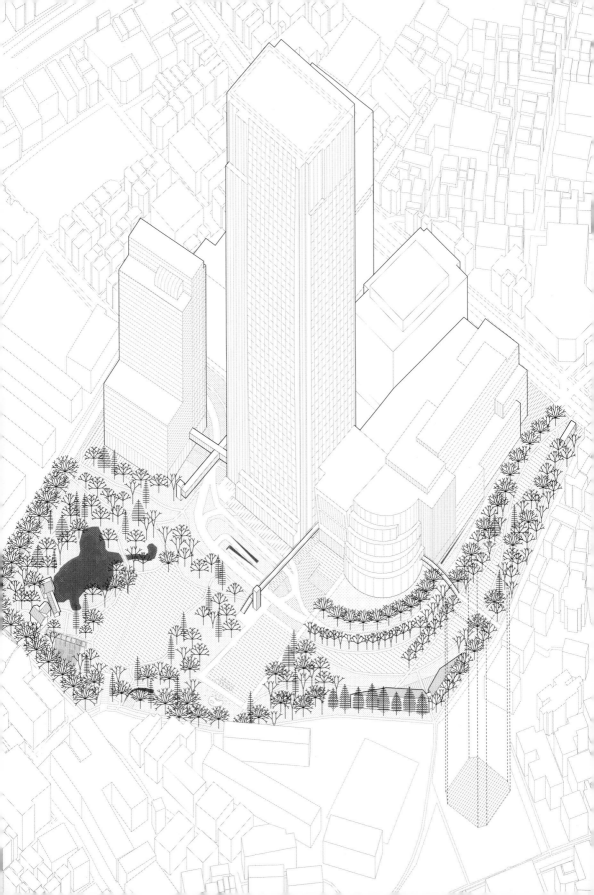

New Forms of Public Space

Contemporary urban redevelopments are changing the face of public space in Tokyo. Since the 1980s there has been an explosion in the number of privately owned public spaces, or POPS. Zoning rules incentivize the production of POPS by offering increased volume and height in exchange for setbacks or publicly accessible open spaces. The character of these new spaces varies greatly depending on the developer responsible for their creation.

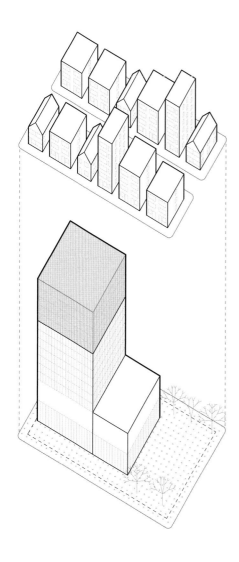

Zoning rules incentivize developers to aggregate parcels and produce privately owned public spaces in exchange for density bonuses

A low-rise design gallery by Tadao Ando in a corner of POPS in Tokyo Midtown. Photo © Kenta Hasegawa

Shibuya Scramble Square
Developers: Tokyu Corporation/East Japan Railway/Tokyo Metro

The plaza between Shibuya Crossing and Shibuya Station is scheduled for an overhaul with the ongoing large-scale redevelopment of and around the station. The plaza will expand, and adjacent streets will be narrowed, easing the flow of pedestrians. An entry canopy designed by SANAA will connect the plaza with elevated train platforms.

Shibuya Crossing from above. Photo © Kenta Hasegawa

Five Major Developers

Each of Tokyo's major developers has different character and corporate structure. Some, like Mitsubishi and Mitsui, are part of sprawling corporate conglomerates known as *zaibatsu*, which operate in realms as diverse as banking, entertainment, logistics, and manufacturing. Others, like Mori Building, are more narrowly focused on real estate. Examining a representative project site of five of the most significant developers in Tokyo, both before and after development, reveals the differences between them in approach and outcome.

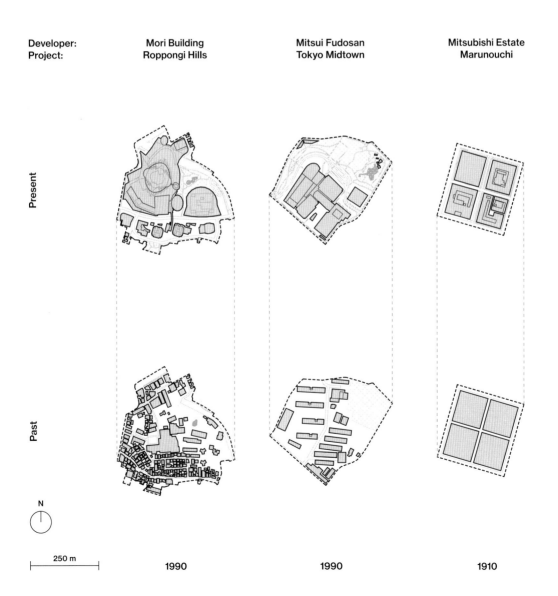

Developer:	Mori Building	Mitsui Fudosan	Mitsubishi Estate
Project:	Roppongi Hills	Tokyo Midtown	Marunouchi

Present

Past

N

250 m

1990   1990   1910

**Tokyo Met. Gov't
Nishi-Shinjuku**

**Tokyu Corp.
Shibuya**

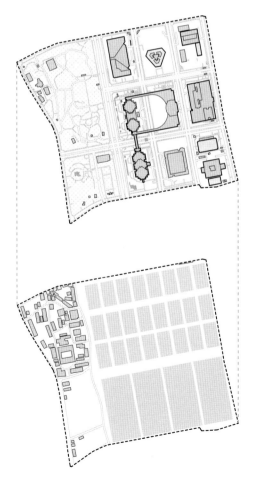

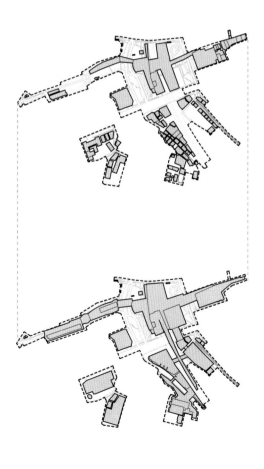

1950

1980

Methods of Agglomeration

When comparing the work of major Tokyo developers, one finds that some projects exist as intermittent nodes within the city fabric, while others are designed to aggregate together into enclaves. For instance, Tokyu Corporation, a private operator of regional rail systems, structures its developments around its rail stations, with commercial interests such as grocery and department stores set in residential areas and prime office space located at transit hubs. Mitsubishi Estate, by contrast, has concentrated some of its developments in contiguous zones of the city.

Developer: Mori Building   Mitsui Fudosan

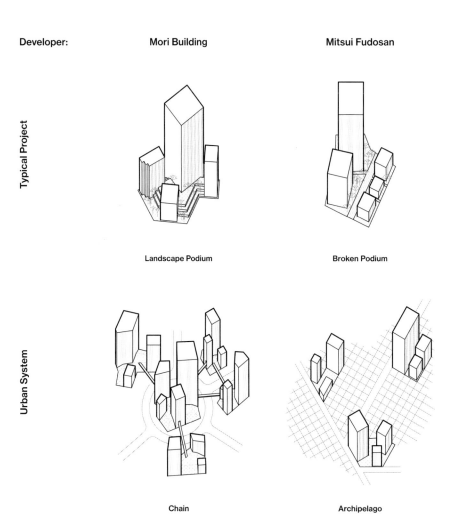

Typical Project

Landscape Podium   Broken Podium

Urban System

Chain   Archipelago

Mitsubishi Estate

Conventional Subdivision

Tokyo Met. Gov't

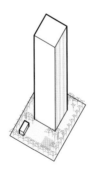

Tower and Plaza

Tokyu Corp.

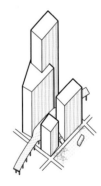

Station Node

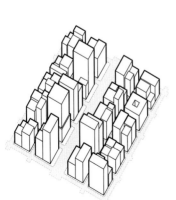

Conventional Grid

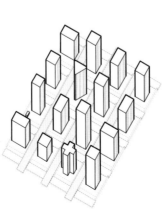

Woven Grid

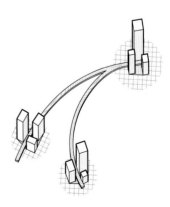

Transit Line

The Growth of Urban Development

High-rise developments began to appear in Tokyo in the late 1960s. In the following decades, skyscraper construction was concentrated in Shinjuku and areas near Tokyo Station. More recently, regulatory changes, including the 2002 Urban Renaissance law, have greatly expanded the areas in which these structures can be built.

Ikebukuro

Nakano

Shinjuku

Meidaimae

Shimokitazawa

Shibuya

Osaki

Urban Renaissance Zones

■ City Center Hubs
■ Mixed Use Urban Zones

3 THE IDEA OF NEIGHBORHOOD

How can living in one of Tokyo's neighborhoods provide an experience of the city that is distinct from that of the new urban enclaves—an experience rooted not only in greater social interaction but also in a culture of care?

In contrast to the recent phenomenon of large-scale private real-estate developments, Tokyo has always had an abundance of small-scale districts or urban villages. While these do not necessarily have the community affiliations of the Western notion of neighborhood, with its implicit links to neighborliness, that situation may be changing as various areas of the city seek ways to strengthen or define their local identities and, in the process, reaffirm their neighborly characteristics.

So far, many such initiatives have been primarily developed at the grassroots level without a more systematic investigation of neighborhood morphologies or how they might be modified to produce a different set of spatial experiences. Such strategies require the investigation of the potentials of a neighborhood at a microscale.

What can be learned from such studies? How might the history of a neighborhood provide clues as to its future course of development? How might such studies be of use in other contexts? How might describing or promoting the story of a neighborhood help reaffirm the inhabitants' sense of belonging? What are the challenges that local activists face in their attempts to transform their local communities, and how best to address them? These are only some of the questions raised by the twin concepts of neighborhood and neighborliness.

INVENTING NEIGHBORHOOD IN TOKYO

● JORDAN SAND

Introduction: A City of Neighborhoods

Even as the Japanese population shrinks, Tokyo continues to grow, and to grow skyward, with thirty-nine of its fifty tallest buildings all constructed since the millennium and over a dozen major development projects presently underway, all with towers in the range of 200–330 meters. Yet, at the same time, anyone who has walked more than a few blocks from a major rail station in Tokyo will tell you that it is a city of small and intimate neighborhoods. This is the conundrum of modern Tokyo and a sign of both its fragility and its resilience. It has also been an object of fascination for over a century.

Journalist Peter Popham captured the contrast vividly in describing a visit to architect Takamitsu Azuma's Sky House in Aoyama:

> Lacking the structure of straight, intersecting lines that roads impose, Azuma's Aoyama assumes a different form, something closer to a spiral, or several circles, each nesting inside a larger one. The image that comes to mind is that of a nut or an egg. On the outside is the high concrete of Aoyama Dori—the hard shell. Within is the street of shops, but in a sense this is no more than the space inside the walnut shell or the white of the egg. It's within this, cradled by it, that is to be found the heart of the matter, the egg's yolk, the kernel. The shopping street's deepest, most basic function is to serve as a mediating space between the roaring, ten-lane city and that soft yolk, the community's kernel, the little lane…Other cities have their quiet streets, their oases of tranquility, but they are usually quiet because they are peripheral. Tokyo's quiet parts are quiet because they are central.[1]

Popham's image of the nested layers created by avenue, shopping street, and lane recalls the concept of *oku*, or spatial depth, that Fumihiko Maki proposed in the 1970s as a distinctive feature of Japanese urbanism and dwelling space.[2] *Oku* continues today to be a useful tool for thinking about Japanese architectural traditions. Yet we needn't depend solely on deep cultural patterns to explain Tokyo's neighborhoods. Some features derive clearly from the political structure of Edo, the city's precursor under the rule of the Tokugawa shogunate (1600–1868); others from the effects of modern planning and exigencies of real estate. And some are readily found in cities outside Japan as well. In fact, the very idea of a unique micro-spatial order in Tokyo itself has a history, and it is only in the past generation that many Japanese urbanists have come to view it positively. As Japan transformed into a postindustrial society in the 1970s and 1980s, the density and irregularity that had once been viewed as evidence

1   Peter Popham, *Tokyo: City at the End of the World* (Tokyo: Kodansha International, 1985), 48–49.
2   Fumihiko Maki et al., *City with a Hidden Past* (Tokyo: Kajima Institute Publishing, 2018), 154–170.

of Tokyo's planning failures came to be championed instead as manifestations of a unique indigenous urbanism. This perspective has proved durable since. Typically, as in Yoshinobu Ashihara's characterization of Tokyo as an "amoeba," the logic of Japanese city building is presented as an antithesis to Western urban planning.[3] Yet Tokyo, in reality, is far from unplanned. Development and construction have been managed through a large urban bureaucracy and complex layers of national and local regulation for over a century. What Tokyo lacks is the immediate legibility of a grid city like New York or the uniform building lines of European cities built between the late eighteenth and twentieth centuries.

Among the modern planning features that have shaped Tokyo's neighborhoods and kept the neighborhood scale alive is a building code that set the minimum street width at four meters. Four meters is barely wide enough for two compact cars to pass but not wide enough for street parking or sidewalks, so bicycles and pedestrians dominate many streets. Since setbacks are required only when a house is entirely rebuilt, thousands of streets that were originally footpaths remain even narrower than the regulation four meters. Height restrictions set by strict sunlight laws in the 1970s have kept many districts with narrow streets low-rise. To these modern features one may add the persistence of a strong tradition of wood construction in Japan (the majority of building permits in Tokyo were for wood structures until the mid-1980s) and the very small typical lot size. All of these factors help make for intimate-feeling neighborhoods.[4]

The English word "neighborhood" has no precise and natural equivalent in Japanese. The closest term, *kinjo*, denotes a locality and captures the spatial component of "neighborhood" adequately, but lacks the element of community, or "neighborliness," suggested by the English word. Architecture scholars Hiroshi Zaino and Teiji Itoh have theorized *kaiwai*, a native Japanese word with a long history, as an evocation of locality strongly inflected by human occupation and use, but *kaiwai* does not suggest a bounded social unit (Itoh calls it an "activity space").[5] Japanese sociologists have been left to devise new terms to translate "neighborhood," such as *kinrin shakai*, literally meaning "neighboring society," but the social-scientific artificiality of terms like this has kept them from becoming common parlance. The description of Tokyo as a city of neighborhoods thus does not readily emerge from Japanese writing on the city.

"City of neighborhoods" nevertheless expresses a truth rooted in both the historical morphology and the history of social relations in a large part of the city. The commoner districts of Edo, packed tight into the area between the castle and the Sumida river, including Kanda, Nihonbashi, and Ginza, were divided into blocks called *cho*, each of which was entered through gates that were guarded at night. Unable to manage the entire city directly, the shogunate granted property-holding households broad autonomy in managing the *cho*. Each *cho* became a self-contained social unit, in which neighbors depended on one another and were governed by local community leaders. Within the block, shophouses lined the main streets while tenement rowhouses, providing minimal shelter to the households of shop clerks, laborers, and the city's large floating population, lined narrow back alleys that were often little more than a meter wide (FIG. 1). In 1868, the newly founded Meiji government removed the gates and guardhouses, but this basic morphology, of shops in front with narrow alleys and tenements behind, persisted in working-class districts of the modern city (FIG. 2). It was reproduced in new industrial working-class areas east of the Sumida as well. In Edo, the label *shitamachi*, meaning "downtown" or "low city," originally referred to the commoner blocks between the castle and the Sumida, but subsequently came to apply to these new districts as well.

As Henry D. Smith has shown, rather than a "city of neighborhoods," the dominant trope of Tokyo from the late nineteenth century through much of the twentieth was that of a "city of villages."[6] The village trope served to convey a range of meanings. It modulated over time, from a spatial trope in the nineteenth and early twentieth centuries to a social one in the mid-twentieth century, then back to a spatial one in the late twentieth century. Beginning in the 1870s and continuing until after World War I, Western visitors repeatedly described Tokyo as an aggregation of villages. Unpainted and small, the majority of houses looked rustic, while the estates of the wealthy were hidden from view. On the other hand, greenery was plentiful, particularly in the *yamanote*, the higher ground on the west side of the city that was formerly occupied by the feudal ruling class. When Ulysses Grant visited Japan on a world tour in 1879, his official chronicler wrote of the capital:

> It is hard to realize that Tokio is a city—one of the greatest cities of the world. It looks like a series of villages, with bits of green and open spaces and inclosed grounds breaking up the continuity of the town. There is no special character to Tokio, no one trait to seize upon and remember.[7]

One senses that what these Westerners saw first was an absence. The city lacked the monuments, squares, and vistas of baroque and neoclassical urbanism. Few buildings stood over two stories or displayed ornament. Until Tokyo Station was completed in 1914, there was no one building or space to serve as

3   Yoshinobu Ashihara, *The Hidden Order: Tokyo through the Twentieth Century* (Tokyo: Kodansha International, 1996).
4   On the history of planning law in Japan, see André Sorensen, *The Making of Urban Japan: Cities and Planning from Edo to the Twenty First Century* (London: Routledge, 2002).
5   Hiroshi Zaino, *Kaiwai: Nihon no toshin kūkan* (Tokyo: Kajima shuppankai, 1978).
6   Henry D. Smith II, "Mura [birejji] to shite no Tokyo: Henten suru kindai Nihon no shuto zo" [Tokyo as a 'village': Changing perceptions of Japan's capital city], in Hiroyuki Suzuki et al., eds., *Shiriizu Toshi-kenchiku-rekishi 6: Toshi bunka no seijuku*, (Tokyo: Tokyo University Press, 2006), 201–237.
7   Smith II, "Mura [birejji] to shite no Tokyo."

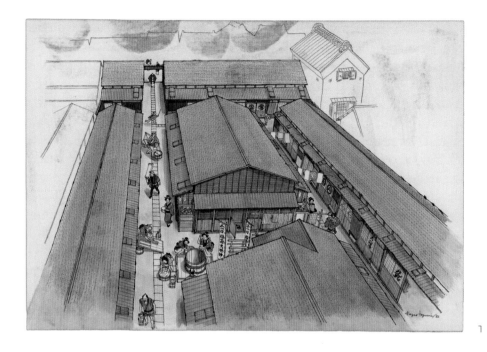

1

2

| 1 | Rendering of Edo tenements. Image reconstructed by Obayashi Corporation © Kazuo Hozumi | 2 | Rows of modern slum housing built on the periphery of Tokyo in the early twentieth century, showing the same wooden tenement structures as the Edo tenements. Source: *Tokyo-fu gakumu-bu shakai-ka ed, Tokyo-fu gunbu (rinsetsu gogun) shudanteki furyo jutaku chiku zushu* [Pictorial collection of the substandard collective housing areas in the five peripheral counties of Tokyo] (Tokyo: Prefecture of Tokyo, 1928) |

the visible city center (as Roland Barthes would later note, the fact that the imperial palace occupies a vast, heavily wooded area, most of which is off-limits to the public, gives Tokyo its "empty center"). Without grand boulevards or conspicuous markers, the sprawling, multi-nodal metropolis appeared village-like. What Isabella Bird in 1878 called Tokyo's "monotony of mean-ness"[8] was not uniformly condemned, however. Rather, it communicated to Westerners that the city's true charms lay hidden. The 1914 *Terry's Guide* wrote that the "outwardly modest, even tawdry" houses often concealed beau-tiful miniature landscape gardens; the authors also admired the "quaint, doll-like houses" along the canals of *shitamachi*.[9] Thus, the intimate scale of Tokyo's neighborhoods, both in the cottages and gardens of *yamanote* and amid the narrow streets and waterways of *shitamachi*, had a picturesque appeal that contributed to its "villagey-ness" in Western eyes.

The Urban Village as Social Problem

A different conception of Tokyo as a city of villages emerged in social science after World War II. In the wake of defeat, Henry Smith wrote, "many Japanese intellectuals began to rethink the social structure of prewar Japan in search of the roots of fascism, a search that led directly to a new scrutiny of the relation-ship between city and country in modern Japan." The village-like quality of Tokyo here manifested itself not in the city's landscape or living spaces but in the mentality and social organization of its residents. Political thinker Jiro Kamishima saw urban Japanese as still mired in the feudal hierarchical habits that he perceived as the essential traits of native rural tradition. In his classic 1950s study of a Tokyo neighborhood, British sociologist Ronald Dore took a more benign view, but asserted similarly that "many features of the system of social relations prevailing in the Tokugawa village are still preserved in the city."[10]

One concrete source for this perception of Tokyo neighborhoods as socially akin to premodern villages was the neighborhood associations, called *chonaikai*. These associations had emerged from local initiatives throughout Tokyo in the first decades of the twentieth century. They were not run by the old elite of Edo property holders, nor were they controlled by the state.[11] Nevertheless, to postwar Japanese intellectuals, they had several features that appeared to define them as traditional, or "feudal," and village-like. Member-ship was not voluntary, as all households in the district were expected to participate; management was patriarchal, since by default senior males repre-sented their households; and while remaining nominally autonomous, the

8   Smith II, "Mura [birejji] to shite no Tokyo."
9   Thomas Philip Terry, *Terry's Japanese Empire* (Boston, New York: Houghton Mifflin, 1914), 129, 134.
10   Ronald P. Dore, *City Life in Japan* (Berkeley: University of California Press, 1958), 378.
11   Sally Ann Hastings, *Neighborhood and Nation in Tokyo, 1905–1937* (Pittsburgh: University of Pittsburgh Press, 1995).

3

| Akabanedai *danchi* housing blocks, Tokyo, 1962. Icons of modern living in the 1960s and 1970s, *danchi* were also criticized for lacking the kind of spaces that encouraged strong relations among neighbors. Photo courtesy of the Urban Renaissance Agency

associations functioned primarily as cooperative partners to local and national government. During the war years, the national Home Ministry made the *chonaikai*, in combination with the new state-created *tonarigumi*, a smaller neighborhood unit nested under it, a vehicle of propaganda and a tool of mutual surveillance. After the war, Occupation authorities dissolved the *tonarigumi*, while the *chonaikai* lived on as voluntary groups (even though all households were still nominally assumed to be members). Thus a modern local organization, originally grassroots, came to embody what appeared to be the legacy of the city's village past.[12]

Fusing the Social and the Spatial

Sociologists and urban policymakers who viewed the conservatism of the old neighborhood associations critically groped for ways to foster a more progressive, genuinely voluntary urban community. Many felt that it had never existed in Japan and needed therefore to be invented anew. Reflecting the sense that voluntary community lacked indigenous roots, the term they used was *komyuniti*, a neologism transliterated from English. The state Economic Planning Agency sponsored a "model community" program in the early 1970s, offering successful municipalities (including sub-units within the metropolis) funding for community centers and other facilities intended to support an "open community" defined by locality, based on equality and mutual trust, and free to all participants. Urban community thus found new expression as an alternative to a form of traditional Japanese community that was seen as backward and oppressive.[13]

The new thinking about urban community influenced architects and urban researchers as well. The most striking case was that of Shigebumi Suzuki, a professor of architecture at the University of Tokyo and one of the designers of the country's first nationally-sponsored public housing, the famous *danchi* of the 1950s. Although *danchi* housing blocks, with their modern conveniences and their promise of greater family privacy, were enormously popular among new white-collar households in the 1950s and 1960s (FIG. 3), by the beginning of the next decade, their novelty had worn off. Critical intellectuals regarded *danchi* as sites of social atomization and alienation. Suzuki himself came to absorb this criticism, and set out to test empirically the spatial and architectural features that fostered intimate community.

To test the spatial-social nexus, Suzuki and his students turned to Tsukishima, a working-class district built in the early twentieth century on a landfill island near the mouth of the Sumida River (FIG. 4). Constructed en

---

12   For an ethnographic study of a Tokyo *chonaikai* in the 1980s, see Theodore C. Bestor, *Neighborhood Tokyo* (Stanford: Stanford University Press, 1989).

13   Jordan Sand, *Tokyo Vernacular: Common Spaces, Local Histories, Found Objects* (Berkeley: University of California Press, 2013).

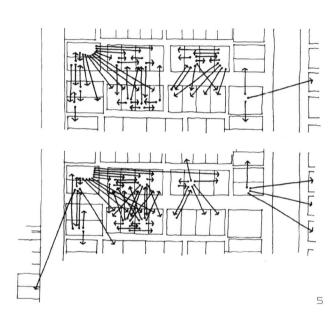

4

5

4 | Alley in Tsukishima. Signage, laundry, and copious potted plants show how the residents treat the alley as common living space rather than as a public street. Photo courtesy of the Chuo City Kyobashi Library

5 | Diagrams of neighborly intimacy in Tsukishima. The images above and below show the same rows of houses sharing an alleyway. The arrows in the top image indicate responses to the question, "Who would you ask to look after your house if you were going out, and vice versa?" The arrows in the bottom image indicate responses to the question, "At which houses would you drop in for tea?" Source: Shigebumi Suzuki et al., *Ie to machi: jukyo shugo no ronri* (Tokyo: Kajima shuppankai, 1984), 147

masse as model factory-workers' housing, the Tsukishima blocks exhibited
a uniform, rectilinear version of the classic *shitamachi* morphology, with identi-
cal two-story wood-built rowhouses facing one another across alleys of roughly
three meters' width. This uniformity leant itself to surveying. The Suzuki team
interviewed residents, studying neighborly behaviors such as sitting out in the
alley together, asking neighbors to watch the house, and exchanging tea and
gifts, then mapped and tabulated their answers. The intimacy that residents'
responses revealed, Suzuki proposed, correlated with architectural features
of the housing, beginning with the scale of the alley space, and including the
facts that houses opened directly onto it and that sliding doors could be left
open without obstructing passage. Indeed, many residents, it was also found,
never locked their doors.[14] (FIG. 5)

    In the longer history of Tokyo tropes, Suzuki's turn from the design of
public housing blocks to the analysis of *shitamachi* alleyways represented a turn
in the "city of villages" story from the social conception of the village back to
the spatial one, which once again cast Tokyo in a positive light (in keeping with
this trend, Peter Popham's chapter on the backstreets of Aoyama was titled
"The Village Dream"). Put another way, this turn marked the emergence of
"neighborhood" as a critical locus of Tokyo urbanism. Naturally, Tokyo had
always had neighborhoods. But it was from the 1970s onward that architects
and a range of other intellectuals—soon to include historians and preservationists—began to locate values unique to the city in them. Fumihiko Maki's
Miegakure suru toshi (original publication 1975; translated subsequently to
English as *City with a Hidden Past*) contributed significantly to this trend in
the architecture field. Maki had not been an orthodox Metabolist, but it is
nevertheless noteworthy that a member of the Metabolist group and a student
of Kenzo Tange chose to turn his attention and his students' energy toward
the study of micro-scale spatial characteristics of Tokyo's neighborhoods in this
period. At least in visual terms, if not programmatically, it was a sharp contrast with the movement's advocacy of megastructures. Subsequently, architecture historian Hidenobu Jinnai would extend this reading of Tokyo with
a similar kind of neighborhood-level spatial analysis rooted in a historical
typology of Edo-Tokyo houses and street spaces.[15]

    Shitamachi emerged in the same years as an icon of Tokyo tradition,
taken up in particular by local government as a form of place branding.[16] The
Shitamachi Museum was founded in 1981, one of the city's first museums of
local everyday life. The *shitamachi* neighborhood image has continued to evolve
and accrue value in the years since through other museums and exhibits,
as well as through print, film, and television. *Shitamachi* did not function as

14   Shigebumi Suzuki et al., *Ie to machi: jukyo shugo no ronri* (Tokyo: Kajima shuppankai, 1984).
15   Hidenobu Jinnai, Fumio Itakura, Hosei Daigaku, *Tokyo no machi o yomu* (Tokyo: Sagami shobo, 1981);
        Hidenobu Jinnai, *Tokyo, A Spatial Anthropology* (Berkeley: University of California Press, 1995).
16   Theodore Bestor, "The Shitamachi Revival," *Transactions of the Asiatic Society of Japan*, 4th series, vol. 5 (1990): 71–86.

a spatial trope alone. Like London's East End, it drew upon a wealth of historical associations with working-class culture, ranging from small-shop manufacturing to local dialect and popular revue theater. But it became increasingly
spatialized, until any Tokyo neighborhood of narrow streets and wooden rowhouses could claim *shitamachi* status. These features were themselves becoming
rarer, as land sharks descended on mom-and-pop shops and old tenement rows
during the real estate bubble of the late 1980s, seeking to assemble parcels
of land large enough to redevelop into *manshon* (reinforced concrete apartment
buildings) or office buildings of ten stories and more. Architectural and social
studies of *shitamachi* and *shitamachi*-like neighborhoods thus flourished as these
places rapidly disappeared. Tokyo offered another example of Michel de
Certeau's classic dictum: "the ethnologist and the archaeologist arrive at the
moment a culture has lost its means of self-defense."[17]

Inventing Neighborhood in Yanesen

And yet it was also in the bubble years of the 1980s that one of the city's most
remarkable and successful experiments in local place-making appeared. The
quarterly local history magazine *Chiiki zasshi: Yanaka, Nezu, Sendagi*—abbre-
viated *Yanesen*—began publication in late 1984. *Yanesen* was a homespun operation. The three women who founded and edited it did most of the writing
themselves. Interviewing neighbors and digging in local libraries, they composed
a vernacular history of these three adjacent districts, excavating forgotten
places and rendering them visible again through stories and hand-drawn maps.

The Aizome River, a narrow waterway that had flowed through the
valley between the three districts, was paved over in the 1930s. Its name,
which means "Indigo Dye River," reflected the fact that it had been lined with
dyers' shops that used the water in the dying process (and also dumped waste-
water, changing the color of the stream). By the 1980s, the only vestiges of this
once-flourishing craft industry were one shophouse from the late nineteenth
century and the shell of an old ribbon factory. But the meandering path of the
road that had replaced the river hinted at its former life. In the magazine's
third issue, *Yanesen* did a feature on the road, using its local nickname, "Snake
Street," tracing the history of dyers in the area, and including a sketch showing its entire length, marked with shops and houses of historical interest (FIG. 6).
In a later community event, residents were invited to add more sites of interest to a blown-up version of the drawing. As a result, the nickname became
widely known, along with the fact that the street had once been a river lined
by dyers' workshops. After the millennium, several young arrivals in the neighborhood opened tiny craft boutiques and restaurants along Snake Street,
taking advantage of the pedestrian traffic it had come to attract. A preservation movement was launched for the ribbon factory, long since defunct and

completely undistinguished in aesthetic terms, but made meaningful again as a repository of local memory.

Every issue of the magazine also included a map of the whole district (FIG. 7). The editors took a minimum of advertisements and required that they be hand-drawn, so that, unlike most magazines, *Yanesen* depended on over-the-counter sales and subscriptions rather than advertising revenue. Shops that agreed to sell the magazine (from small handmade wooden racks) were marked on the map, along with places about which stories had been printed. The operation was kept local by the editors' decision to print in the area and only to sell the magazine in shops to which they could deliver copies by bicycle. The entire process created a dense network of local places and participants built around a locally crafted publication telling stories of special meaning to people living in or connected to the area. When the land sharks came, the growing sense of local identity also helped galvanize residents against indiscriminate redevelopment.

Through alley surveys, preservation campaigns, and oral history, *Yanesen* conjured into existence a neighborhood that had not been called a neighborhood before. The three districts, Yanaka, Nezu, and Sendagi, were separate municipal units and straddled two of the city's 23 wards. The shared history of certain places, like Snake Street, together with a Kevin Lynchian sense of rough district boundaries based on topography and major thoroughfares, connected them, but only loosely. The magazine editors might have chosen a different configuration of localities—and other adjacent districts were both considered and sometimes included in stories—but the success of the magazine in community-building cemented these three as a single place. *Yanesen* the magazine begat "Yanesen" the toponym, which became increasingly popular from the 1990s, used by shops, visitors' guides, and occasionally municipal government. The experience of *Yanesen* also built the foundations for local cultural events, preservation groups, and innovative adaptive-reuse projects that have made the area both a center of community activism and a tourist site.

Yanaka, Nezu, and Sendagi were not part of the traditional working-class *shitamachi*, but they possessed the small street scale, low-rise wooden housing, and dense and irregular network of alleys associated with *shitamachi*, having survived relatively well through the disasters and rapid redevelopment that transformed most of Tokyo in the twentieth century. The forging of a local identity in part through the survival of these features encouraged outsiders, as well as some natives, to think of Yanesen as a typical *shitamachi* neighborhood. This loose application of informal place names—neither "Yanesen" nor "*shitamachi*" has an official definition—reflects the expanded

---

17   Michel de Certeau, *Heterologies: Discourse on the Other*, trans. Brian Massumi (Minneapolis: University of Minnesota Press, 2010), 123.

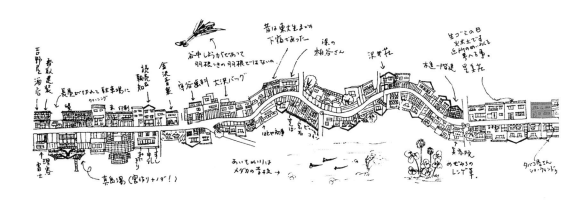

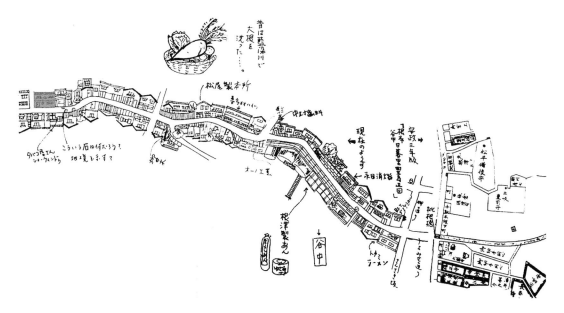

Map of "Snake Street" (originally the
Aizome River), *Yanesen* 3 (1985): 5-7

frame in which Tokyoites have come to experience and understand "neighbor-hood." One could say that through concrete placemaking efforts like the creation of Yanesen, and simultaneously through popular discourse about these places, the neighborhood idea, combining a particular kind of space and a community of neighbors, has found its own indigenous form in Tokyo.

The Kampung Dream: Tokyo in Asia

As Tokyo neighborhoods became both objects of study and sites of community mobilization, Japanese urbanists recognized that the kinds of spaces they now valorized were not unique to Tokyo. Hidenobu Jinnai turned attention away from the formulaic comparison of Japan and the West, in which a no-tional "West" was taken as normative, by celebrating the "Asianness" or "ethnic" character of Tokyo.[18] Architectural theorist and ethnographer Shuji Funo turned to study of neighborhoods in Southeast Asian cities, collaborating with Jonah Silas of Indonesia's Kampung Improvement Program.[19] Funo found in the Southeast Asian *kampung* (Malay *kampong*) not only the marks of urban informality or the problems of third-world poverty, but the combination of indigenous architecture tradition, a flexible building system in local materials, intimate scale, and strong local ties that constituted the "village dream" of Tokyo's rediscovered neighborhoods.[20]

Like architects and preservationists in Tokyo after the 1970s, Funo's interest lay in the physical and spatial features that made for a strong sense of neighborhood. The negative view of traditional local institutions that had preoccupied Japanese sociologists in the previous generation played no role in this assessment of Asian urban commonalities. There is an interesting irony in this. Indonesia has come to pride itself in what is sometimes called the "*kampung* spirit," represented in mutual aid activities at the block level. These activities are organized around the smallest unit of urban administration, the RT (*rukun tettanga*), neighborhood associations that involve all households. The RT derive directly from local organizations created by the Japanese military throughout Java in 1944. In fact, until not long ago, many residents of Jakarta and other Javanese cities old enough to remember the Japanese occupation knew the neighborhood associations by the Japanese name *tonari-gumi*. The Japanese occupiers had created them to enforce mutual surveil-lance and facilitate labor extraction, but they served post-liberation regimes equally well and became an accepted part of city life. However, in the studies of Funo and Silas and subsequent researchers, the "*kampung* spirit" is tied more to a particular type of urban space, a space that has resonances with the

18   See Hidenobu Jinnai and Haruo Hirota, eds., *Process Architecture no. 72: Ethnic Tokyo* (January, 1987).
19   Shuji Funo, Naohiko Yamamoto, and Johan Silas, "Typology of Kampung Houses and Their Transformation Process," *Journal of Asian Architecture and Building Engineering* 1, no. 2 (2002): 193–200.
20   Shuji Funo, *Kanpon no sekai* (Tokyo: Parco shuppankyoku, 1991).

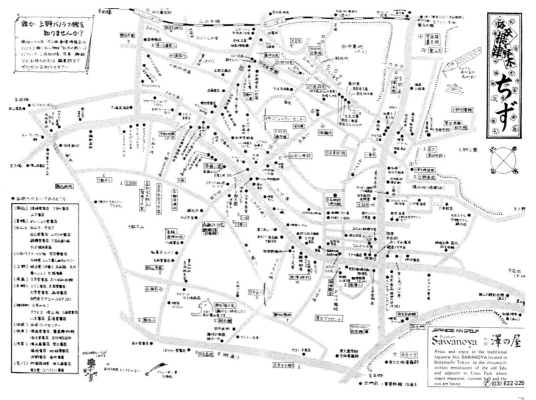

7 | District map of the Yanesen districts,
Yanesen 10 (1986): 18-19

surviving old alleys of Tokyo. This architectural affinity, rather than the Japanese role in constructing the institutions of Indonesia's *kampung* solidarity, animates interest in the idea of a shared Asian urbanism.

The built environment of Indonesian cities (which predates the Japanese occupation) doubtless contributed substantially to the "villagey" character of *kampung* life. Yet in institutional terms, Indonesia's urban neighborhoods share with Tokyo's neighborhoods roots in non-voluntary local associations that Japanese social scientists had once viewed as a problematic "feudal" legacy. In Tokyo, this criticism led urbanists to look for the elements of neighborhood community in the physical environment instead of in social institutions; in Indonesian cities, the physical and the social were viewed as a natural and harmonious pair—despite the fact that the social institution in Indonesia was, even more clearly than in Japan, a product of government fiat.

This is in no way meant to disparage the work of architects and researchers in Tokyo and elsewhere who have gone to the back alleys and *kampungs* in search of the architectural and spatial ingredients of good neighborhood. Whatever social, political, and institutional factors have also played a role in sustaining local community in Asian megacities, there is no question that these spaces offer the formula for a livable urbanism that has tran-scended the vicissitudes of war and reconstruction, colonialism and independence, rapid industrialization and, at least in Tokyo's case, subsequent deindustrialization. Small lots and the flexibility of low-rise mixed-use neighborhoods built with inexpensive local materials also permit frequent rebuilding with limited gentrification.[21]

Since the millennium, special easements have facilitated enormous high-rise developments in certain designated sites around Tokyo, sometimes called "island universes" because of their sharp disjuncture with surrounding blocks. The visual contrast between these new districts and their neighbors brings the value of Tokyo's older spatial model more plainly into view. One need only imagine how deleterious to Tokyo life it would be if similar easements were granted in neighborhoods that remain low- and middle-rise, or if all narrow streets were widened for automotive traffic. Although it lacked visual glamor, from the nineteenth century until the end of the twentieth, Tokyo offered a distinctive model for urban livability—one still worth learning from today.

---

21   Benjamin Bansal, "Urban Space as a Factor of Production: Accounting for the Success of Small Factories in Postwar Tokyo," *Social Science Japan Journal* 23, no. 2 (October 20, 2020): 281–298.

THE POSTWAR BLACK MARKETS AND THEIR LEGACY

SEIJI M. LIPPIT

At the end of World War II, Tokyo lay in smoldering ruins, devastated by a relentless Allied bombing campaign that burned much of the city to cinders, killing and wounding hundreds of thousands of residents and leaving millions homeless. The shocking vista of the sprawling capital city reduced to a vast flatness, stretching limitlessly in all directions, is one of the indelible images of the time. From the ashes of the imperial capital would eventually emerge the contemporary metropolis of Tokyo and the postwar nation-state of Japan, shorn of its multiracial, multilingual empire and reconfigured around a phantasmal conception of a mono-ethnic nation that was, in turn, projected back into history.

In the immediate aftermath of the war, however, before the construction of the postwar nation and its capital could get fully underway, throughout the city (and indeed throughout the country's major urban areas), a singular type of economic, social, and cultural space known as the black markets (*yamiichi*) proliferated, expanding rapidly to fill the empty spaces in the urban landscape as well as the gaps in the fractured apparatus of the state and the economy. These markets, which began appearing just days after the end of the war in August of 1945, fulfilled the vital role of offering a way for people to obtain the daily necessities of life such as food, clothing, and household goods at a time when most stores were bombed out or empty. Yet they also came to take on an outsized symbolic role in the cultural imagination by marking, in an extremely visible way, the collapse of the imperial state and society, while also providing dynamic and chaotic signs of an alternative future.

A Space of Reconfigured Consciousness

They were referred to as black markets because they sold goods outside the system of government-established price controls that had been in effect since the early days of the war. Government rations continued to be distributed to households after the war, but they were sorely inadequate for subsistence, as starkly shown in 1947 by the death of a judge who perished of malnutrition after refusing to eat black-market food, relying only on rations.[1] Beyond food and household items, all manner of other goods were available for purchase, including alcohol (sometimes the homespun variety known as *kasutori*, which could prove lethal), drugs, and firearms, as well as a wide range of American commodities that, in many instances, circulated in Japan for the first time via the black market. John Dower notes that beyond consumer goods, a variety of manufacturing materials, including "coal, coke, gasoline, lumber, cement, plate glass, *tatami* straw matting, pig iron, rolled steel, galvanized steel, copper sheeting, aluminum, tin, electric wire, electric motors, fertilizers, industrial chemicals (sulfuric acid, caustic soda, soda ash), mechanic oil, rubber tires, farm equipment, alcohol, paints, dyestuffs, textiles, paper" were also available

1   See John Dower, *Embracing Defeat: Japan in the Wake of World War II* (New York: Norton, 1999), 99–101.

for purchase.[2] Additionally, the burgeoning unlicensed sex trade, formed in large measure around the massive presence of Occupation troops in the capital city, was also associated with the black markets and served as a significant route for American products to enter the marketplace, as payment was often made in goods rather than currency.[3]

Of course, the black market as a general space of illicit exchange had existed long before the war's end, and physical marketplaces selling contraband items had also operated in the city, especially following natural disasters such the Great Kanto Earthquake of 1923. In fact, Kosei Hatsuda argues that the black markets are a latent yet essential function of the city that comes to the surface at moments of crisis, such as in the aftermath of earthquake or war.[4] Yet the scale of the black markets in postwar Japan was something new, along with their impact on public consciousness and discourse. The markets were ubiquitous, and generally acknowledged to be a necessary part of economic and social life in the aftermath of the war, even as they typically operated in defiance of the law. An Asahi newspaper column of 1947 stated that the black markets constituted "the microcosm of Japan today."[5] In an influential essay, writer Ango Sakaguchi listed the *kamikaze*-pilot-turned-black-marketeer as one of the symbols of Japan's "decadence," along with the desanctified emperor and the war widow who has taken on a new lover, each marking the process of falling away from wartime ideology as well as the first step toward a reconfigured identity.

The Evolution of Black Markets

The markets in Tokyo were located adjacent to major train stations, with the largest found along the Yamanote Line, the city's main commuter line that runs in a loop around central Tokyo. The areas surrounding train stations had been cleared through forced evacuations as fire breaks during the war, thus creating space for the markets to take root, and of course the trains themselves functioned as important conduits for both consumers and commodities. As Masakazu Ishigure writes, to a degree rarely seen, the historical development of Tokyo has been fundamentally shaped by its extensive network of rail and subway lines; chief among them is the Yamanote.[6] Stations along the Yamanote Line serve as terminal points for train lines extending out to the suburbs and thus function as destination points for consumers coming into the city to shop as well as crucial transfer points for commuters changing to subways and other transportation lines in the city. In addition, stations such as Ueno, the location of one of the largest markets in the city, were important gateways to farmlands outside the city, and provided a transit route for black market produce to enter the city as well as for buyers on *kaidashi* "shopping excursions" to venture into the countryside, where they often bartered personal items for precious rice and other produce (FIG. 1).[7] The city's physical markets in effect existed as material nodes in the larger black-market economy that permeated the nation.

In the early days, the "markets" were sometimes nothing more than individuals spreading out their personal belongings to sell on the sidewalk (including, for example, ex-soldiers selling military helmets for use as cooking pots at a time when any household items made of metal had been requisitioned by the military) or farmers and others bringing produce from rural farmlands to sell in the city. Other markets were more organized from the beginning, managed by groups known as *tekiya* that had traditionally controlled street sales in the city. In many cases, such markets occupied public or private land without legal permits, leading to various civil disputes and police raids. Violent turf wars among rival gangs and clashes with police were prominently portrayed in the media and became a mainstay of cultural representations of the black markets, as seen in two of Akira Kurosawa's best-known postwar films, *Yoidore tenshi* [*A Drunken Angel*], 1948 and *Nora inu* [*Stray Dog*], 1949. The latter film, which traces a police detective's descent into the city's underworld in search of his stolen pistol, includes key footage of Tokyo's markets shot on location.

The first organized markets were makeshift collections of carts and reed-wall stalls, temporary and ephemeral configurations of space that over time developed into more durable wooden structures clustered together. The opening of Jun Ishikawa's celebrated short story, "The Jesus in the Ruins" (1946), provides a memorable description of the fluid and transitory quality of the markets:

> Under the blazing sky of a hot summer sun, amidst choking dirt and dust, a cluster of makeshift stalls has sprung from the land, and like a weed that grows in a clump, it has sent out its tendrils to cover the earth. The stands are partitioned by screens made of reeds, each pressing so hard upon the next there is scarcely room to breathe, let alone move. And as for the occupants, if there are those who flog their various and sundry household goods by simply setting them out on the ground, and those who spread kimonos or things to wear across tables, by far the vast majority are people with food to sell. They operate out of their carts, openly taking out white rice and serving it to the public in defiance of the law.[8]

2   Dower, 116.
3   In Akiyuki Nosaka's short story, "American *Hijiki*," the narrator recounts his experience as a youth of taking goods given to Japanese women by American soldiers, including a "half-pound can of MJB coffee and a can of Hershey's cocoa," and trading them for cash at a Korean-run café in Osaka. Akiyuki Nosaka, "American *Hijiki*," trans. Jay Rubin, in *Contemporary Japanese Literature: An Anthology of Fiction, Film, and Other Writing Since 1945*, ed. Howard Hibbett (New York: Alfred A. Knopf, 1989), 442.
4   Kosei Hatsuda, "Toshi to shite no yamiichi," in *Yamiichi bunka-ron*, ed. Mitsuo Ikawa, Takumi Ishikawa, and Hideyuki Nakamura (Tokyo: Hitsuji Shobo, 2017), 41.
5   Cited in Hatsuda, "Toshi to shite no yamiichi," 47.
6   Masakazu Ishigure, *Sengo Tokyo to yamiichi* (Tokyo: Kajima shuppankai, 2016), 16.
7   See Dower, *Embracing Defeat*, 95.
8   Jun Ishikawa, "The Jesus of the Ruins," in *The Legend of Gold and Other Stories*, trans. William J. Tyler (Honolulu: University of Hawai'i Press, 1998), 72.

1

1   A busy district with stalls and stands made
of wood and reed screens near the train
station of Ueno, 1946. Photo © Shunkichi
Kikuchi, courtesy of Harumi Tago

Ishikawa's description of this market near Ueno Station captures many of the tropes and images typically associated with the black markets, including their seemingly spontaneous emergence from the scorched earth of the city and their unrestrained proliferation throughout the ruined landscape. As he writes in a subsequent passage, "It is also what comes in the wake of war and its fire: a city in ruins, the burnt-out shell of a metropolis."[9] By the end of Ishikawa's story, the lively and cacophonous market has completely vanished, having been shut down by the police, leaving behind only a "cold, white desert."[10]

Beyond providing necessities for daily survival, the markets also served to absorb the massive unemployment produced by the end of the war and the implosion of the imperial state.[11] Those active in the black markets included returnees from overseas territories and battlefields, such as soldiers and settlers, as well as former subjects of the Japanese empire, particularly from China and Korea, who remained behind in Japan after the war. Although the majority returned to their homelands, hundreds of thousands remained in Japan due to various factors, often with nowhere else to turn for employment than the black markets. Their liberation from empire also meant that they were bereft of legal status in occupied Japan. As Akito Sakasai writes, for resident Korean writer Tal-su Kim, the black markets serve to frame the "borderline space" not only between imperial and postwar Japan, but also between Japan and Korea, the in-between space occupied by Korean and other colonial subjects who remained in Japan in a state of exclusion and precarity.[12] In turn, the association between the markets and former colonial subjects became a common aspect of the black markets' portrayal in the media.

In this way, we can see the markets as a key component in processes of decolonization in the immediate postwar period, facilitating the transition away from the state-regulated wartime economy, while also absorbing various remnants and fragments of empire left in the wake of its collapse. They also served as a key site of intersection and exchange between occupier and occupied, although in the immediate aftermath of the war any mention of Allied involvement in the black market, including any accounts of "fraternization" between Allied personnel and Japanese women, was strictly prohibited by Occupation censors.[13] In various cultural representations, the markets emerge as a dynamic space in which multiple temporalities came into conflict, including memories and traces of the imperial past that were often excluded from public discourse, the destitution and ruination of the present, and visions (whether idealized or dystopic) of the future.

---

9   Ishikawa, 73.
10   Ishikawa, 79.
11   See Kazuo Okochi, *Sengo shakai no jittai bunseki* (Tokyo: Nihon Hyoronsha,1950), 224–26. See also Hatsuda, "Toshi to shite no yamiichi," 40.
12   Akito Sakasai, "Monogatari no naka no yamiichi," in *Sakariba wa yamiichi kara umareta*, ed. Kenji Hashimoto and Kosei Hatsuda (Tokyo: Seikyusha, 2016), 189.
13   See Jay Rubin, "From Wholesomeness to Decadence: The Censorship of Literature under the Allied Occupation," *Journal of Japanese Studies* 11, No.1 (Winter 1985): 93.

2

3

2 | The black market in Shinjuku undergoing demolition, 1950-1951. Courtesy of the Tokyo Metropolian Archives collection *Kukaku seiri jigyo kiroku shashin* [Photographic Documentation of Land Readjustment Work], film 012

3 | Black market in Shinjuku, 1949, that stretched along the railway lines. Following the land readjustment plan instated by the municipality of Tokyo, the market was destroyed. Eventually the Shinjuku East Exit Side Shotengai [shopping street] grew up in its place. Photo © Asahi Shimbun

Impact on Postwar Tokyo

As the nation's economy began to revive toward the latter years of the Occupation, and as the state relaxed price controls, the need for the markets lessened. After increasingly frequent police raids and attempts to curtail the presence and power of the *tekiya*, it was ultimately the orders issued at the behest of Occupation authorities in 1949 to remove street stalls that marked the end of the black markets' dominance of city streets. By spring of 1950, the large-scale removal of these markets from the areas adjacent to stations was well underway (FIGS. 2, 3), a process that continued in some form for years. Yet despite the relative brevity of the era of the black markets, their impact on the development of postwar Tokyo was significant, and their traces remain visible to this day. As Kenji Hashimoto and Kosei Hatsuda write, many of the major commercial and entertainment districts (*sakariba*) of contemporary Tokyo trace their roots back to the postwar black markets.[14]

These include Ikebukuro, a district currently dominated by railway-owned department stores Seibu and Tobu, and which was the site of one of the city's most extensive black markets on the western side of the station. The Ikebukuro markets persisted in some form until the accelerated urban reconstruction and development leading up to the 1964 Tokyo Olympics.[15] Akihabara, which played a key economic and cultural role in postwar Tokyo as the site of some of the largest electronic retailers in the city and later the locus of an *otaku* subculture centered on anime and video games, was also the former location of a black market specializing in electronic parts.[16] Traces of those original stalls can still be seen in the narrow alleyways and stalls selling a dizzying array of electronic components, located inside buildings close to Akihabara Station, just beyond the neon facades of the large retailers. Shibuya was also a major black-market site. Situated close to a significant residential complex for American soldiers, Shibuya was home to a "labyrinth" of bars and restaurants in makeshift structures, as well as the site of a violent confrontation between Taiwanese gangs and police that galvanized the state's campaign against the markets.[17] The extensive markets there helped to spur the postwar development of Shibuya (FIG. 4), as it became a center of youth-oriented consumer culture and one of the most popular shopping and entertainment districts in the city.

Yet in terms of their impact on postwar Tokyo, the markets of Shinjuku can perhaps be considered paramount. In the city of Edo as well as in the early decades of Tokyo's history, the center of popular life was located in the *shita-machi* (downtown) area of the city, located between the palace and the Sumida

14   Kenji Hashimoto and Kosei Hatsuda, eds., *Sakariba wa yamiichi kara umareta* (Tokyo: Seikyusha, 2016).
15   See Kosei Hatsuda, "Tokyo no sengo fukko to yamiichi," in Hashimoto and Hatsuda, *Sakariba wa*, 45–47.
16   See Kaichiro Morikawa, *Shuto no tanjo: Moeru Akihabara no tanjo* (Tokyo: Gentosha, 2003).
17   See Akihito Aoi, "Shibuya: Yamiichi kara wakamono no machi e," in Hashimoto and Hatsuda, *Sakariba wa*, 88–101.

4

Black market stretching from Shibuya
towards Roppongi, 1945, photographed
four months after the end of the World
War II. Letters of "bread" and "beefsteak"
can be read on the shop curtain or paper
signage. Photo © Shunkichi Kikuchi,
courtesy of Harumi Tago

River to the east, historically the locale of the merchant class. Yet the aftermath of the Great Kanto Earthquake of 1923, which devastated the *shitamachi*
section, saw a sizable migration of residents westward and the concomitant
growth of suburbs on the western outskirts of the city. This process provided
the impetus for the development of Shinjuku, whose station serves as terminus for suburban train lines and that became the largest commuter hub in the
nation.[18] The trend was greatly accelerated after the war, which once again
was marked by the destruction of *shitamachi* Tokyo, and Shinjuku emerged as
a dominant commercial, entertainment, and cultural zone of the city. What
is generally acknowledged as the nation's first black market opened in Shinjuku
on August 20, 1945, only five days after the end of the war, heralded by a newspaper advertisement placed by the Ozu Kanto Group calling for goods from
manufacturers who have "naturally converted to peacetime production."[19]

    Located on the east side of the station, the Shinjuku Market was one
of four major markets surrounding the station (FIG. 3) that made Shinjuku
a vibrant locus of economic activity in the immediate postwar period. Fumiko
Hayashi's novel of occupied Tokyo, *Ukigumo* [*Floating Clouds*] (1951), contains
a vivid description of these markets. When the novel's heroine, Yukiko, returns
to Tokyo from Japanese-occupied Indochina after the war, she encounters
a strikingly transformed cityscape:

> Shinjuku, which she had not seen in many years, was as crowded as
> ever. The fact that she did not see one face she knew made Yukiko
> feel that she was walking the streets of a foreign city […] When she
> turned right alongside the building, she came to a series of alley-
> ways where the wares of one roadside vendor after another were lined
> up. Sardines by the handful were fished out of kerosene cans and
> offered for sale. There was bean-jam candy in little glass-lidded boxes.
> There were vendors selling tangerines heaped up in pyramids, ven-
> dors selling rubber-soled shoes, vendors who laid out rows of frozen
> squid at five yen apiece. Along every alley, such roadside markets
> overflowed in the roadway. In the desolate rubble left by the firebomb-
> ing, dirty street children clustered, taking long drags on cigarettes.
> Yukiko bought some tangerines at twenty yen a pile, clambered atop
> the rubble, and sat down. She peeled a tangerine and ate it. All the trou-
> blesome old ways of life had been smashed to bits, she thought. This
> gave her a cool, refreshing feeling.[20]

18   Jordan Sand, *Tokyo Vernacular: Common Spaces, Local Histories, Found Objects* (Berkeley and Los Angeles:
       The University of California Press, 2013), 33.
19   Cited in Kenji Ino, "Yamiichi kaihoku koto hajime," in *Tokyo yamiichi koboshi*, ed. Kenji Ino (Tokyo: Sofusha,
       1978), 15.
20   Fumiko Hayashi, *Floating Clouds*, trans. Lane Dunlop (New York: Columbia University Press, 2006), 64.

5

5 | A "folk guerrilla" crowd at a rally organized
by the Beheiren [Citizens' Federation
for Peace in Vietnam] filled the west exit
plaza of Shinjuku Station in May 1969.
Photo © Asahi Shimbun

For Yukiko, the Shinjuku markets are a completely novel sight, registering the complete transformation of the city and the destruction of the old order through war and occupation, which has rendered Tokyo as almost a "foreign city."

The markets in Shinjuku were known for their eating and drinking establishments, and they became a favorite haunt of writers, artists, and intellectuals. Some traces of these markets still exist today, such as the Omoide Yokocho (Nostalgia Alley), an alleyway tucked away adjacent to Shinjuku station, where small *yakitori* shops survive in the shadows of towering office buildings and hotels. The Goruden-gai (Golden Town), a block of small drinking houses located a short distance from the station, retains heavy traces of the narrow, wood-construction drinking houses of the postwar markets. Originally situated on the east side of the station and moved to its present location after the cleanup of roadside stalls in 1950, it has been a favored destination for generations of writers and artists. More generally, Shinjuku developed into the city's most prominent *sakariba*, home to a massive concentration of restaurants, bars, and boutique and department stores, as well as the city's largest red-light district.

In the 1950s and 60s, Shinjuku became the locus of Japan's counter-culture, a notable site of avant-gardist artistic practice as well as of political activism, from protests against the renewal of the US-Japan Security Treaty in the late 1950s to the anti-Vietnam War protests of the late 1960s and early 1970s. As Jordan Sand has written, during this time a series of political clashes centered on areas adjacent to Shinjuku Station, involving a contestation over the communal use of public space for political expression and action.[21] In particular, the newly created West Exit Plaza on the west side of Shinjuku station (the site of one of the major postwar markets) became the staging ground for a wide range of activists, who appropriated the transit space for a new type of engagement with the city and its residents, setting up regular "guerilla" folk song performances and political debates and encounters with commuters passing through the area (FIG. 5).[22]

Sand notes that at stake in these actions was the development of a new spatial practice, the creation of a sense of "commons" that existed independently of the state and thus differed from prior examples of public protest that took place in state-sanctioned public spaces such as Hibiya Park.[23] In these contestations, centering on the rights of the populace to communal property, we can see echoes—now primarily political rather than economic—of the struggle over the occupation and appropriation of land that took place in the immediate postwar period in the same area. In fact, historian Kenji Ino

21   See Jordan Sand, *Tokyo Vernacular*, 25–53.
22   Sand, 36.
23   Sand, 33.

called the black markets the originary "liberated zones," a space of (ultimately unrealized) democratic potential where "nationality, class, status, place of origin, and education were not questioned."[24]

Palimpsest of Borderline Space

In this sense, although the black markets are generally seen as ephemeral and transitional spaces that expanded astonishingly fast and then faded just as quickly, their impact continued well beyond their heyday. The markets constituted both temporal and spatial borderlines that marked the interval between the extensive, multiethnic empire and the formation of a national collectivity organized around conceptions of ethnic homogeneity. As borderline spaces, they occupied a contradictory position within the topography of postwar Tokyo. On the one hand, the markets can be seen to have facilitated the transition away from the imperial state and wartime economy toward the social and economic structure of postwar Japan. On the other hand, absorbing the fragments of empire, including returnees from overseas territories and former colonial subjects, they served as containers of an imperial past that, while excluded from the postwar national imaginary, never entirely disappeared from the Tokyo cityscape.

Both of these conflicting characteristics continued to shape the sections of the city where black markets once thrived. As mentioned previously, a number of such sites developed into commercial and entertainment centers of the city that were emblematic of the postwar recovery and, later, the supercharged economic growth powered by a dynamic consumer culture. At the same time, areas such as Shinjuku became the locus of counter cultural movements, protests, and avant-gardist practice, absorbing politically and socially marginalized groups.

In addition, areas associated with black markets have, in recent decades, emerged as the most prominent ethnic enclaves in contemporary Tokyo. As scholars have pointed out, the development of these enclaves has been largely driven by recent migration, particularly from mainland China (following normalization of relations between the two countries and the latter's economic reforms of the 1970s), yet they also formed against the historical backdrop of the postwar markets.[25] In particular, the prevalence of low-rent apartments in these areas, a holdover from the black market era, helped to enable the assimilation of immigrants into the city, where housing is typically difficult for outsiders to secure.

This historical legacy is especially notable in Toshima Ward's Ikebukuro, the location of what has come to be referred to as Ikebukuro Chinatown. Ikebukuro station is the second-largest commuter hub in Tokyo, connecting heavily used private suburban railways to the city's transportation network, and it was the site of one of the largest black markets in Tokyo. Compared to other parts of the city, in Toshima Ward the redevelopment of the postwar markets and the apartment buildings that sprouted up around them occurred relatively late, and the persistence of these rental units provided a means for absorbing immigrants to the city, both from the countryside and abroad.[26] As Jamie Coates has written, in recent years, the ward has emphasized the city's history as a major black market site in touting its development as a "free culture city," recasting what was often a source of denigration and discrimination into a positive value within the rapidly globalizing economy and consumer culture.[27]

Subject to repeated cycles of destruction and reconstruction, including in the 1923 earthquake and the aerial bombardment of WWII, Tokyo has sometimes been described as a city without memory, one that seemingly lacks a substantial connection to its past in the material environment. The black markets appear to embody this transitory, ephemeral quality, yet they also underscore the complexity of the city's relation to its history. As Hatsuda argued, the markets can be seen as an essential aspect of the city that typically remains obscured from view, but which comes to the surface in moments of crisis. Located precisely in the spatial and temporal interstices between collapse and renewal, the black markets served as receptacles for those excluded or marginalized in the reformulation of national collectivity after the war, while also helping to facilitate the city's evolution and transformation through successive stages of history.

24   Kenji Ino, "Yamiichi kaihoku koto hajime," in *Tokyo yamiichi koboshi*, ed. Kenji Ino (Tokyo: Sofusha, 1978), 33.
25   See Junko Tajima, "Chinese Newcomers in the Global City Tokyo: Social Networks and Settlement Tendencies," *International Journal of Japanese Sociology* 12 (2003): 68–69, 72–73; Jaime Coates, "Ikebukuro In-Between: Mobility and the Formation of the Yamanote's Heterotopic Borderland," *Japan Forum* 30, no. 2 (2018): 170–172.
26   Coates, 171.
27   Coates, 178–180.

REVITALIZING THE COMMUNITY OF THE CHO

● HIROTO KOBAYASHI

Throughout history, the lifestyles of people who gather and dwell in cities have undergone dramatic transformations. We are living in one such epoch. When we look at urban life today from the standpoint of "community," we see major changes afoot in the relationships among, and spaces created by, people living together in neighborhoods—the local communities that are so intimately linked to our satisfaction with daily life. Cities are losing long-nurtured systems and formats of community, and with them the richness of lives rooted in a neighborhood and the relationships that thrive there.

I believe that there is wisdom to be found, as well as values we would do well to incorporate into contemporary life, in the forms of community that are on the verge of disappearing in Japan today. What are the formats and systems of these vanishing communities? By examining them in detail here, I would like to offer a basis for contemplating how cities will change from now on, how we can deal with those changes, and what they signify for us.

The Dilution and Fragmentation of Relationships

One contemporary phenomenon that continues to have a profound impact on urban life is the loss of local culture caused by the degradation of neighborhoods in the wake of large-scale redevelopment projects, which are still touted as engines of urban economic growth. In September 2021, for example, the Yaesu/Nihonbashi/Kyobashi district on the east side of Tokyo Central Station was the site of 16 massive redevelopment projects in progress; over the next 15 years or so these will produce a battery of high-rise office buildings with a total of three million square meters of floor space. Behind this activity is the determination of the government and major developers to transform the area into a mecca for global business concerns. Projects like these currently underway in many parts of downtown Tokyo are an extrapolation of the urban development schemes undertaken by the national and local governments during the economic boom years of the 1960s and 1970s. In today's neoliberal economic climate, such projects are carried out by private entities and are heavily skewed toward office functions that promise high profit margins. The result is the rapid metamorphosis of the cityscape on a massive scale. Meanwhile, deregulation in the name of public benefits and convenience is altering the environment of these development sites and the neighborhoods around them.

The district east of Tokyo Station is the city's old merchant and artisan quarter. It dates back to the founding of Edo in the early seventeenth century, when it was designated as an area for the homes and businesses of merchants who migrated to the new seat of the shogunate from the imperial capital of Kyoto and its neighboring province, Omi (now Shiga Prefecture). One of the hallmarks of this district is the number of *shinise*, "long-established houses" that have been in business since that time and survive to this day. Hence it is

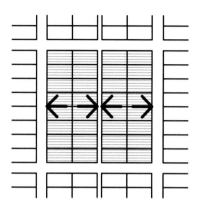

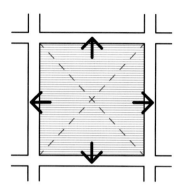

Nimen-machi (two-sided block)
A *machi* consisted of a square block, about 121 meters per side, with a narrow street passing through the center. Each *nimen-machi* was composed of up to 32 lots (four from east to west by eight from north to south), depending on the class of the residents

Shimen-machi (four-sided block)
The rigid division of lots in the nimen-machi dissolved as houses began altering their orientation to face the nearest major street, thus forming a *shimen-machi*

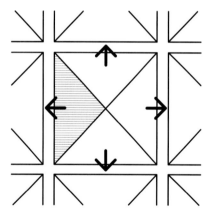

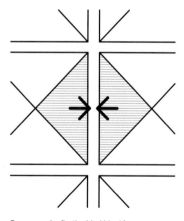

Katagawa-cho (one-sided block)
As the relationship of each house to a particular street became more pronounced, the blocks were redefined and renamed from *machi* to *cho*

Ryogawa-cho (both-sided block)
Houses facing each other across the same street formed communities known as *ryogawa-cho*

1

1   Evolution of the concept of community from *machi* to *cho*. Source: Hiroto Kobayashi, "*Cho*: A Persistent Neighborhood Unity Maintaining Microculture in Japanese Cities: Analyzing the Relationship between Social Structure and Urban Form," (PhD diss., Harvard University, 2003), 16

known for the longstanding and deep-seated ties of its inhabitants to one another and to the land they live on. When a large-scale urban renewal project comes to a historic neighborhood like this one, it transmutes not only the shape of the urban space, but also the very culture of the neighborhood. That impact can disrupt the community of locally rooted human relations and destroy the unique culture it has nurtured.

Another contemporary phenomenon is the direct connection with the rest of the world engendered by the spread of the Internet. As we have seen during the coronavirus pandemic that began in 2020, the ongoing digitization of information has accelerated the digitization of human connections as well, so that networks formed by individuals are now linked globally, unfettered by space or time. This trend has, however, also triggered a sharp decrease in people's direct interactions with one another as well as with specific places or spaces in the city. Our relations with real people and places are rapidly attenuating. On the other hand, the same trend may be said to have increased our personal appreciation of the appeal and significance of real places and spaces.

The remodeling of Japan's urban spaces is thus transforming its cities on both the "hard" and "soft" level in the name of convenience and economic efficiency. But this change comes at the price of obliterating the diverse relationships nurtured by those spaces to date. What can the history of the Japanese form of community teach us as we strive to address this situation?

Cho of the Low City, Machi of the High City

When the imperial capital of Heiankyo (today's Kyoto) was laid out in the late eighth century, the planners took their cue from the grid pattern used in Chinese cities. The capital was composed of blocks called *machi*, which were ringed by earthen walls and moats that enclosed the residences of the nobility and others of high social status, as well as those of commoners. Initially the houses in these *machi* had entrances onto the streets only on their east or west sides, a configuration known as *nimen-machi* (a "two-sided" block) (FIG. 1). In the twelfth century, however, markets began to proliferate along the city's streets and become important places of public commerce. People began opening their residences to the streets on all four sides of the *machi*, tearing down the walls and filling in the moats. This marked the advent of the "four-sided" block, or *shimen-machi*.

By the thirteenth century, a sense of solidarity had developed among houses facing the same street, leading to the subdivision of the *machi* blocks into four sections known as *katagawa-cho* or "one-sided" blocks. Now a row of houses on one side of a street constituted a single community unit. The change in the appellation of these blocks from *machi* to *cho* (different pronunciations of the same *kanji* character 町) signified a change from the enclosed,

2

3

Utagawa Hiroshige, *The Prosperity of the Odenmagai Street in the Eastern Capital*, 1843-1847, showing an Edo-period *shitamachi* block in *ryogawa-cho* format. Courtesy of the National Diet Library

3 Utagawa Hiroshige, *Kasumigaseki no kei*, [View of Kasumigaseki] from the series *Edo Meisho* [Famous Places in Edo], ca. 1840-1842, depicting samurai mansions, Buddhist temples, and Shinto shrines in an Edo-period *yamanote* neighborhood. Courtesy of Tokyo Metropolitan Library

inward-facing *machi* to the outward-facing *cho*. The fourteenth century saw the emergence of *ryogawa-cho* ("both-sided" blocks) in which houses facing each other across a street formed a community unit. In times of war and social unrest, these communities banded together to protect their homes and livelihoods.

The *ryogawa-cho* format, centered around a street flanked by rows of houses, evolved into the template for communities in Japan. When Tokugawa Ieyasu became shogun in 1603 and built a new de facto capital in Edo, the *ryogawa-cho* pattern was transplanted to Edo's merchant district, where it survives today in the area known as Tokyo's *shitamachi* ("low city") (FIG. 2).

There is a second template for neighborhoods in Tokyo, however. This one is modeled on the blocks laid out in the city's hilly *yamanote* area, a "high city" often contrasted with the "low city" of the *shitamachi*. During the Edo period (1603–1867), the higher ground of the *yamanote* was occupied by samurai mansions as well as Buddhist temples and Shinto shrines. Unlike the residences of the merchant and artisan classes in the *shitamachi*, the estates of these mansions, temples, and so on were surrounded by walls and shut off from the streets, forming their own worlds within those walls. Streets did not function as common spaces shared by the houses fronting them as in the *shitamachi*, but as boundaries separating estates from one another. In that sense, the enclosed, territorial character of living spaces in the *yamanote* resembled the *machi* of medieval Heiankyo, where the blocks were isolated by streets on all sides according to the Chinese model. Therefore, we can say that Tokyo traditionally consists of two types of socio-spatial zones—the *cho* of the *ryogawa-cho* format exemplified by the merchant and artisan quarters of the *shitamachi*, and the *machi* exemplified by the estates of the *yamanote* (FIG. 3).

In the old imperial capital of Kyoto, you can still see how the street passing through each *cho* continues to function in the management of buildings and the maintenance of human relationships. If you visit a *cho* in Kyoto early on a summer morning, you will find its residents sweeping and tossing water on the section of the street in front of their house. These actions not only keep the pavement clean and cool, but reflect the responsibility felt by each member of the community for the well-being of the common space of the *cho*. At the same time, the ritual is an implicit assertion that the street in front of one's house is part of one's territory. In other words, the range of pavement one splashes with water is an indicator of the extent of one's connection with the *cho* community (FIG. 4).

On dry winter evenings, members of each block association will take turns walking around their *cho*, beating wooden clappers and calling out, "Fire watch!" for fire prevention purposes. The shouting serves not only to encourage vigilance against conflagrations, but also to announce one's membership in and service to the closed community of the *cho*.

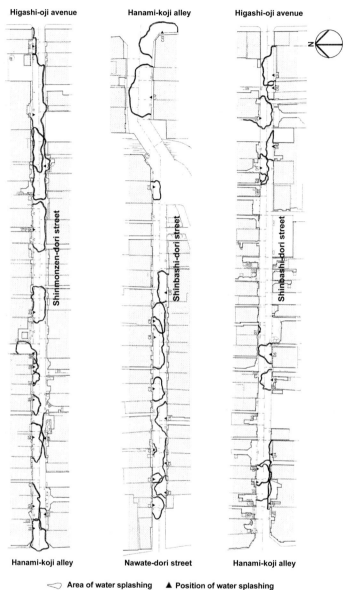

Higashi-oji avenue   Hanami-koji alley   Higashi-oji avenue

Shinmonzen-dori street

Shinbashi-dori street

Shinbashi-dori street

Hanami-koji alley   Nawate-dori street   Hanami-koji alley

▽ Area of water splashing   ▲ Position of water splashing

△ Entrance/exit of neighboring house   ▨ Built area

4 Results of a survey of "water-splashing" territories along streets in Kyoto in Hiroto Kobayashi and Junzo Munemoto, "A Study on How Residents' Territorial Recognition and Neighborhood Social Structures Relate to Spatial Understanding: Through Research on the Behavior of Cleaning and Spreading Water (*uchimizu*) on Streets," in *The Collection of the Research Reports from the Kinki Branch, the Architectural Institute of Japan*, Vol. 38 (1998): 209-212

In this manner, members of the *cho* community utilize the intermediate space *(ma)*[1] of the street to cultivate solidarity in thought and action and form a social organization rooted in the land they share. The street thus creates the community and helps maintain it. Traditionally, the street gave birth to invisible networks of people and spaces, nurturing a distinctive culture in every neighborhood, however small. The communities that arose from such microcultures became the defining constituent elements of their locale, and in the aggregate they created the *chonin* (literally "*cho* people") culture of the Edo-era *shitamachi*.

From Fragmentation to Reconnection

When downtown neighborhoods are subjected to redevelopment today, such projects are typically planned in block units. As a result, the streets that once linked the *cho* communities become demarcation lines that isolate those blocks from the rest of the neighborhood, just as in the *yamanote* pattern. This fragmentation risks the eradication of the microculture that makes a neighborhood unique.

Future urban development schemes, including large-scale redevelopment projects, must take into consideration the organization and layout of the *cho*—communities that have been a real, albeit barely visible, presence nurtured by the neighborhood. An understanding of the system of relationships and connections that comprise the *cho* is crucial to the success of the measures required to reinforce—not destroy—them. In short, we must prevent the boundaries of redevelopment projects from turning into barriers that break up the *cho*. To this end it is imperative that we construct a framework for personal interactions that will reinforce connections among the people of a neighborhood, as well as spaces that facilitate such interactions. This framework must be one devised with the participation and approval of local residents.

In order to build, maintain, and develop a community, it is not enough to simply ensure the safety and security of its residents. One must also consider the following measures as means to that end: the perpetuation of seasonal festivals and other events that enlist community participation; ensuring equity among residents through the transfer of air rights, a concept only recently incorporated into urban redevelopment schemes in Japan; and preservation of the neighborhood's existing ambience. All of these demand urban development strategies and administrative measures based in the local community and its traditions.

Let me cite the example of the Ginza district of downtown Tokyo, for which I serve as an adviser on community development. Ginza-dori, the area's

---

[1]   Literary critic Takeo Okuno writes that a keen Japanese sensibility about relationships is evident in the use of 間 *ma* (which may also be read as *kan* or *ken*), meaning an interval or "space between," in words and phrases that express relations between elements, such as 時間 *jikan* (time), 空間 *kukan* (space), and 世間 *seken* (society).

main thoroughfare, has been an interface between Japan and the rest of the world since the Meiji era (1868–1912). Today it is still the country's premier shopping street, able to attract customers and name-brand businesses from around the globe. The reason is simple: Ginza-dori's open, pedestrian-friendly ambience makes it a pleasurable place to visit. Street-level shops line the avenue, each projecting its own colorful image. To enhance the Ginza's vitality, the district hosts numerous events that offer opportunities for local proprietors and visitors to mingle. On one of Ginza-dori's "pedestrian paradise" days, a practice that originated here, the street is closed to traffic and throngs of people can be found strolling along it, window-shopping as they go. Drawing tourists, families going out to eat, and single shoppers alike, Ginza-dori is a space that embraces a wide range of activities (FIG. 5).

The shop owners who watch over the district say that they come to the Ginza every day like farmers coming to till their fields. The analogy speaks to the pivotal role their neighborhood plays as a source of sustenance in people's lives. The local community development council has established an ordinance that prohibits high-rise construction and maintains the human scale of the district. The interactions the street fosters between visitors to the Ginza and those doing business there are the engine that gives this *cho* its life force and ensures that it will be passed on intact to the next generation.

5

Ginza-dori on a "pedestrian paradise," 2008. Photo by the author

Revitalizing the Street

In the society of the future, we can anticipate that the practice of "dwelling" will not be limited to one location, but that people will move their base of livelihood at frequent intervals. Since a city is an aggregation of the day-to-day lives of many people, this increasing fluidity will necessitate a fundamental rethinking of the concept of urban community development. In a society where people no longer "settle down," what form is to be taken, what role is to be played, by the human and spatial aggregation that is a place-based community? In my view, the socio-spatial zone we call the *cho* is a useful model for the renewal of the urban environment under these circumstances. As our society ages, and as households and individual residents become increasingly isolated, incorporation of the framework for personal and spatial connections represented by the *cho* is more essential than ever.

In the post-corona era, downtown business districts, where the largest redevelopment projects hold sway, will inevitably see a drop-off in office leasing, their most lucrative source of rental income. The search is now on for urban functions that will make up the difference. If the *raison d'être* of a city is to cultivate new cultures from the brew of people, information, and capital gathering there, then what we will desire of cities in the future is not a place to work, but a place to gather. The shared space[2] of the street, with its power to bring people together and nurture a locally rooted microculture, offers great hope as a catalyst for that purpose.

The lower stories of buildings facing the street can be used for a variety of activities. A street space in the *ryogawa-cho* format stimulates all manner of interactions among people and things, and these in turn can generate new values. One of the controversial aspects of large-scale developments is their tendency to eradicate small alleys and the side streets that pass through a block. That problem can be solved if, instead, such streets are preserved or restored in the development process, allowing them to continue to function as arteries linking neighborhoods.

As an intermediate space rooted in a neighborhood, the street is a pivotal presence amid the spaces that have sustained urban culture in Japan. Streets serve as *ma*, openings in the crowded fabric of the city. Since ancient times, people have gravitated to these open spaces to make connections, find their identity, and create something they are proud of. This traditional means of creating a local culture can be applied to the community development of the future. The people who gather there will generate the conditions for the birth of a new urban culture, a city of the future with a distinctly Japanese flavor.

---

2   Whether in human or spatial relations, "public" and "private" are treated by Western thinkers as being in an oppositional, dualistic relationship. In Japan, however, "public" and "private" are treated as poles of a gradational relationship, with "shared" relations residing along the spectrum between them.

INITIATIVES IN YANESEN

● MAYUMI MORI

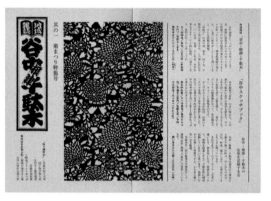

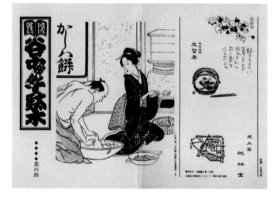
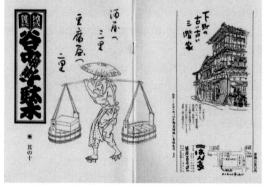

1 | Covers of the early issues of the maga-
zine *Yanaka, Nezu, Sendagi*, 1984-1986.
Courtesy of Yanesen Kenkyukai

In October 1984, I and two other young mothers living in an old Tokyo neighborhood called Yanesen launched a local magazine titled *Yanaka, Nezu, Sendagi* (FIG. 1) [the full names of the three districts comprising the nickname "Yanesen"] to record memories of our neighborhood with the aim of preserving its history, culture, scenery, and people. That first 1984 issue had only eight pages of text. Themed around the Edo- and Meiji-era Chrysanthemum Festival, which we and other residents revived on the grounds of the Daienji temple, it featured our neighbors' histories, traditional songs, and editors' essays exploring the stories of Kasamori Osen, a teahouse maid who was the belle of Yanaka during the Edo period (1603–1867), and the *kiku ningyo* (chrysanthemum dolls) of Dangozaka, which were a popular attraction up to the end of the Meiji era (1868–1912). The 1,000 copies we printed to distribute on the day of the festival sold out, and we kept reprinting it until we had sold 16,000 copies of the issue.

The history of Yanesen arguably begins in the middle of the Edo period, when the city of Tokyo's predecessor, Edo, had a population of a million, making it the largest city in the world. About 70 percent of the city's area was given over to residences for the samurai class, while another 15 percent belonged to temples and shrines. Commoners, who made up 90 percent of the population, occupied the remaining 15 percent of land. The districts of Yanaka, Nezu, and Sendagi were located on the outskirts of the city proper at the time (FIG. 2).

The basic layout of this trio of neighborhoods has remained substantially the same since then, as have their distinct personalities. Very generally speaking, Yanaka is a town of temples, Nezu is a valley enclave of artisans and merchants, and Sendagi is a hilltop residential area. The corporate warriors who are today's equivalent of the samurai live up on the hill (Sendagi), the shopping streets are down at the bottom (Nezu), and the alleys that branch off from there are dotted with old row houses occupied by artisans, entertainers, and other practitioners of a freelance lifestyle (also Nezu). Yanaka is still full of temples, which lease out much of their land to builders of apartment houses and single-family dwellings.

The samurai class that lived in the *yamanote*, or upland, districts of the city during the Edo period prized loyalty, filial piety, and obedience to authority, and made much of family lineage and educational background. The commoners who lived in the lower *shitamachi* neighborhoods, on the other hand, gave greater weight to community and personal relations, and were more concerned with mutual assistance than with social status or organizational affiliation. This contrast in values prompted the *shitamachi* merchants—who prided themselves on their refined tastes—to ridicule the ways of *yamanote* residents, many of whom were samurai from the provinces posted to the *daimyo* mansions there, as boorish and "provincial."[1] Due to the strict caste system enforced by the Tokugawa Shogunate, samurai were allowed to kill commoners with impunity.

However, when the samurai ran out of money, the merchants got their revenge by lending them funds at high interest. A popular saying among the merchants at the time was, "Why should we fear a two-sworded samurai when we skewer sardines for dinner?"

Vestiges of those times persisted well into the modern era in Yanesen. In the 1980s the area still had plenty of pawnshops, as well as 15 public baths. As Shikitei Sanba (1776–1822) vividly described it in his comic novel *Ukiyoburo* (Ukiyo Bath) (FIG. 3), the Edo-era bathhouse was not just a place to cleanse the body, but also a community center of sorts where locals exchanged all kinds of information. Even in the subsequent Meiji era, a time of rapid modernization, few households could afford their own private bath, and even prominent residents like the novelists Mori Ogai and Natsume Soseki, who both lived in Sendagi, frequented the public bathhouses.

Today every home can heat its bath in no time with natural gas, yet somehow that seems like a waste of water and energy. Not too long ago, a gas line near my house ruptured and the ward office handed out free public-bath tickets to everyone in the affected area. In that sense, the two remaining bathhouses still have an important role to play in emergencies. Yet gentrification of the neighborhood proceeds apace without regard for the quality of life of elderly people of modest means, who have no choice but to move from their bathless old apartment houses into publicly owned nursing homes.

Alleys and Row Houses

In 1883, modernization came to this part of Tokyo in the form of Ueno Station, a major train terminal that was the point of disembarkation for people arriving in the capital from Tohoku, the northern region of the country. After the Tokugawa Shogunate ceded political power to the emperor in 1867, provincial lords in the north who supported the Shogun rebelled against the new imperial government in a civil war that lasted until the battle of Hakodate in May 1869. Though the rebellion was quelled, the government knew that another might erupt if steps were not taken to improve the lot of the impoverished Tohoku region. The new railway served to transport produce and other goods from Tohoku to Tokyo, as well as people: the capital needed laborers from the north to help build it into a modern metropolis.

Ueno Station was the terminal not only for trains from Tohoku, but also from Nagano and Niigata. The people arriving on them were hired by merchants and artisans to work as maids and factory workers, and many gravitated to the alleys of Yanesen, which adjoined Ueno, for lodging. Those who became successful in Tokyo built cheap housing for rent here, particularly to accommodate later arrivals who often depended on the good graces of predecessors from the same village to find work. With employment agencies located in Ueno (and the station nearby if circumstances compelled one to skip town), it was a convenient location.

Although we editors had originally intended to have our neighbors, who were also lifelong residents of Yanesen, write their own stories, they were reluctant to do so, and so we began recording their oral histories in 1984—to date, we've collected several thousand. Later, during the 1990s, we conducted research and interviews on the alleys and row houses of Yanesen—their layout, design, and living conditions. *Nagaya*—long rows of small homes with adjoining walls—lined narrow, secluded streets (FIG. 4). We residents of Yanesen lived a quasi-communal lifestyle, borrowing miso or soy sauce or rice from each other when we ran out, cooking extra portions of stew and tempura to share with neighbors, and passing out potatoes and apples delivered from their hometown. It was a sharing culture.

For alley residents, the entire neighborhood was home. When I went out on one interview, an old lady living next door to the house I was visiting appeared, took out some sweets from the cupboard, and served me tea. When I went back to return some documents to the interviewee, I found the same lady there taking a nap—she had just lost her husband and was taking a break from the hustle and bustle of the funeral in progress at her own house. Residents blithely remarked that they never had to worry about burglars because there were always people awake in the homes facing the alley twenty-four hours a day—either someone up until three in the morning, or someone waking up then. Adjoining row houses usually had their second-floor laundry platforms connected to give everyone more space to hang up their wash.

These backstreet row houses had no yards. However, residents would place potted plants in the narrow space between their wall and the street and grow whatever they liked there. There was no dearth of local events, like the morning glory market, the Chinese lantern plant market, and the revived Chrysanthemum Festival, where one could purchase potted plants. When we surveyed these roadside gardens, we found many plants that were not merely ornamental: edibles like perilla, bitter melon, sponge gourd, and laurel, as well as cosmetic or medicinal herbs like horsetail for polishing fingernails and aloe vera for bug bites. One resident laughed off the lack of garden space by quipping, "I'm just renting my garden out to Rikugien"—the spacious Edo-era formal garden not far from Yanesen. People without baths at home would make similar jokes about loaning their tub to the local bathhouse.

After I married in 1979, I lived in a Yanesen *nagaya* that had survived the firebombing of Tokyo in 1945. The house where I grew up in the 1950s and 1960s was also a *nagaya* in a different part of Yanesen, and the culture at that time was similar. The people next door were like our relatives, and since

I   *Daimyo* is generally translated as "feudal lord." As the feudal lords of each province were compelled to spend every other year in Edo with their vassals, each of them also owned a mansion in Edo.

2   The Yanaka, Nezu and Sendagi districts (marked with white lines) in Edo. *Edo Kiriezu, Owariya Seishichi edition*, a detailed wood-block print map of Edo, published in 1849-1862. Courtesy of the National Diet Library

3   Shikitei Sanba, *Ukiyoburo*, Volume 2 (Edo: Edo Shorin, 1809), illustrating a women's bath as a social gathering place. Source: National Diet Library

4

Old rowhouses in Yanaka, Tokyo, photo-
      graphed in 1985. Courtesy of the Tokyo
      Metropolitan Government

my mother was busy as a dentist, I would go to the neighbors' place after school, eat a snack, and do my homework there. The lady of the house was a full-time housewife, but she would go shopping for dinner ingredients for my mother. Dozaka Market, the little marketplace right across the way, boasted a butcher, a fishmonger, a greengrocer, a tofu shop, a dumpling shop, and a confectioner.

On the other hand, the house next door lacked a bathtub, so the three children living there took their baths at our place. We were also the first family to get a television set, so neighborhood kids would gather at our house from late afternoon until suppertime to watch the cartoons and dramas of those early days of TV. The back alleys were a child's paradise because cars never passed through, so we played tag, hopscotch, baseball, cards, and marbles right in the street. I feel lucky to have grown up in such a happy environment.

Pros and Cons of Convenience

In the 1980s, big money began to flow into the neighborhood. A large Summit supermarket opened, offering one-stop shopping for everything from groceries to toilet paper. Then, in the 1990s, chain convenience stores began to pop up here and there. Nowadays most of them are open 24 hours, selling magazines, newspapers, underwear, socks, stationery, umbrellas, coffee, and more. You can make photocopies there, or purchase train and concert tickets. Students, singles, and company employees working overtime at the office have all become convenience store regulars.

These stores have, in fact, become de facto community centers. They are the perfect place for students coming home late after club activities at the nearby middle or high school to grab a snack. And around 11 in the morning, the elderly people living alone in the neighborhood gather there and check in on each other. Because they're open all night and can provide shelter in an emergency, the stores are also popular with women worried about their safety on dark streets.

Yet these same convenience stores and supermarkets are responsible for the fact that only 20 sake shops remain out of a previous 60, and only two tofu shops where there were once 23. There is nothing as tasty as freshly made local tofu, but most people buy theirs at the supermarket now, and the factory-made variety keeps longer in the refrigerator. Meanwhile, people concerned with obtaining fresh organic produce order their food from a co-op or a home delivery service.

The Bubble That Hasn't Burst

Around 1986, land prices in Yanesen began to rise, real-estate sharks moved in, and condominiums sprang up along the main thoroughfares. Some of these streets are flanked by steep cliffs, so people in the neighborhoods sandwiched between the cliffs and the rows of new buildings were deprived of sunlight and subjected to the wind gusts generated by the new high-rises. Inheritance and property taxes also rose, causing an exodus of elderly residents to the homes of children living in the suburbs. In Yanesen, they had enjoyed access to daycare services, poetry and calligraphy clubs, and familiar hospitals and clinics. Many of the elderly passed away not long after moving out of town and losing all of these community bonds. And with funerals held so far from home, few, if any, of their friends were able to attend.

These were the circumstances that spurred us to publish a magazine devoted to chronicling memories of our neighborhood for 26 years, from 1984 to 2010—94 issues in all. (We also published three issues of an English-language edition, titled *Yanesen*.) During this same period we also participated in the struggle to protect the residence rights of local people from developers, and to preserve historic buildings in the area like the Ichida, Yasuda, and Denchu Hirakushi residences.

The inheritance tax is meant to be an equalizing measure to prevent the consolidation of wealth in the affluent class. However, land prices in Tokyo are so steep that the tax, even on a small house of a hundred square meters or so, is prohibitive. In order to pay the tax, the heirs have no choice but to sell off some or all of an inherited property. The result is the loss of many old houses and trees to developers. In the process, family documents, memorial tablets, books, and artwork are discarded as well. Though Japan's late-1980s real estate bubble burst in 1992, and the banks that had financed the land sharks and driven lower-income people out of their homes were called to task, most of them survived with the help of mergers and taxpayer-funded government subsidies.

From 2010 or so, young people, those around the age of my generation's children, began to take an active part in the life of the neighborhood. This also marked the end of an era of huge public structures by big-name architects like Kenzo Tange and Tadao Ando. Young architects opened offices in Yanesen and embarked on projects renovating and repurposing old houses. Other youthful entrepreneurs proved adept at renting storefronts on the cheap and opening new retail businesses selling used books, T-shirts, shoes, brushes, bags, handmade clothing, or woodwork. They also developed their own network of contacts. One product of this solidarity was the establishment of the Yanesen Community Development Fund, which finances the preservation and renovation of old houses, giving new life to structures that would otherwise have been demolished.

During the coronavirus pandemic of 2020 and 2021, local eating and drinking spots were hit hard by government mandates to shorten their hours and forgo selling alcohol. Many proprietors attempted to make up for the loss of income by offering takeout food. Several establishments in Yanesen teamed up with the Tokyobike bicycle shop and launched the Yanesen Delivery service. Staff with time on their hands volunteered to deliver dishes prepared by participating businesses for a fixed price of 500 yen per order. This service expanded the customer base for area restaurants and bars as residents began to help them out by buying locally. It also facilitated exchanges of information via Twitter. Meanwhile, the foreign tourists who thronged Yanesen before the pandemic had dwindled nearly to zero, so Sawanoya, an inn catering to visitors from abroad, made its rooms available to Japanese locals working remotely. It also opened two of its attractively appointed private baths to overjoyed residents in a neighborhood that had lost the last of its public bathhouses.

Despite rumors that land prices would plunge after the conclusion of the highly unpopular Tokyo Olympics, Yanesen's popularity remains undiminished and its land prices continue to climb. Factors include the failure of government economic policies and the growing gap between the super-rich and the ranks of temporary workers unable to earn no more than 2 million yen (US$ 17,500) a year. With Otemachi, Japan's financial center, only ten minutes away by subway, developers in Yanesen are trying to attract power couples working for downtown corporations.

The bubble-era system persists today: banks lend money to developers, who continue to erase the neighborhood's collective memory. We are on the verge of reliving the nightmare of past decades. Just recently, criticism has been leveled at a plan to tear down the stone walls in a beautiful, leafy old residential area to make way for a condo, and another plan to build a condo right next to the Asakura Museum of Sculpture, a nationally known landmark and registered cultural property.

Until now, the government's stance has been to permit any development that conforms to the Building Standards Law and the City Planning Act. One reason is the prospect of long-term tax revenues from wealthy young families purchasing condos. Virtually no measures have been enacted to preserve the history, culture, and ambience of local neighborhoods, and residents have begun to realize that, as things stand now, it is impossible to protect their townscapes. Granted, the national government has systems to protect cityscapes and historical heritage. However, the Tokyo Metropolitan Government offers no such support.

What is needed now is to apply these government initiatives to downtown metropolitan neighborhoods like Yanesen, and to implement mechanisms for district planning and mutual agreement on building standards by residents. Improvement of the local government's system of support for residents' initiatives is also needed. Without these measures, Tokyo will lose its historic neighborhoods. That would be a tragedy not only for local residents, but also for the tourist industry and the world at large.

THE DILEMMA OF DEVELOPING A NEIGHBORHOOD

● CONVERSATION III WITH MASAMI KOBAYASHI

1

2

●   MOHSEN MOSTAFAVI: Shimokitazawa, as I gather, is a town that has a unique subculture brewed from a mix of grassroots theatre, music, and fashion, and it's favored by young people. For quite some time, you've been leading a movement there against large-scale development, and you documented the process in the book *The DNA of Shimokitazawa*. First, can you tell us how you became involved and what you did?

●   MASAMI KOBAYASHI: In a nutshell, a conflict broke out seventeen years ago between some of the residents and the municipality of Setagaya (where Shimokitazawa is located) over a major urban planning project involving the center of town, which included widening the main streets. This street-widening project was bundled together with a plan to remove the railway crossing the street as part of a district scheme for easing traffic around the train station. The plan also follows the Tokyo government's policy of building a network of urban arteries around the city center, a policy dating back some 50 years. So some residents raised their voice against street widening, as it would harm the urban fabric of the neighborhood.

    In Japan, the value of land is linked to the width of the street that it's facing. So, the wider the street, the higher the price of the land facing it; and the property tax is likewise higher. Therefore, both land-owners and developers have a vested interest in street widening, as does the government.

    The municipality promised the shopkeepers along the main streets that they would relax the building height limit if the shopkeepers agreed to the new district plan (including street widening), and that the relaxed volume limits would be more than what is normally granted. This deregulation would enable landowners or developers to build seven to ten stories instead of the current five, all for having their prop-erty line set back 50 centimeters from the current street edge. You can imagine that the jump from five to seven to ten stories would easily affect the atmosphere of the neighborhood.

A Conflict Between Economics and Culture

○   KAYOKO OTA: Shimokitazawa is one of the towns that developed around railways that carry workers living in the outskirts to the center of Tokyo. Typically, these towns have one or more shopping streets called *shoten-gai*, which stretch out from the station and penetrate the residential quarters around it. So the conflict over the street widening divided the residents or landowners in the central area (who can benefit from the project) from

3

4

3	The last greengrocer in Shimokitazawa, which closed in 2013	5	Examples of the adaptive reuse of an old house as a café or shop can be found all over Shimokitazawa
4	A *shotengai* shopping street is a social mixing space. Photo © Momo Yago	6	Pre-development congestion around the Shimokitazawa railway station. Photo © Momo Yago

5

6

Two-story wooden structure shop buildings, a typology common before World War II

Four- to five-story reinforced concrete shop buildings, typically built from the 1950s to the 1970s

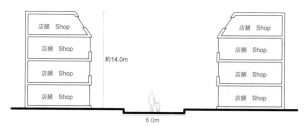

Since 2010, shop building heights of up to seven stories are permitted, with the stipulation that the building front be set back 0.5 m and 2.0 m from the street

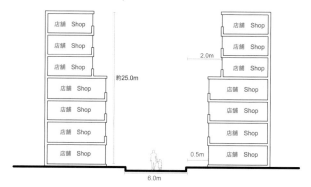

7

7 | The relationship between street width and building height in a commercial district. Courtesy of Greenline Shimokitazawa

those living further out as well as visitors who were attached to the character of Shimokitazawa.

●   That's right. The municipality gave an incentive to the main street merchants' association with the height deregulation, something that the residents living outside the district planning area opposed. When the plan became known to the public in 2004, some opposing residents came to my office for help. I responded by having my university lab research the possible consequences of the street widening. Apparently, the impact would be enormous. It was clear that the plan would spoil the character of a neighborhood that had, until now, maintained a human scale and intimate atmosphere.

    This research and public discussion led to forming the nonprofit organization Shimokitazawa Forum in the same year.[1] We organized a number of seminars and workshops with the residents and specialists with a view to formulating a counterproposal. We appealed continually to the municipality, but they were stubbornly resistant. The street-widening act was officially approved by the Urban Planning Committee of the Setagaya municipality in 2006. You can imagine how shocked we were. But we didn't give up working against the plan until the election of liberal mayor Nobuto Hosaka five years later, who drastically changed the municipality's approach. Now the execution of the plan has almost stopped.

●   So, you and your team have been working on this movement for seventeen years. That's quite a long time. Can you tell us exactly what is it that people tried to protect?

●   Before the modern age, Shimokitazawa was a farmland. When a large part of central Tokyo was destroyed by the Great Kanto Earthquake in 1923, many people moved in this area. Houses were built quickly and without proper urban planning; two private railway lines came to run through this area and opened stations, which made street widening unnecessary.

    As you mentioned, what really makes Shimokitazawa special is its strong subculture, first sown by Kazuo Honda when he opened the first theater in 1982. Soon, similar "off-off-Broadway" theaters and live music clubs followed, then came cheap sewing shops, and so on. Along the way, various synergies contributed to the organic growth of Shimokitazawa's unique culture, which is firmly rooted in an intricate, human-scale urban fabric (FIGS. 3, 4, 5, 6).

---

1   Shimokitazawa Forum was renamed the Association to Think about the Odakyu Line Site in 2008, which became the nonprofit organization Greenline Shimokitazawa in 2011.

Instigating as an Alternative Form of Development

● In the long process of your team's engagement in the neighborhood, I assume you also thought of alternative development models to revitalize the neighborhood. In other words, beyond protecting a neighborhood, do you think we can also instigate, start something?

● Well, that's also an important part of our activities that the nonprofit organization is working on. After the new mayor arrived in 2011, the organization shifted its focus to thinking about how to "instigate" people to manage the neighborhood autonomously. It had already been decided that the Odakyu Electric Railway, which runs the Odakyu line, would move the railway track (that crosses a main street) underground instead of elevating it. So our grassroots organization took the initiative of thinking about how to reuse the long strip of land that would be left after the track's relocation.

To develop ideas for using the new land, we continued to work closely with residents and specialists from various fields (including urban planning and architecture) as well as representatives from the municipality. We made a public call for ideas. At the end of the process in 2012, we compiled the citizens' land-use recommendations[2] and presented them to the mayor.

● That's impressive. I assume the recommendation included residents' requests for new forms of urban institutions in the neighborhoods—a library, kindergarten, or other kind of public spaces, even small-scale ones. These can be considered to be alternative forms of development that enhance the sense of community. Were such needs articulated?

● Yes, there were all kinds of requests that came from the residents through workshops and public calls, and some of these were represented in the aforementioned recommendation. Basically, based on what we learned from the Great East Japan Earthquake about how important open spaces are for evacuation (especially in a densely built area), our proposal was to keep the number of new buildings to a minimum. And these new buildings should be institutions for public use, such as libraries of different kinds, large open spaces where temporary performance stages or markets can be held, a community farmland, coworking facilities in small glass boxes surrounded by woods, and so on. We also wanted to express our strong desire that these facilities be surrounded by vegetation: to fill the site with as greenery as possible (FIG. 8).

A Channel for Demands

●   I think that's really great. So, your organization instigated from scratch, building a system of empowering residents so that they could be engaged in the discussion of demands, of what's missing. Which brings me to more questions. If, for example, we wanted to enhance the neighborhood's characteristics by adding facilities for the citizens, who would we talk to? If we made a list of things and asked for discussion or advice, is there a local district planning office to take it to? Do you present your ideas at a community center? How would you begin to engage people in the conversation about what's missing in the neighborhood, what it needs, what would improve their lives?

●   Well, that's really the problem. The whole public process of making decisions and planning new institutions, even on a small scale, is so inaccessible that it prevents the public from understanding and being engaged in the process. It's not that the information is unavailable, but in effect, residents are barely aware of the urban planning rules and the master plans for public works. They are also unaware of the vision for shaping the whole district. What's missing is a mechanism that works to enhance the public discussion of the urban planning visions and takes a neutral stance in mediating between the residents and the local government. I think that's the role our organization has come to assume.

    Our action started with my students and myself making models and computer-simulated renderings of the municipality's plan so that the residents can really understand what's going on. We then organized a series of design charrettes involving local people to develop counter-proposals for the municipality; then we held workshops and symposiums that were open to the public.

○   So through the actions taken by your organization, the needs of the residents are made public and reflected in the ongoing developments by Odakyu?

●   Yes, if not entirely.

●   But how are the voices of the residents actually reflected in designing new institutions in Odakyu's plans?

●   For example, the public space in the original plan that was provided along the long strip after the railway track (FIG. 9) was hardly large enough

2   "Citizens' Plan of the Land Use of the Former Odakyu Railway Land," proposed by Greenline Shimokitazawa.

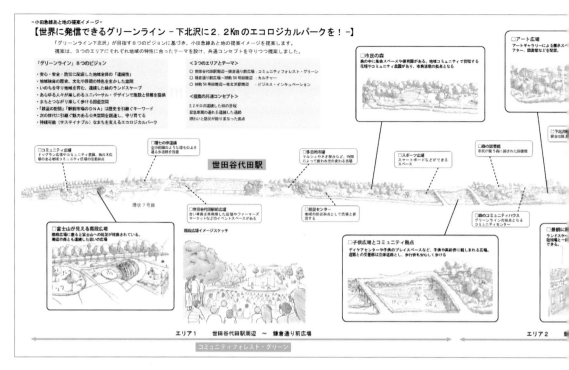

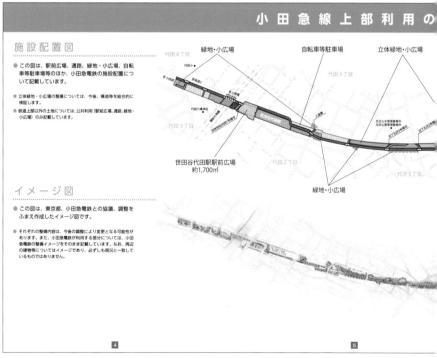

8 | Greenline Shimokitazawa, "Citizens' Plan of the Land Use of the Former Odakyu Railway Land," a recommendation presented to the mayor of the Setagaya municipality in 2012

9 | Setagaya City (municipality), "Layout of facilities using the space above the Odakyu Line railway (Zoning Plan)," published on November 25, 2013. Provisional zoning of the former railway

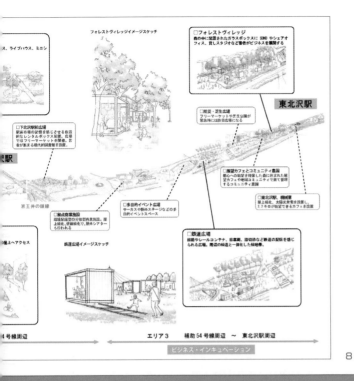

track site agreed upon by the Setagaya
municipality and Odakyu Electric Railway in
2013; https://www.city.setagaya.lg.jp/
mokuji/sumai/003/002/002/d00129740.
html, accessed March 1, 2022

to form a continuous pedestrian passage. But, fortunately, the Odakyu company has listened to the neighbors and incorporated their requests (the pedestrian passage is a good marketing strategy) but only to the extent that it didn't cut into their profits (a pedestrian passage does not generate any income).

● The model for Odakyu's development of smaller-scale projects on the line referred to your team's proposal?

● Yes, I would say so. Originally, Odakyu was planning to build to the full FAR (floor-area ratio) as developer. But they eventually asked the major corporate design firm Nikken Sekkei and my design office to create building guidelines. We suggested an alternative: to make the whole development more village-like and walkable, which is very much in line with the citizens' recommendations from 2012. The railway track disappeared in 2013, and a succession of small-scale developments on the long strip began. Tsubame Architects and other small design offices were assigned to design some of the segmented plots.

As it turns out, Odakyu's development seems to be following our proposal in that the whole development aims for a village-like atmosphere with small-scale, low-profile buildings for public use with a lot of open space and abundant green throughout. We are very happy to see that.

Beyond Opposing Conditions

● What do you think are some of the key lessons you have learned from your involvement with the local citizens of Shimokitazawa?

● Well, on the negative side, we learned how rigid and inflexible the public administration system is through the process of negotiating with them. But on the positive side, we are beginning to see people making claims or voicing ideas about urban planning issues. I also have a little hope for the area management movement emerging among young people, which is sometimes a kind of tactical urbanism. Young people seem to enjoy the urban movement, getting together and working together. I think I'm more optimistic than before.

○ It seems that your initiative in the movement since 2005 has been instrumental in empowering the residents to be more engaged in the future of their neighborhood. Compared to the rest of Tokyo, where people tend to think of high-rise condos on the waterfront as a desirable place to live, Shimo-kitazawa locals seem to be more literate in urban development.

●   In fact, urban planners and designers like me think that tower condos are a risky form for living environments since they lack social connectivity or a sense of community with neighbors outside the building, but as you know, developers want to make these towers to maximize profit. It's our profession's task, I believe, to change the orientation of housing in general into something less risky, more low profile, and more connected to the surrounding urban fabric.

●   I'd also like to ask you: as an urban planner, what are your recommendations for the current state (or dilemma) of urbanism in Tokyo, apart from the housing issue you just referred to? What would you say regarding the gap between large-scale, mixed-use developments and, for example, high-density wooden housing districts?

●   I would say that we should keep the urban tissues to a human scale, as evident from people's desires for as a walkable city. But I do understand that making tall buildings is inevitable for the economy. So the question is how to accomplish these two aims together and address the risks of combining two opposing conditions. The city of Vancouver has made a model for us in that it has achieved a fine balance of high-rise building complexes with low-rise rowhouses. I believe it's possible to find a way to negotiate between conflicting purposes.

    Additionally, one type of space that we should explore and activate for urban development is the residual or unused infrastructure spaces, as well as land that was purchased by the government and reserved for future road development. It's quite interesting to think about giving such spaces a new value. The new development underway along the former railway tracks, or under another, elevated, railway in Shimokitazawa, offers one typological role model for shaping the future of Tokyo.

NEIGHBORHOOD ELEMENTS

● JAPAN RESEARCH INITIATIVE TEAM

At 8 p.m. on Thursday, March 10, 2022, the Kasai Shoten liquor store in Nakano officially closed for business. Unofficially, it remained open for several more hours as throngs of loyal customers pleaded for one last drink, then another and another. People stood bundled against the cold, warming their hands and cups of rice wine on glowing electric heaters. Older people clustered on the rickety chairs and tables that spilled out from the shop and filled the narrow alley. Children dressed in pajamas played nearby, expending the last of their energy before being sent back to the small houses and apartments that surround the shop. After several decades of service as a neighborhood watering hole and meeting point, the Kasai Shoten liquor shop would be vacated, along with more than 30 of the surrounding buildings. In their place would rise a single twenty-story condominium tower.

Next to the liquor shop is a rusted iron pump. This relic of an earlier era still functions, and locals use it to water their plants and clean tools. Buckets, shovels, plastic dinosaurs, and rubber balls lie strewn around the pump, the collective belongings of neighborhood children. Three meters away is a small shine marking the site of an even older stone well. Both are symbolic and spatial artifacts of the neighborhood. The alleyway widens slightly near the well, creating a small space in front of the pump and the liquor shop. It was this space that was full to bursting on the night the liquor shop closed.

Old wells, or *furuido*, are a common feature of back alleys in Tokyo's older neighborhoods. Although modern plumbing systems have superseded them, these wells were once daily necessities. So integral to neighborhood life was this shared infrastructure that it remains embedded in modern language: the phrase *idobata kaigi* (literally, "well-side chat") is roughly equivalent to the English phrase "water cooler conversation," though its connotations are domestic rather than professional. Many of the old wells that once proliferated across Tokyo have been paved over or swallowed up by large buildings, but others linger on. Some are neglected, others have found second lives as water sources for gardens or decentralized fire-suppression equipment. In some neighborhoods, the wells and the small spaces they define are cared for and used as gathering places.

Furuido 古井戸
Old well

Once a vital part of everyday life in Tokyo,
these wells are no longer used for drinking
water. They have found a second life
as water sources for gardening and fire
suppression, and the small spaces they
define remain neighborhood landmarks

Old wells are one of many spatial elements that have structured Tokyo neighborhoods over the centuries. Some, like *yatai* food stalls, are almost entirely lost to time. Others, like station-front bus plazas, are of relatively recent vintage. Some seem incidental, others play an obvious role in the routines of Tokyoites, but all help define the visual and social landscape of the city. The drawings that follow form a visual glossary of these neighborhood elements.

The recent proliferation of large-scale developments in Tokyo has been concentrated in central districts, which include some of the city's oldest neighborhoods. Much attention has been paid to the charismatic buildings that are lost in these redevelopments—the old homes, public baths, and worn wooden shophouses. Less visible, but perhaps more important, is the loss of the complex pattern of ownership, organization, and use that undergird these neighborhoods. Earthquakes, fires, war, and prevailing local attitudes have made change the only constant feature of Tokyo's architectural character. But the streets, alleys, spaces, and public features of these neighborhoods have proven surprisingly resilient; they have safeguarded the character of the city through successive waves of destruction and demolition, at least until more sweeping methods of urban transformation began scraping entire districts down to bare earth.

Against this onslaught, what purpose do traditional neighborhood elements have in the future of Tokyo? Who, if anyone, will ensure that they have

The old well next to the Kasai Shoten liquor store in Nakano, a district west of Shinjuku. People congregate in front of the shop on its final night. Photo © Don O'Keefe

one? Should designers concern themselves with only the newest features of Japanese urban life (shopping malls integrated with rail stations, for instance), or is there still a role for older, less commercial forms of urban organization? Can aging elements of Tokyo's urban identity be rediscovered, refurbished, or even replicated without resorting to empty nostalgia?

Some recent efforts suggest that they can. On the Nihonbashi River in central Tokyo, there is an effort underway to rehabilitate neglected spaces known as *hashizume hiroba*—small plazas that lie on either side of a bridge. They were natural points of concentration for commerce and communication throughout the Edo era, since any pedestrian crossing a river would have to pass by. The construction of the Tokyo Metropolitan Expressway in the 1960s covered over the Nihonbashi River, and highway exit ramps occupied the once-vital public spaces. An ongoing effort to reroute the highway through an underground tunnel will free these spaces, again making them places for pedestrians to meet. These bridge-edge plazas may be an old form of public space, but they are not antiquated. In the post-COVID era, these distributed gaps in the core of the metropolis may be more valuable than ever.

In Ebisu, a district in south central Tokyo, a group of independent business owners collaborated to create a new *yokocho*, a type of commercial alleyway. Unlike its precursors, which feature structurally independent shops, the Ebisu Yokocho fills the vacant shell of a former supermarket. The authenticity of the Ebisu Yokocho is a topic of debate among aesthetes, but its commercial success at least indicates the continued appeal of this long-running neighborhood feature. It also demonstrates that the elemental building blocks of Tokyo neighborhoods are not only relics to be preserved or restored, as in Nihonbashi's riverside plazas. They can also be created anew. In *FiberCity 2050*, architect Hidetoshi Ohno's manifesto for the future of Tokyo, he proposes that narrow residential alleys known as *roji* be transformed into strands of greenery, weaving an ecological network into the fabric of the city. Other designers have proposed radical reimaginings of the neighborhood elements shown in these drawings. Few have been realized, but the contemporary interest in the social and spatial role of these elements attests to their relevance.

Which brings us back to the rusted iron pump next to the Kasai Shoten liquor store. The neighborhood's fate is decided, and none of the existing buildings will survive. But before the last properties were sold to the developer, the residents extracted a promise. When the new tower opens, the Kasai Shoten liquor store will reopen with it. And near the shop, in a small patch of open space next to the tower, will be a new well with a new pump for people to gather around.

—Don O'Keefe

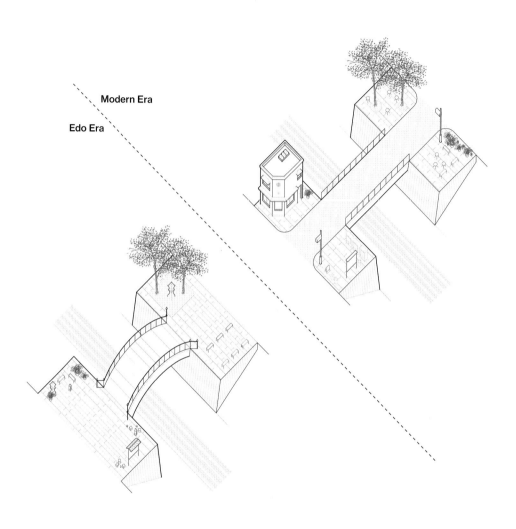

Modern Era

Edo Era

 Hashizume Hiroba 橋詰広場
Bridge-edge plaza

These small spaces located at the head of
a bridge were once common. Contemporary,
automobile-dominated streets have cut
them in two, reducing their area and utility.
Some remain public spaces, though many
have been partially filled in by public
restrooms or storage buildings

 Afuredashi あふれだし
Overflowing objects

The array of items found in front of
buildings soften the boundary between
public and private spheres

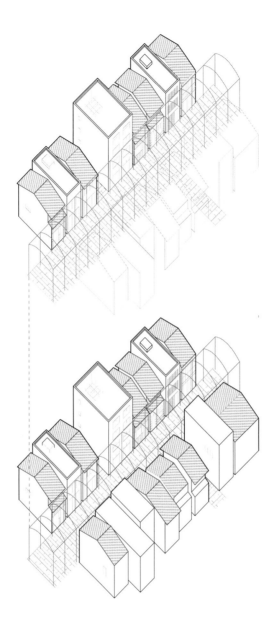

↑
Shotengai 商店街
Local shopping street

Many neighborhood shopping streets, which typically terminate at rail stations, have struggled economically in recent decades. Merchants' associations often coordinate street fixtures like light posts, paving, and planters, and some are covered by freestanding canopies

→
Gadoshita ガード下
Development under elevated rail tracks

[Photo] A wide array of programs can be found under Tokyo's elevated rail tracks called *Gadoshita*, including shops, restaurants, parking, art galleries, offices, storage, student housing, hotels, and grocery stores. Photo © Jiji Press Photo

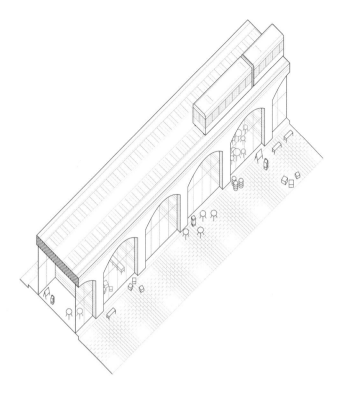

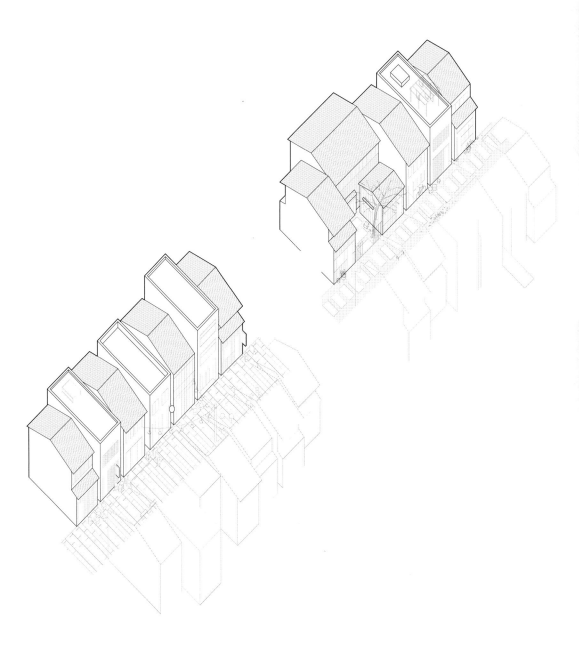

Yokocho 横丁
A commercial alleyway

Yokocho is an alleyway that goes from
the main street to the side, typically lined
with bars and restaurants. Though the use
of the term is decreasing along with the
disappearance of such alleys, urban
redevelopment has begun to revive this
form of intimate space

Material storage

Small batches of building materials, such as
lumber, steel pipe, and PVC, are stored in conspicuous locations in Tokyo. This unnamed phenomenon
is another recurring neighborhood element,
along with countless others excluded from this
provisional glossary

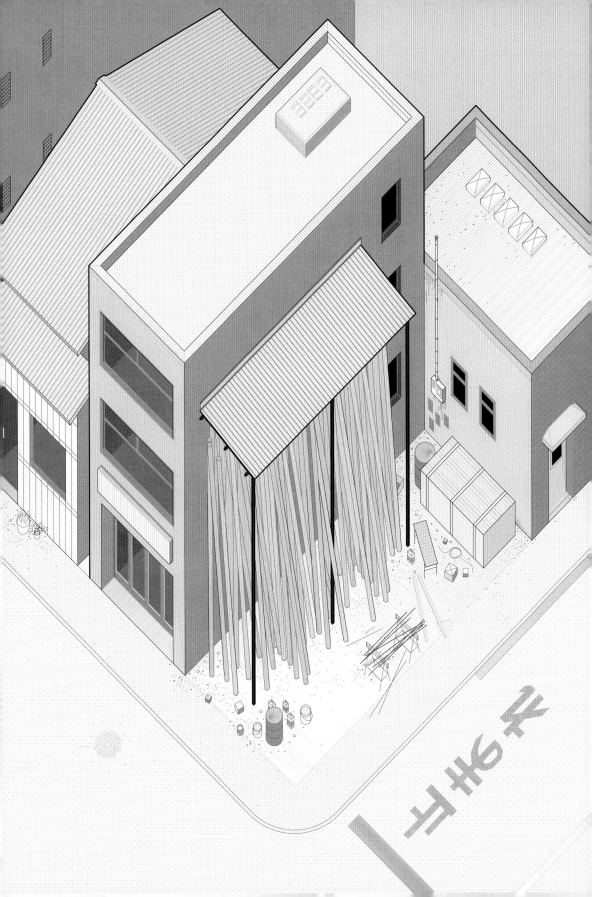

④ ARCHITECTURE AS URBANISM

Is it possible to plan large-scale developments in a more collaborative manner, as public and private partnerships? Can such collaborations represent the rights of the city's inhabitants while also benefiting from the expertise that private companies have garnered over the decades?

Alternatively, can small-scale projects be envisaged as part of a larger urban strategy? Can individual buildings be curated—accumulated, grouped together as clusters of ideas, resources, and efforts—in ways that transcend the impact of localized singularities, thereby helping change an old neighborhood into a contemporary urban district shared by its inhabitants?

Innovative projects are being realized in different parts of the city by a talented group of developers, designers, and planners. But these smaller architectural interventions tend to be conceived as singular occurrences rather than deliberate strategies.

Tokyo seems to be missing the will to imagine its future as a phenomenon at the intersection of the political and the spatial. Instead, and as a result of neoliberal policies, the political has been supplanted by capital as the key factor in shaping the city's spatial characteristics.

But perhaps a more participatory and inclusive form of planning and negotiation would enable not only Tokyo, but also other cities around the globe, to consider alternative developmental options both at the macro and the micro scales. The advantage of such an approach would be to imagine and evaluate projects and proposals within relational and networked frameworks, rather than as isolated and privatized artifacts. How would such ideas transform our understanding and knowledge of architecture and urbanism? Might such a framework change the role of architecture from scenography to urban intervention? How can architecture be considered to be urbanism?

DEVELOPMENT AFTER A SHIFT IN VALUES

● TSUBAME ARCHITECTS

1 | Tsubame Architects, Bonus Track, Tokyo, 2020. The new development in Shimokitazawa contrasts with the large-scale development in the Nishi-Shinjuku CBD visible in background. Photo courtesy of Tsubame Architects

The standard template for urban development projects in Japan has been to invest in space in front of or atop train stations frequented by commuters—the ultimate prime real estate in any Japanese city—and stack as many floors there as possible. Developers have always taken it as a given that residents prioritize convenience over all else. Urban development of this sort has ruthlessly laid waste to the traditional townscapes, shopping streets, and bar-lined alleys that gave these neighborhoods their character, replacing them with mass-produced, cookie-cutter station plazas—or so it is said in facile critiques of the work of developers.

Our view, however, is that as long as development is here to stay in our society, architects should be able to do something creative with it. Ironically, it was the advent of the coronavirus that brought this point home to us. There have been signs since around 2010, as our present-day information infrastructure began to settle into place, that commuting to work or school would become less imperative. However, the pandemic accelerated a transformation in many people's living conditions, and a lifestyle in which home and workplace are in close proximity is increasingly the norm. This trend has created a need for a different kind of urban development.

The coronavirus pandemic has exposed the flaws of the modern city and its pursuit of economic efficiency through the differentiation of spaces according to function. In the cities of the future, architects will find ways to exercise their creativity in places that have been traditionally undervalued: areas midway between train stations; mixed-use neighborhoods at the interface between differently zoned districts; places where foot traffic is impeded by natural barriers or those created by public works projects. And, ideally, these newly developed spaces should be managed by the people who live there.

Such an approach implies a new direction to be taken toward a lifestyle centered around movement on foot, one where people's lives are grounded in the neighborhood where they reside and work. This new center of gravity should grant people a greater degree of freedom in their mode of living than the model we know of rigid adherence to a single template of development.

Preserving the Appeal of a Neighborhood

Our first effort to devise a form of urban development that departs from the conventional model is Shimokitazawa Bonus Track (FIG. 1). Shimokitazawa sits at the junction of two of Tokyo's major privately owned commuter lines. Several shopping streets radiate from Shimokitazawa station, linking the surrounding residential neighborhoods together. The complex topography of the area is one factor contributing to the maze of narrow streets running through the shopping district, which supports many small colorful retail shops as well as the theaters and music clubs that have made Shimokitazawa a popular gathering place for young Tokyoites. Even past the edges of the commercial district, some houses have been converted into stylish cafés, forming a distinctive mix of homes and small businesses that gives Shimokitazawa an air of freedom and diversity. However, this very charm has driven a surge in rents in recent years, and big chain stores have begun to replace the funky little shops. The neighborhood is in danger of losing its old ambience.

Meanwhile, the Odakyu line, one of the two railways that intersect at Shimokitazawa station, has been moved underground, and the railway company has been developing the land where the tracks used to run. The goal of Bonus Track, which is part of this redevelopment project, is to foster an environment conducive to the launching of small businesses by individual proprietors and thereby give birth to a new shopping street that preserves the traditional charm of Shimokitazawa.

A New Development Policy

When we were commissioned to draw up a master plan for development of this strip of track bed, we began by contemplating the underlying principles for the plan. Our vision was of development that would promote the transformation of the site into a new center of gravity for Shimokitazawa while doing away with the negative elements that past development had brought to the area. The following principles were intended to help realize that vision:

1   Create continuity by emulating the scale and elements of the existing neighborhood so as to avoid forming spatial barriers between it and the development site.

2   Facilitate the entry of individual owners and young proprietors of new businesses, as well as the sustainability of their shops, by optimizing the number of businesses on the site while keeping rents low by reducing each tenant's floor space.

3   Create a living-working environment so that tenants are encouraged to view themselves as actors with an interest in nurturing the site.

4   Assign management of the site to a team of tenants and local residents, rather than a single management company.

Putting these principles into practice can, we believe, ensure the growth here of a locally autonomous, symbiotic, convivial community, rather than a site gentrified purely with an eye to maximizing its market value—i.e., with only the interests of the developers in mind.

The 49 Percent Margin

The site is located a few minutes' walk from Shimokitazawa station at a point precisely midway between two stations. Approached on foot, one can see that the lot sits astride the boundary between the commercially zoned shopping district and a residential area zoned for detached housing. Since it occupies the old railway bed, all the buildings adjoining the site face away from it. Also, since the tracks now run directly beneath it, only two-story wood- or steel-frame structures are permitted here. Some 3,000 square meters in area, it is essentially a narrow gap in the cityscape (FIG. 2).

The western half of the lot is designated for residential use, so commercial buildings are not permitted, but combined home-and-business structures are. Customarily these consist of a shop on the ground floor with living quarters above—in other words, a living-working arrangement. It occurred to us that building such units here would be the perfect strategy for knitting the bifurcated neighborhood back together. To this end, we decided to incorporate small alleys into the site that would maintain the balance of the surrounding residential streets.

Placing work and living places close together not only engenders a lifestyle-friendly environment, but also, if done in the standard shop-cum-dwelling format, has the advantage of legally permitting the use of up to 49 percent of a residentially zoned lot for nonresidential purposes. By putting this 49 percent margin to effective use, one can transform a residential area into an entirely different environment.

Moreover, if people who achieve a certain degree of success with their business here can be encouraged to expand by utilizing vacant structures in the immediate vicinity rather than moving out and leasing larger commercial spaces elsewhere, then one can achieve a synergy between the business incubation process and the use of empty housing stock. We hope that Bonus Track can serve as a role model for the active utilization of vacant houses elsewhere in the neighborhood.

Creating Continuity by Learning from the Neighborhood

The Bonus Track complex consists of four buildings of living-working (SOHO) units and a central commercial building. Three of the SOHO buildings are row-house structures, each with three adjoining ten-*tsubo* units divided into dwelling and shop spaces of five *tsubo* each (one *tsubo* is 3.31 square meters). The central building contains shop spaces of varying heights and ranging in area from 50 to 140 square meters, as well as spaces that supplement the small shops, including a shared-use gallery, a lounge, toilets, and a trash disposal area (FIG. 3).

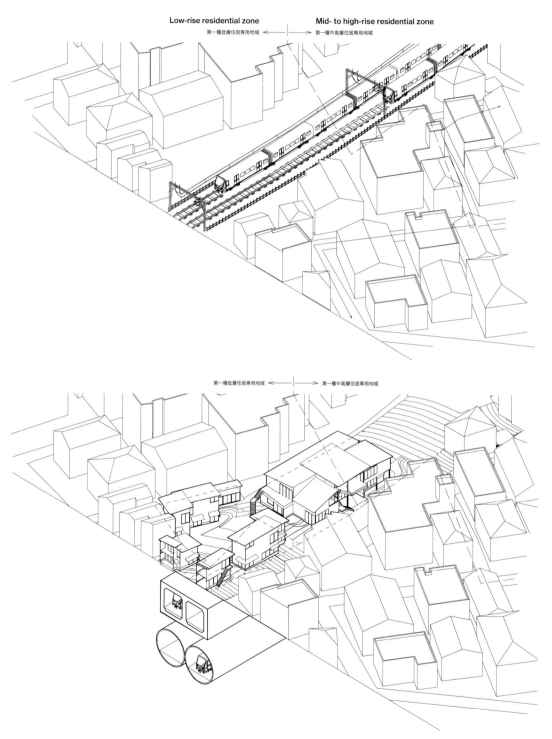

Low-rise residential zone   Mid- to high-rise residential zone
第一種低層住居専用地域 ←   → 第一種中高層住居専用地域

第一種低層住居専用地域 ←   → 第一種中高層住居専用地域

2 | The railway that used to run through the neighborhood of Shimokitazawa (top) and the Bonus Track development after the railways were relocated underground (bottom). Courtesy of Tsubame Architects   2

This layout is designed not only to facilitate tenancy by young people, but also to ensure that business at the site is not confined only to its tenants. Events are held weekly in the courtyard, gallery, or lounge to attract people from the neighborhood and beyond. Thus the purpose of these facilities is not just to meet tenants' needs, but to stimulate economic interaction with the wider community.

We want Bonus Track to be a place that the tenants themselves develop and nurture, just as people have done with Shimokitazawa at large. The district's alleys are a natural incubator of unique, homey spaces where shopowners have remodeled their buildings and set up counters and furniture outside. In a kind of reverse engineering, we wanted to support "legal" measures taken to replicate the neighborhood's motley, liberating charm.

We therefore formulated a remodeling-friendly framework within which tenants can carry out their own renovations. The buildings, with abutting lean-to roofs, segmented exterior walls, and frame-exposed interiors, are designed so that each unit is intentionally incomplete. Scattered throughout them are unfinished elements—exterior walls, eaves, concrete counters—with which the tenant can tinker (FIG. 4). Our position is that of an "interior design control center" whose job is to support this system by actively promoting renovations and advising tenants on what remodeling methods are feasible (FIG. 5).

Self-Governance by Tenants and Local Residents

There are very few trees in this part of Shimokitazawa, and neighboring residents asked that the Bonus Track site include some greenery. Accordingly, we created a verdant landscape based on the concept of "a shopping street in the woods." We also did away with lease lines, allowing each shop to place furniture and signs outdoors as they like. This exterior space thus serves as a shared courtyard that helps compensate tenants for the small floorage of their shops, as well as a "public" park of sorts for area residents, despite its being privately owned by a railway company (FIG. 6, bottom).

The trees and shrubs in this space are maintained by a gardening club formed of local residents (rather than a management company), an indicator that the space is already beginning to function as an incubator of civic pride. Although this arrangement necessitates the inconvenience of do-it-yourself maintenance, it is also liberating—an example of the "benefits of inconvenience." It also reduces management costs for the owner, so the idea of entrusting maintenance to the community may prove attractive as a strategy for community development.

As is the case with its outdoor space, Bonus Track is distinguished by an emphasis on self-governance that is built into its organization. The railway company that owns the property does not directly manage it. Instead, a management company, Sanposha, leases the entire site from the owner and rents the individual units out to the tenants. Sanposha was launched by

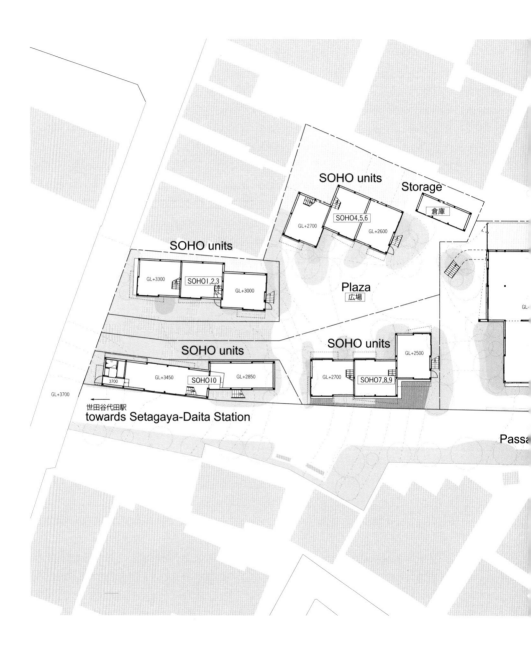

SOHO units

Storage
倉庫

SOHO4,5,6
GL+2700   GL+2600

SOHO units

GL+3300   SOHO1,2,3
                        GL+3000

Plaza
広場

GL+

SOHO units   SOHO units
                                                GL+2500

SOHO units
                    GL+2700   SOHO7,8,9
GL+3450 SOHO10   GL+2850

3700

GL+3700
世田谷代田駅
towards Setagaya-Daita Station

Passa

Tsubame Architects, Bonus Track. General
plan. Courtesy of Tsubame Architects

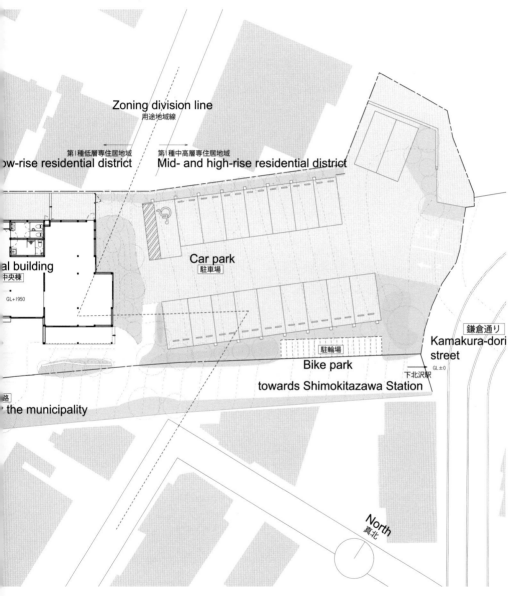

Zoning division line
用途地域線

第1種低層専住居地域   第1種中高層専住居地域
ow-rise residential district   Mid- and high-rise residential district

al building
中央棟

GL+1950

Car park
駐車場

駐輪場
Bike park
towards Shimokitazawa Station

鎌倉通り
Kamakura-dori
street

下北沢駅   GL±0

the municipality

North
真北

全体平面図 1/300   3

1   No lease line is set in the outdoor space so that leasers can freely place their signage and furniture
2   Exterior wall surface with siding can be finished with any material
3   Handrail can be used as a balcony or a flower bed
4   Eaves can be finished by each tenant
5   Rails can be used to hang signs or store curtain
6   Ceiling is basically bare. Wiring racks and lighting fixtures are installed using suspension bolts provided for the A work
7   Interior walls are basically column-exposed and can be finished over structural plywood
8   Countertop can be finished over reinforced concrete

4 | Tsubame Architects, Bonus Track.
Perspective section. Courtesy of Tsubame
Architects

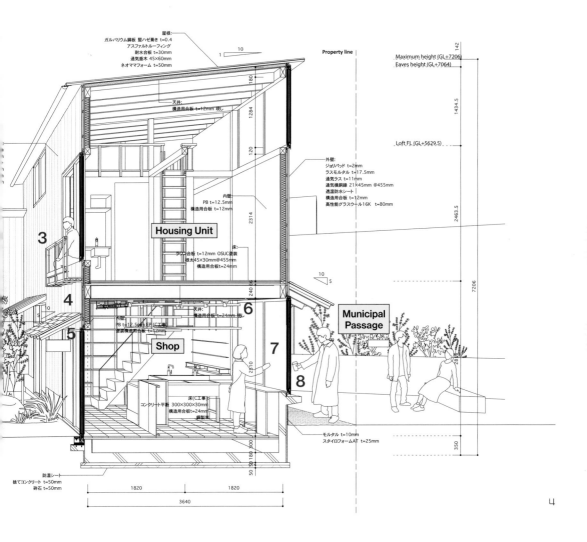

屋根:
ガルバリウム鋼板 堅ハゼ葺き t=0.4
アスファルトルーフィング
耐水合板 t=30mm
通気垂木 45×60mm
ネオマフォーム t=50mm

1 _____ 10

Property line

Maximum height (GL+7206)
Eaves height (GL+7064)

天井:
構造用合板 t=12mm 現し

Loft FL (GL+5629.5)

内壁:
PB t=12.5mm
構造用合板 t=12mm

Housing Unit

外壁:
ジョリパッド t=2mm
ラスモルタル t=17.5mm
通気ラス t=11mm
通気横胴縁 21×45mm @455mm
透湿防水シート
構造用合板 t=12mm
高性能グラスウール16K t=80mm

床:
ラワン合板 t=12mm OSUC塗装
根太45×30mm@455mm
構造用合板 t=24mm

3

10 ____ 5

天井:
構造用合板 t=24mm 現し

4

6

Municipal
Passage

5

内壁:
PB t=12.5mm EP (C工事)
素地構造用合板 t=12mm

Shop

7

8

床(C工事):
コンクリート平板 300×300×30mm
構造用合板 t=24mm
鋼製束

モルタル t=10mm
スタイロフォームAT t=25mm

防湿シート
捨てコンクリート t=50mm
砂石 t=50mm

1820   1820

3640

5

5 | Tsubame Architects, Bonus Track. The development under construction (left column) and after completion with optional finishes chosen by the tenants (right column). Photo © morinakayasuaki

the longtime proprietor of a local bookstore and the founder of *greenz*, a web magazine on community development.

What is important is that the managers are not just the "landlords" of the complex, but also local residents, one a shopowner and the other a community development activist. These multifaceted roles enable them to be flexible decision makers who can generate an atmosphere conducive to active participation by tenants and neighborhood residents in the development of the site.

The Architects' Strategy

As part of our effort to make the Bonus Track concept a reality, we have taken on a role that is broader than the usual one for an architects' collective—three roles, in fact. Besides collaborating with the property owners on the design of the architecture, we also worked with them to draw up rules for the remodeling of tenant spaces as well as the management of common areas. Additionally, we have taken an active part in encouraging renovations by consulting with individual tenants and checking their designs. In short, our participation did not end with the completion of the complex; if anything, our role in this project is like that of a town doctor, responding to the ongoing needs of the tenants and their neighbors (FIG. 7).

Earlier we referred to "'legal' measures," but in practice, when users express a wish to do something that bends the rules a bit (such as spreading a tarp over the central courtyard between the buildings to keep the rain out), we try to respond to each request on its own merits. In other words, the rules of operation are flexible and always open to improvement. We view this as a constructive kind of collective learning process for us, the users, and the neighborhood.

In addition to conventional architectural design work, we also engage in "post-production"—designing the operation and use of buildings after their completion. Alternating between these two tasks has enabled us to successfully develop projects and then further improve them through continued engagement with the buildings we design. It was thanks to this experience that we were able to tackle a project like Bonus Track, where it was not immediately clear how to develop the site. Upon receiving a request to help draw up a plan, we worked with the owner to identify requirements for the design, which led to our commission to design the site and, subsequently, to design the operating rules for the complex.

Although Bonus Track opened almost concurrently with the government's emergency declaration to combat the coronavirus, it has grown day by day into a flexible and robust venue for community life. Taking the long view, this experiment in creating and sustaining a "pedestrian zone development model" should provide a template for a new kind of development in the post-corona era.

6

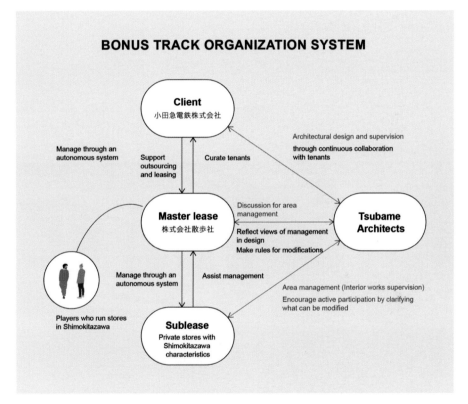

TAKING THE INITIATIVE IN NEIGHBORHOOD REVITALIZATION

● MITSUYOSHI MIYAZAKI

1

Yanaka Ginza shopping Street. Photo
© Jade Miles, courtesy of japanjourneys.jp

I manage an architectural design office as well as several community spaces in the Yanaka district in northeastern Tokyo. Yanaka is a neighborhood of temples—seventy or more. Spared the worst of the firebombings that leveled much of Tokyo during World War II, it is also full of narrow alleys lined with wooden buildings dating back to the 1910s through the 1930s. Today Yanaka is a multifaceted ecosystem with a mix of homes, small businesses, artisans' workshops, and art galleries. Because this ambience makes it a rarity among Tokyo neighborhoods, Yanaka has been attracting growing numbers of tourists, both domestic and foreign, for the past decade or more.

This trend has spawned a number of issues for Yanaka, however. Its rapid metamorphosis into a sightseeing destination has led to symptoms of over-tourism. Yanaka Ginza (FIG. 1), the main shopping street, is losing businesses that cater to the daily needs of local residents as aging proprietors retire and their shops convert to souvenir outlets in response to tourist demand. Meanwhile, there is little community spirit fostered between older residents and the younger people moving into the area. Moreover, those who have inherited real estate in Yanaka tend to live elsewhere, so the number of vacant houses is growing, and with it increasing concerns over public safety and fire prevention. The Great East Japan Earthquake of 2011 was also a stark reminder of Yanaka's vulnerability to natural disasters, with its predominance of narrow streets and old wooden structures.

Street widening and building reconstruction projects proceed apace, fueled by subsidies from the local government. The danger with this approach to urban improvement is that it threatens to eradicate the very charm that makes Yanaka Yanaka. An example is the ongoing loss of the wooden buildings that, together with the alleys, form Yanaka's unique urban identity. These are being relentlessly replaced by prefab homes made with steel frames and autoclaved lightweight concrete (ALC) walls in the name of fire resistance and privacy. Many residents find this trend disturbing, but they are faced with an either-or choice between maintaining old housing stock and allowing Yanaka to become a new town that looks like any other.

The Neighborhood as Hostelry

My current activities in Yanaka are also a consequence of the earthquake of 2011. Due to that disaster, Hagi-so, the wooden apartment house (FIG. 2) I lived in at the time, was slated for demolition. As a sort of funeral for the building I decided to hold an arts event there, "Hagiennale 2012." Some 1,500 people showed up over the course of three weeks, a sight that awakened the owner of the building to its true value. When I proposed remodeling the apartment house into a "multiuse cultural mini-complex," the owner assented. The

2

3

2 | Hagi-so apartment house before renovation. Photo courtesy of Hagi Studio

3 | Hagi Studio, HAGISO, 2013. Front view after the renovation. Photo courtesy of Hagi Studio

upshot is that HAGISO (FIG. 3) opened in 2013, with the owner and I sharing the costs of its management.

Subsequently I proposed the concept of treating the entire neighborhood as a hotel complex, with HAGISO serving as the reception desk, a still-standing public bathhouse down the street as the bathing pool, and a vacant house converted to guest rooms. Our team began by building HANARE,[1] (FIGS. 4, 5, 6, 7, 8) a hotel, and TAYORI,[2] a café and deli situated on a back street. We then added a bakery, TAYORI BAKE,[3] (FIG. 9) as well as a rental classroom space, KLASS,[4] for local residents to use. Ultimately HAGISO gave birth to seven satellite facilities, all within walking distance. The program for each was developed by contemplating its role in the larger neighborhood scheme, along with conditions at the site and the wishes of the owner. All of these facilities are under our direct management and were acquired through the same series of steps: contacting the owner of a vacant building in the area, negotiating with the local government, identifying a new role for the building to play in the community, presenting our proposal to the owner and obtaining permission, designing the renovated facility, and signing a lease with the owner.

HAGISO is a typical postwar wooden house, the sort that can be seen throughout Tokyo, and somewhat symbolic of Japan's impoverished days after the war. When we began renovating the old Hagi-so apartment house, few of our neighbors could see the sense in preserving this type of building. But our project was worthwhile, we thought, precisely because its purpose was not to simply preserve a structure for its cultural value, but to put a building that had no such discernible value to optimum use.

HAGISO has engaged in a highly diverse menu of activities, ranging from operation of a café-bar and a contemporary art gallery to hosting concerts, picture-book readings for local children, and meetings between neighborhood association stalwarts and new residents, as well as organizing hybrid bar/performance events (FIG. 10). Our flexibility enables us to provide venues for all manner of community-oriented activities in a way that a typical modern cultural facility cannot.

In the course of these activities, we have been approached by local land or building owners who, after observing and participating in HAGISO's events, expressed interest in having one of their properties put to similar use. The revitalization of a building like Hagi-so, which they had viewed as a worthless piece of real estate, spurred them to reconsider the potential of

1   This HANARE (hotel) is designed with various elements intended to enhance guests' enjoyment of the Yanaka district.
2   "Dining Post Office TAYORI" prepares and sells food items made with ingredients delivered directly from all over Japan. It also has a mailbox to encourage correspondence between food producers and customers.
3   TAYORI BAKE squeezes a bakery (kitchen and shop) for small confections into a space of less than 17 square meters between the houses on a residential street.
4   Neighborhood Classroom KLASS is a place where residents can teach and learn.

4

5

7

6

8

4	Old generic wooden house before the renovation into HANARE. Photo courtesy of Hagi Studio
5	Hagi Studio, HANARE, 2015. After renovation. Photo courtesy of Hagi Studio
6	HANARE. Entrance. Photo courtesy of Hagi Studio
7	HANARE. Interior renovation. Photo courtesy of Hagi Studio

8	HANARE in the Yanaka neighborhood. Photo courtesy of Hagi Studio
9	Hagi Studio, TAYORI BAKE, 2019. Front view. Photo courtesy of Hagi Studio
10	HAGISO. The wooden skeleton is left to create a space for exhibition and gathering. Photo courtesy of Hagi Studio

9

10

11

12

13

14

| 11 | Walkway in a cemetery of an old Buddhist temple in Yanaka. Photo © Linda Lombardi |
| 12 | Neighborhood around HANARE and HAGISO. Photo © hyo |

| 13 | HAGISO. Small outdoor lounge between the house and the street. Photo courtesy of Hagi Studio |
| 14 | Hagi Studio, TAYORI, 2017. Approach through an alley. Photo courtesy of Hagi Studio |

property of their own that they had seen no point in preserving. In this way, new facilities have continued to spin off from HAGISO.

An Experiment in Dissolving Boundaries

Basically, our objective is to revitalize a neighborhood by sharing our vision with local building owners. Creating a number of facilities in such buildings (however small in size) and dispersing them throughout the area can help ensure the preservation of the neighborhood's identity—one that would be lost if entrusted solely to top-down infrastructure management by government authorities. By enlisting the active cooperation of the owner from the outset of a project, we foster a relationship in which, instead of merely interacting as landlord and tenant, we are partners rowing the same boat. The fact that many owners have become true allies in this undertaking, reducing or even forgoing rent despite the economic hardships they have faced during the pandemic, testifies, I believe, to the effectiveness of this approach.

Much of the Yanaka district is owned and leased out by temples and other large landowners who generally maintain a big-picture attitude vis-à-vis the neighborhood, while the residents, who rarely own the land they live on, are relatively unconcerned about becoming owners themselves. When they share our vision, owners with this sort of perspective can make decisions that are not predicated on maximizing their return from each property. Residents, for their part, are not fixated on the prerogatives of land ownership, and hence are more amenable to cooperating on projects that transcend such boundaries. Because people in Yanaka are less obsessed with what constitutes "their" property, it is possible, for example, to install a community garden along a back alley, or to build a bench on a tiny strip of land that belongs to no one in particular.

Thanks to this outlook, coupled with the abundance of tiny, often blind alleys that define Yanaka, the district is blessed with optimum conditions for intimate communications among neighbors (FIGS. 11, 12). However, these conditions are deteriorating year by year. Lots not owned by the big landlords often get subdivided when they change hands, and the owners of new homes built on these lots; we also have new business tenants who tend to be concerned only with their own profits. These owners and tenants are sending an increasingly loud message into the neighborhood that boundaries do matter.

In making Yanaka the focus of our activities, our aim is to break down physical and emotional boundaries in the district, create conditions that are conducive to dynamic and diverse interactions among its residents, and thereby nurture an urban environment with a healthy metabolism. As the HANARE model demonstrates, reorganizing the scattered resources of a neighborhood can give birth to a spirit of local cooperation and solidarity that transcends the specific interests of individual people or businesses.

In the process of expanding our points of contact with the neighborhood, we have developed physical spaces that convey a clear message in favor of dissolving boundaries. Our experiments include utilizing Yanaka's alleys to create outdoor spaces where people can congregate (whether or not they are patrons of the facilities they adjoin); designing facades that are just striking enough to stand out from the general townscape without being too jarring; and, in terms of indoor space, designing interiors that add an element of surprise, and hence extra depth, to the urban environment. This might be called a subliminal strategy of transforming the Yanaka experience while preserving it (FIGS. 13, 14).

Showcasing Long-Term Value through Practice

What does it mean for an architect to take on risks in a neighborhood project? For one thing, it means taking the initiative rather than waiting for a client to appear with a request to help solve the neighborhood's problems. The project of resuscitating structures that give a neighborhood its unique identity—those street-corner buildings that define the mood of their entire block, the old buildings miraculously spared the wrecking ball so far—reveals its intrinsic value. The combination of architecture and the uses to which it is put seems to be a winning one. However, if a project is to have a significant impact on a community, the architecture must take into account the urban context even as it guides users toward a new way of interacting with it. In short, function and design must complement one another.

We also wish to demonstrate that in the long term, the practice of effectively utilizing the empty buildings that are the historical resources of a community will increase their neighborhood's value more than any attempts to maximize short-term gains. Buildings and development projects that ride on the coattails of a temporary boom in tourism often end up destroying the very appeal that drew attention to the neighborhood, as Yanaka itself has experienced. It is crucial that neighborhood preservation practices showcase not only their cultural value, but also their contribution to the overall urban environment of the neighborhood, including the livelihoods of the people living and working there. Today the results of these grassroots-style efforts are gaining recognition, and we are receiving requests to undertake similar all-community projects from municipal governments, railway companies, and the like.

With its big-picture perspective, the project we initiated in the Yanaka district is a departure from typical architectural practice. Even when applied in a top-down manner by government entities, I believe that this same methodology yields more successful results than ad-hoc development driven by the logic of the market. Sustainable revitalization of a neighborhood is possible when one taps into the human relationships and motivations that derive from intimate interaction with the community.

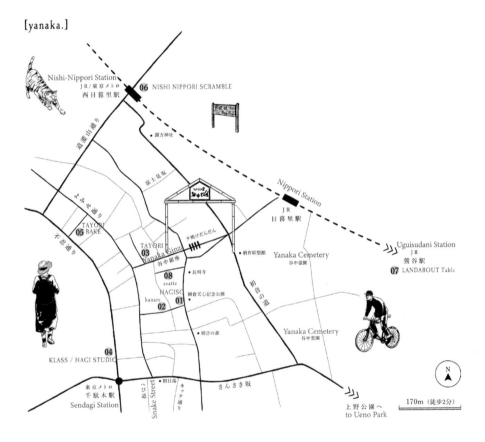

A NARRATIVE FOR EVERY NEIGHBORHOOD

● YOSHIHIKO OSHIMA

A precipitous decline in population, unprecedented in Japan's history. A society that is rapidly growing older and producing fewer children...Perhaps we have been overly naive about the impact of these inexorable trends on our social environment. The collapse of the social security system, the proliferation of abandoned houses, the decline of regional cities—where are the solutions to these social ills that seem to be cropping up one after another? The theories and assumptions of the past, when the economy was booming and the population growing, are of no use at all. We are never going to relive the glories of those heady days.

As architects, we find our profession subjected to a transformation of values that challenges the very purpose of our existence. The transformation is from an era of "making" things to one of "using" them—in other words, the Age of Management. An increasingly important part of the architect's job description, beyond the design of new buildings, is the design of frameworks or scenarios for putting existing buildings (i.e., spatial resources) to work in the service of society. We call this the creation of a narrative design for architecture.

During the years of the postwar economic boom, numerous "new towns" or "bed towns" were built to provide mass housing on the periphery of Japan's largest cities. Lining the streets of these huge developments were row upon row of prepackaged "all in one" houses on separate lots with clearly defined boundaries. Gone were the spaces with ambiguous demarcations—verandas, eaves, courtyards around wells—that provided common gathering places in traditional Japanese villages. The new self-contained homes epitomized the prosperity of the nuclear families spawned by this era.

Nowadays, however, the children have departed from these suburban new towns, leaving only the elderly. As the new towns become old towns, the boundaries separating homes—once symbols of the good life—have turned into barriers to the communication that is all the more critical to maintaining the health of an aging population. Isolation and loneliness are now social problems that erode the quality of life in these communities. Conditions in these aging new towns are a microcosm of what is happening to society on a national scale.

Energizing the Latent Values of a Neighborhood

Why did the suburban new towns turn out this way? Because they were not designed as *neighborhoods*. Municipal governments and developers simply supplied large numbers of houses, and neither they nor anyone else attended to the physical environments of these places to ensure that they could adapt to changes in the people or society dwelling there. For the past ten years or so, we have grappled with many of the issues facing these new towns. Essentially, our

| 1 | The Hoshinotani Danchi collective housing next to the Zama station before renovation. Photo courtesy of Blue Studio | 3 | Hoshinotani Danchi. Vegetable garden in the courtyard. Photo courtesy of Blue Studio |
| 2 | Blue Studio, Hoshinotani Danchi, 2015. After renovation. Photo courtesy of Blue Studio | | |

task has been to come up with models and narratives showing how people might live in the areas one typically refers to as "the suburbs."

Today's suburbs harbor a great number of latent values: a rich natural environment, convenient access via public transportation to metropolitan centers and other suburbs, relatively low population density, a moderately high level of income among residents, most of whom are baby-boomers…the list goes on. And in "new" towns reaching the half-century mark, the torch—in the form of inherited property—is now being passed to a new generation of residents.

What is needed today is a reevaluation of all that potential, and a redesign of the various relationships associated with it. What is the value of living in a place? Perhaps it is to be found in the communication that takes place among the people there. Buildings and city layouts are no more than stage props that provide a setting; it is communication that defines the character of a place, that allows its residents to feel safe and secure, and that, ultimately, makes them proud to live there.

Sharing a *Danchi*

Our "Hoshinotani Danchi Project" for the Hoshinotani apartment complex in the city of Zama, Kanagawa Prefecture, had two objectives. The first was to convert a fifty-year-old *danchi*,[1] originally built to house employees of the nearby railway (FIG. 1), into rental housing for a new generation of families with children. The second was to utilize the *danchi*'s proximity to Zama train station to make it a gathering place for residents of the larger community, both station users and nonusers (FIG. 2).

Since there was quite a bit of space between the buildings in the complex, which are arranged in parallel rows, we decided to convert it into a vegetable garden for rental by seniors throughout the neighborhood (FIG. 3). On the ground floor of the buildings facing the garden we installed a childcare support center and a community café. The balconies of the apartments on the second and upper floors look out over the comings and goings of adults and children using the garden, center, and café. This, in a nutshell, is our master plan for the revival of the Hoshinotani Danchi (FIGS. 4, 5).

The new occupants of the refurbished housing units were primarily single or married commuters, but through the garden and other facilities they have cultivated relationships with other people in the neighborhood. Now, in the sixth year of the project, those relationships have encouraged more and more residents to make this neighborhood their permanent home. Even those

---

1   A type of high-density apartment complex that first appeared in the suburbs of major cities in the mid-1950s during Japan's postwar economic boom. Most *danchi* were built in parallel rows of rectangular blocks five or more stories high. Typically including a dining/kitchen area, bath, and a flush toilet, early *danchi* apartments were considered a model of modern living. As they entered the twenty-first century, however, these complexes faced such problems as aging buildings, high vacancy rates, and aging occupants.

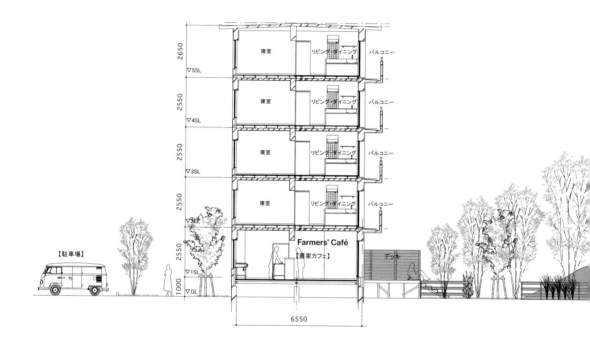

2650
▽5SL

2550
▽4SL

2550
▽3SL

2550
▽2SL

2550
▽1SL

1000
▽GL

寝室　リビング・ダイニング　バルコニー

【駐車場】

Farmers' Café
【農家カフェ】

デッキ

6550

Blue Studio, Hoshinotani Danchi. Section.
© Blue Studio

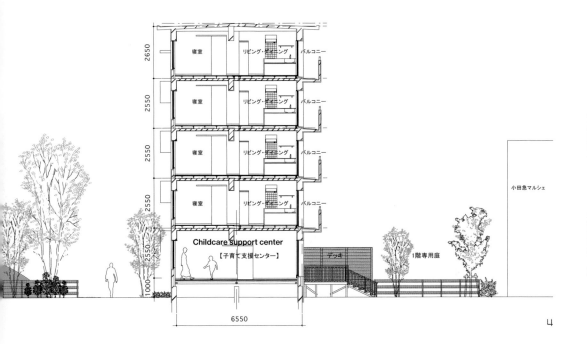

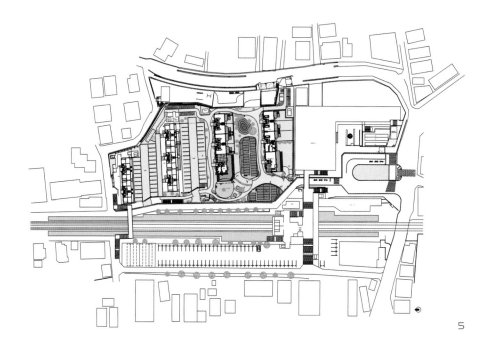

5

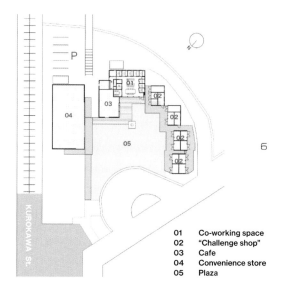

6

01 Co-working space
02 "Challenge shop"
03 Cafe
04 Convenience store
05 Plaza

who come to desire more space than the rental units provide, and decide to become homeowners, tend to purchase houses in the immediate area. Thus the communications fostered by life in this *danchi* now extend to the surrounding neighborhood, creating a circulatory effect throughout the community environment at large.

Sharing a Station Plaza

In the summer of 2019 we opened a commercial complex, Nesting Park Kurokawa,[2] on a plot of unused land in front of a suburban train station owned by the same railway company with whom we worked on the Zama project. The complex includes coworking offices, "challenge shops,"[3] and a café.

Kurokawa is a station on the Odakyu Tama Line, a commuter branch line that was built to connect with a large new town developed in the Tokyo suburbs in the late 1970s. Initially, a shopping mall operated by the railway occupied the site in front of the station. With the flourishing of roadside malls in the 2000s, however, the station mall went out of business, leaving a vacant lot. Nesting Park was a plan to put this site to use.

Because relatively few passengers used Kurokawa Station, the area around it was quiet. For that very reason, however, we thought it was the perfect place for local residents to try out new experiences in the course of their daily lives, and it was with this idea in mind that we developed the project.

Close by the station is the forty-year-old Tama New Town.[4] The first generation of residents in this town were typically baby boomers (or thereabouts), so by now most of them were recent retirees with many years of experience behind them, searching for something they could do close to home for a second, post-retirement career. Meanwhile, the younger generation of thirty-something parents, their child-rearing duties notwithstanding, were probably still seeking fresh challenges in their lives as well. What if we brought the two groups together at this site?

First, we greened up the area in front of the station to harmonize with its woodsy surroundings. Then, in keeping with our concept of "a place between work, play, and home life," we built coworking spaces and shop spaces in a row of wooden one-story structures that look just like log cabins at a campsite. These cabins were subdivided into 15 booths of various sizes, providing rentable retail spaces ranging from 4 to 8 square meters in area (FIG. 6).

The result was a proliferation in the station area of local residents who had previously never spent time there: child-rearing housewives running "select shops" (boutiques offering a selection of brands) during their free

2   http://nestingpark.jp/#MainVisual
3   Shop spaces funded by local governments or public entities to combat the shrinking of communities. Support in the form of rent subsidies and management training is provided to promote retail startups.
4   One of Japan's first and largest "new towns," initially consisting of *danchi* complexes.

7

8

9

10

hours; outdoors-loving retirees serving as instructors in the café's barbecue corner; young farmers collaborating with café operations (FIGS. 7, 8, 9, 10). The site was transformed into a place brimming with activity and lively communications among all these different actors. It was a phenomenon made possible precisely because Kurokawa was a local stop in a residential area; elsewhere, in the commercial districts by train stations at major transit hubs, the rent was too high for small businesses of this sort.

When area residents are able to share a highly public space like a train station, they fill it with activities that give the site a richly local flavor far more charming than the clusters of chain stores that occupy shopping centers connected to the big hub stations.

An Entire Neighborhood as Home

These projects have actually been affected positively by the coronavirus pandemic that arrived in early 2020. The crisis has forced us to diversify the ways we live and work, increasing the amount of time we spend at home and making us more acutely aware of shortcomings in our residential environments. Suburbs previously dismissed as "bed towns" to which workers returned only to sleep have now begun to look like Shangri-las where people can live, work, and play.

In the past, people defined a suburban "home" in the narrowest sense of the real estate to which one could claim ownership. With the pandemic-induced paradigm shift that has occurred in how we live and work, however, it is fair to say that the definition of "home" has begun expanding to include one's entire neighborhood. This in turn has kindled in people a shared desire to expand, distribute, and enjoy the elements that enrich lifestyles throughout their neighborhood.

Thus the suburbs are in the process of changing from places burdened with negative attributes into vibrant, distinct neighborhoods. What makes this possible is the "narrative" of each individual community, and these narratives are bound to grow even more flavorful when the pandemic subsides.

BARRIERS TO SHARING AN URBAN ENVIRONMENT

● RIKEN YAMAMOTO

The theories of urban and housing design that prevailed in Japan after World War II were heavily influenced by the International Congresses of Modern Architecture (CIAM). Japanese architects in those days could not conceive of urban or housing policies outside the framework of CIAM theory.

This was due to the fact that Japan's traditional cityscapes had been entirely destroyed in the war. Until then, most Japanese residences had doubled as places of economic activity, built for working as well as dwelling. These hybrid living-working spaces, as well as the urban configurations that sustained them, vanished in the firebombings of World War II. The US air raids not only obliterated Japan's major cities, but also smaller ones throughout the country. Comprised mainly of low-rise, high-density wooden housing, they were all too vulnerable to the incendiary bombs, resulting in the most thorough destruction of a nation's cities in history. The atomic bombings of Hiroshima and Nagasaki were the final blow.

It was in the aftermath of this devastation that the urban theory of CIAM came into prominence.

The theme of the Second International Congress of Modern Architecture (CIAM II) in 1929 was "The Minimum Dwelling," while that of the Third Congress (1930) was "Rational Land Development." The Fourth Congress (1933) was themed "The Functional City," and the principles later published as the Athens Charter were adopted at this fourth meeting.

The principles articulated in the Athens Charter, along with the housing theories prevalent in Europe during the postwar era, were imported directly into Japan's cities. Urban areas were zoned by function in accordance with the CIAM concept of rational land development, and housing was mass-produced in the "one unit = one family" format of residential units that conformed to the notion of the "minimum dwelling" necessary for family life. Having lost its traditional wooden urban housing in the war, Japan was, if anything, more receptive than Europe to the wholesale adoption of CIAM theory.

What Is CIAM Theory?

CIAM espoused urban planning that divided cities into function-specific zones. In contrast to the traditional Japanese urban configuration of integrated living and working spaces, CIAM completely separated residential areas from areas of economic activity. Cities were divided into exclusively residential, industrial, and commercial zones; hence people dwelling in the residential zone could no longer engage in economic activities there. Housing units existed exclusively for the family and were therefore built solely for the purpose of maintaining family privacy and reproducing labor power. This type of housing had the following characteristics:

1   Each unit housed a single family under a "one unit = one family"
         system of housing supply.

2   Units were entirely standardized, resulting in the standardization of
         families themselves.

3   Each unit was thoroughly shut off from the outside world (i.e., the
         surrounding community), and privacy was prioritized.

4   Units were built so as to minimize interference from neighboring
         units; thus the "one unit = one family" format prevented the formation
         of communities.

5   The "one unit = one family" format envisioned each family as a self-
         contained, autonomous unit. Moreover, the provision of housing
         was predicated on the understanding that it was the role of the house-
         wife to maintain the life functions of the household.

6   In the "one unit = one family" system, the family was a unit of labor
         power reproduction (i.e., of procreation in order to generate new
         labor power).

7   Dwellings were for the purpose of housing workers engaged in
         wage labor.

This highly autonomous "one unit = one family" format was an unfamiliar
framework for Japanese housing up to that point. Nonetheless, these family-
only units were mass-produced to accommodate the large numbers of workers
required to implement the national policy of postwar recovery. The orderly
rows of houses built for this purpose resembled nothing so much as detention
facilities for families. The fact that this housing was defined as part of the postwar recovery effort to help people who had lost their homes during the war
contributed to a strong perception among architects that they were managing
the lives of the residents. This institutionalization of the home was, indeed,
intentional, and became the standard for public housing in Japan.

The Advent of the Condominium

The 1980s saw the wholesale transfer of the housing supply system from the
government to private hands. It was also a decade when the contradictions of
the "one unit = one family" format came into bold relief. The problem was
the excessive insularity of these units. Private developers sought to commodify

the "one unit = one family" concept by selling each unit as a package isolated from its surrounding environment, touting this (excessive) privacy and security as a top selling point.

The sales pitch went something like this: "The world outside is fraught with danger. You can't trust anyone. This residence is guaranteed to protect you from those outside dangers!"

The pitch worked, and the housing sold like hotcakes. Apartment units that promised this extreme degree of privacy and security were dubbed "mansions," which became the standard Japanese term for condominiums.

Around this time, solitary deaths and incidents of domestic violence in the home began to make the news—largely due, I believe, to the isolated nature of life in these "mansions." Architects, too, belatedly began to recognize the fundamental problems of the "one unit = one family" format. It was during this period, the 1980s, that we received the commission for the design of Hotakubo Housing.

Hotakubo Housing: An Experiment in Fostering Community

The first phase of Hotakubo Housing, an apartment complex in Kumamoto, Kyushu, was completed in 1989. The second phase was completed a year later.

This was the first project undertaken during Arata Isozaki's term as commissioner of Kumamoto Artpolis, an urban policy initiative instigated by Morihiro Hosokawa, the governor of Kumamoto Prefecture [ed.: Hosokawa would later serve as prime minister]. The purpose of the initiative was to raise the quality of public architecture and thereby improve urban environments.

The plan called for building 110 housing units on a two-hectare site formerly occupied by one-story "recovery housing" that had been built right after the war. These structures were to be demolished and replaced by five-story apartment houses.

How should 110 households be laid out on this site? What was the optimum plan for each unit? How should one design housing for the benefit of the residents rather than for the profit of the builder—that is, housing meant to serve as a "public asset"? And what, exactly, was a public asset?

We arranged the 110 units around a central open space. There was no gate through which one had to enter the complex from outside (FIGS. 1, 2). In place of a gate, we installed a community room, which would be accessible not only to residents of the complex but also to the whole neighborhood. In other words, anyone using the community room could also use the central space.

Each building has two staircases: one facing the central space and one facing the outer ring road. This enabled residents to freely access the central space directly from their homes. This layout is designed to make the central space an area managed by the residents, not by the prefecture.

1 | Riken Yamamoto & Field Shop, Hotakubo Housing, Kumamoto, 1991. General layout plan. Three buildings with 110 residential units and a "community room" (*shukaishitsu*) surround a central open space. © Riken Yamamoto & Field Shop

2 | Riken Yamamoto & Field Shop, Hotakubo Housing. Aerial view. Photo GoogleEarth

3 | Riken Yamamoto & Field Shop, Hotakubo Housing. System of managing the central open space by the residents. © Riken Yamamoto & Field Shop

2

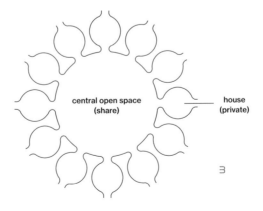

central open space (share) ———— house (private)

3

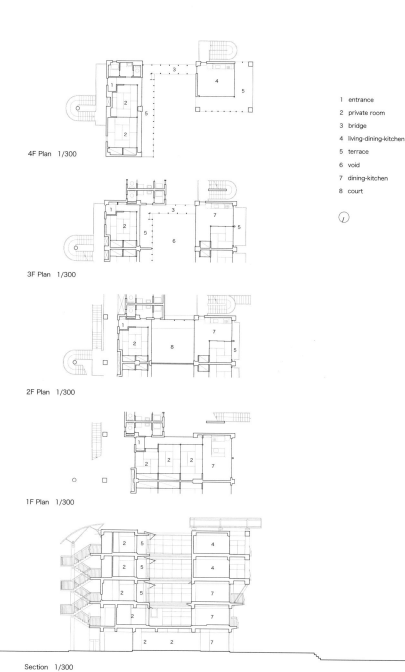

4F Plan 1/300

3F Plan 1/300

2F Plan 1/300

1F Plan 1/300

Section 1/300

1 entrance
2 private room
3 bridge
4 living-dining-kitchen
5 terrace
6 void
7 dining-kitchen
8 court

Riken Yamamoto & Field Shop, Hotakubo
Housing. Plans and section. © Riken
Yamamoto & Field Shop

So who is permitted to enter the central space? That is up to the residents to decide. It is the residents who share this space and who determine how the sharing is to be done (FIG. 3); the layout is designed to ensure that (FIG. 4). We may describe a collective space of this sort, whose usage is defined by its residents, as a "community." Our aim in designing this layout was precisely that—to foster a community relationship among residents.

However, our community-fostering strategy cannot be said to have succeeded. The problem lay in our inability to eradicate the "one unit = one family" bias of the residents, who retained the same attitudes toward privacy reflected in the "one unit = one family" concept that we had seen in the past. Although the central space was clearly designed for self-management by the residents, there was much ambiguity around questions such as how they were to use the space, and how freely. As the architect, I was in a position to encourage discussion of these issues between the residents and the prefecture, which managed the complex, but it turned out to be difficult to initiate such conversations. The complex was designed exclusively for family dwellings, and people living there solely in order to pursue a nuclear-family, consumer-oriented life-style viewed efforts to bring them together with residents outside their immediate families as an incursion on their privacy, and the prefecture saw things the same way.

There is an inherent contradiction in the notion of grouping multiple "one unit = one family" households together. Indeed, this remained an intransigent problem for me in subsequent projects involving multi-unit housing.

Shinonome Canal Court: An Experiment in Promoting Live-Work Housing

Shinonome Canal Court is an apartment complex of 2,000 units that was completed in 2003 in Tokyo's bayside district. The 4.8-hectare site was subdivided into six blocks, each to be designed by a different team of architects. The architects, who included Toyo Ito, Kengo Kuma, and myself, consulted with one another, but we developed our own designs.

I was asked to serve as the master architect for the project by its developer, a semi-public housing agency now known as the Urban Renaissance Agency, or more commonly, UR. They requested that I develop a set of principles for the six participating teams of architects to share in creating the general plan for the project. I proposed that we design housing that was as open as possible to the outside environment. In a workshop setting, the six teams then worked up the designs over the course of discussions about what "open" meant, and what form it might take.

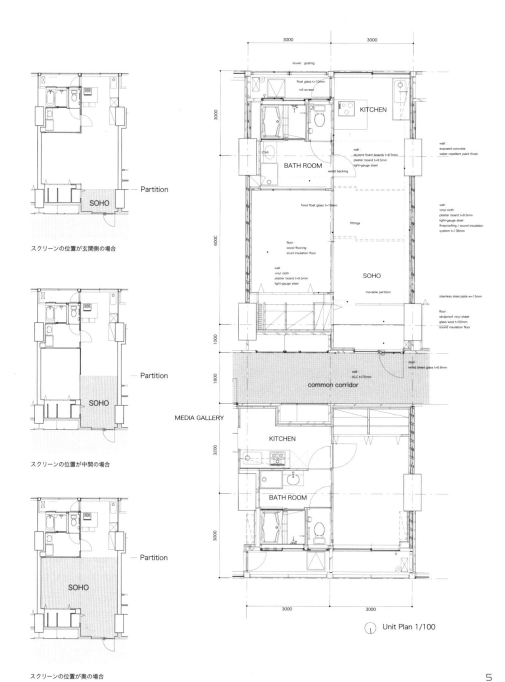

スクリーンの位置が玄関側の場合

— Partition

SOHO

スクリーンの位置が中間の場合

— Partition

SOHO

スクリーンの位置が奥の場合

— Partition

SOHO

MEDIA GALLERY

KITCHEN

BATH ROOM

SOHO

common corridor

KITCHEN

BATH ROOM

Unit Plan 1/100

I also asked the other architects to contemplate housing units that were not solely for families to live in, but that could include workplaces or even retail shops—in other words, integrated living-working spaces.

For Block 1—the "Riken Yamamoto Block," for which I was responsible—I proposed a unit floor plan (FIG. 5) featuring a glass entry door and partition, and an optional workspace located behind it. It was an extremely flexible layout that would allow this space to be used either for family purposes or as an office or shop.

Block 1 shares a second-floor deck with Block 2, the "Toyo Ito Block"— a simple method of creating an enclosed plaza. A community room faces the deck, which provides children with a safe place to play.

Passing through all six blocks is an S-shaped "avenue" lined with shops, restaurants, and daycare centers for children and the elderly. This general plan—as well as our agreement on a unique design of elevations perforated here and there with large apertures that function as terraces for common use in each building—was made possible by discussions involving all six teams as well as the housing agency at our workshops (FIG. 6).

However, the provision of "living-working" style units proved to be a high hurdle, both for the architects and for the housing agency. In principle, Japanese law prohibits the operation of businesses in an exclusively residential zone: the CIAM zoning concept is still alive and well in Japan. The idea is that a quiet environment must be maintained to ensure the privacy of families in a residential zone, and that permitting shops to open risks disturbing that environment. In practice, the living-working option had to be dropped from the actual management of the complex. Residents showed tremendous ingenuity in turning the glass entry doors into "show windows" facing the outside corridor (FIG. 7). However, that was as far as the concept developed, and they were never used as actual storefronts.

UR hosted a jazz festival for residents of the new complex, timed to take place when all of the blocks were occupied. It was a lively event that drew people from the surrounding neighborhood, but some residents of the complex complained about the noise and demanded that such events not be held there again. There have been no jazz festivals at Shinonome Canal Court since then.

Recently, UR has outsourced management of the complex to a private developer, making it even more of a closed environment. Some residents are now covering the glass entry doors with blindfold sheeting. Due to the rules of use imposed by the management company, which now makes all such decisions, people no longer spend time in the common-use terraces interspersed throughout the buildings. The principles envisioned by the architects for living in this complex have been abandoned, and it has become a place that prioritizes privacy above all else, like other conventional housing.

6

7

6   Riken Yamamoto & Field Shop, Shinonome
Canal Court Block 1. General view.
Photo © Riken Yamamoto & Field Shop

7   Riken Yamamoto & Field Shop, Shinonome
Canal Court Block 1. Entrance to a housing
unit. Photo © Riken Yamamoto & Field Shop

How Standardized Housing Standardizes the Family

What was the world like during the heyday of CIAM, during the 1920s and 1930s? In Europe, it was a period of recovery from World War I, as well as of intense economic competition among nations, each attempting to accelerate its own trajectory of progress. Victory in the economic race required an industrious labor force, and housing in the "one unit = one family" format and a system for supplying it were crucial to the reproduction of that labor force.

After World War II, Japan, too, instituted the supply of "one unit = one family" housing as part of a national recovery policy. The standardization of housing in this format in turn contributed to the standardization of the families living there. Communities were subdivided into residential units that functioned as isolated compartments in which to raise children. The sociologists' critique that "community" in Japanese society was merely an illusion acquired the ring of authenticity.

Resident Autonomy

True community demands autonomy by residents. The opposite concept is "management of residents." The CIAM theory of collective housing was, in fact, heavily skewed toward resident management, not resident autonomy.

If an urban environment is to be "shared," then the residents who are to do the sharing must themselves be aware of the necessity of resident autonomy. An urban environment that supports resident autonomy cannot simply be bestowed upon them; they must be the actors who create it. This, however, is difficult to achieve in Japan, because postwar housing policy in this country was implemented with the aim of managing residents. There are daunting barriers to resident autonomy still in place.

Sharing an urban environment does not simply mean creating spaces where people can meet one another by happenstance. These spaces must belong to the residents, and they must be the kinds of places that support resident autonomy. The difficulty of creating such spaces is a challenge we must overcome.

THE CULTURAL CITY

● JAPAN RESEARCH INITIATIVE TEAM

A collage showing the 1946 Bunkyo Academic Cultural District plan superimposed onto contemporary Tokyo. Image © Japan Research Initiative Team. District plan from the Kenzo Tange Archive. Gift of Mrs. Takako Tange, 2011. Courtesy of the Frances Loeb Library, Harvard University Graduate School of Design

Many of Tokyo's recent large-scale developments have appeared in areas such as Marunouchi, Roppongi, and Shibuya. But in the wake of World War II, an idea emerged for a different kind of large-scale development, one that was conceived for another part of the city and that still inspires us to consider alternative forms of urban development.

This large and ambitious urban development proposal would have created a "cultural city" that tied together institutions such as the University of Tokyo, the Tokyo National Museum, and Ueno Park, as well as old neighborhoods including the area now known as Yanesen. The master plan, designed by a team that included a young Kenzo Tange, was conceived to parallel a university city, much like Oxford or Cambridge. The wholesale urban transformation of this Modernist scheme may be anachronistic, but the motivating ideas behind the unrealized project are once again being promoted by a group of scholars, professionals, and local citizens. They argue for the importance of a cultural district for Tokyo—one with a different set of priorities than the supposedly comprehensive urban developments elsewhere in the city.

Ueno Park has been the site of important cultural developments throughout Japanese history. An ancestral ground of the shogun and a popular place for cherry-blossom viewing in the Edo era, Ueno was designated as the first park in Japan soon after modernization began. It became a showcase of national modernization—and westernization—through exhibitions, events, and a growing campus of cultural and educational institutions. Today, these include the Tokyo University of the Arts, National Museum of Nature and Science, the Museum of Western Art (the only project in Japan by Le Corbusier), Tokyo Bunka Kaikan (concert hall), and the city's Zoological Gardens.

Ironically, the park with its myriad buildings, lakes, and greenery has also become one of the city's main locations for the homeless, who have created numerous temporary structures made of cardboard and tarps as shelter from the elements. The recent novel Tokyo Ueno Station by Yu Miri beautifully depicts the life of a homeless man who lives in the park, and sheds light on the contested status of this civic space.

What lessons can we learn from previous proposals for a cultural district including Ueno, and from the conflictual uses of the park itself as a public space shared by all?

Land Use Plan

Proposed in 1946 by a team including Eika Takayama and Kenzo Tange, the Bunkyo Academic Cultural District would have linked Ueno Park, the University of Tokyo, and other institutions northeast of the palace. Plan from the Kenzo Tange Archive. Gift of Mrs. Takako Tange, 2011. Courtesy of the Frances Loeb Library, Harvard University Graduate School of Design

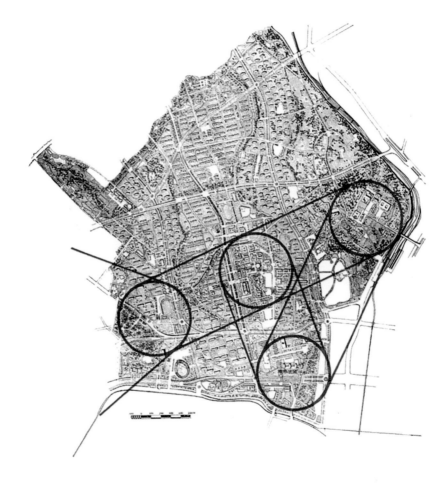

Zone Plan

Bunkyo Academic Cultural District, 1946. Plan from the Kenzo Tange Archive. Gift of Mrs. Takako Tange, 2011. Courtesy of the Frances Loeb Library, Harvard University Graduate School of Design

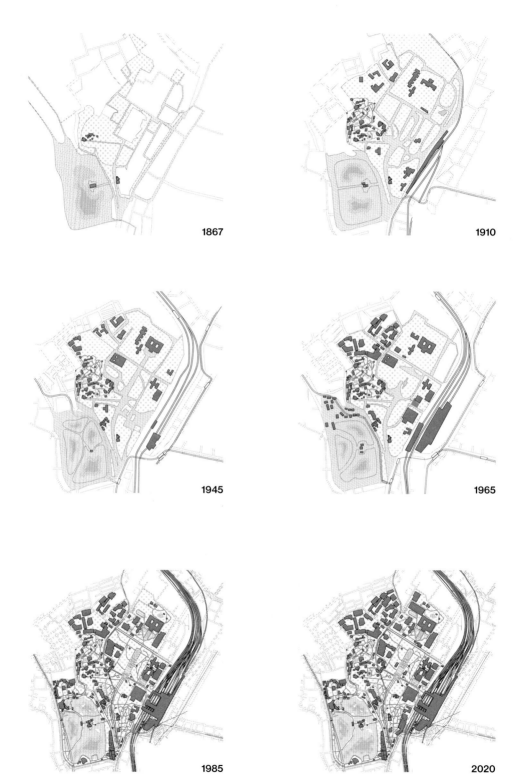

1867

1910

1945

1965

1985

2020

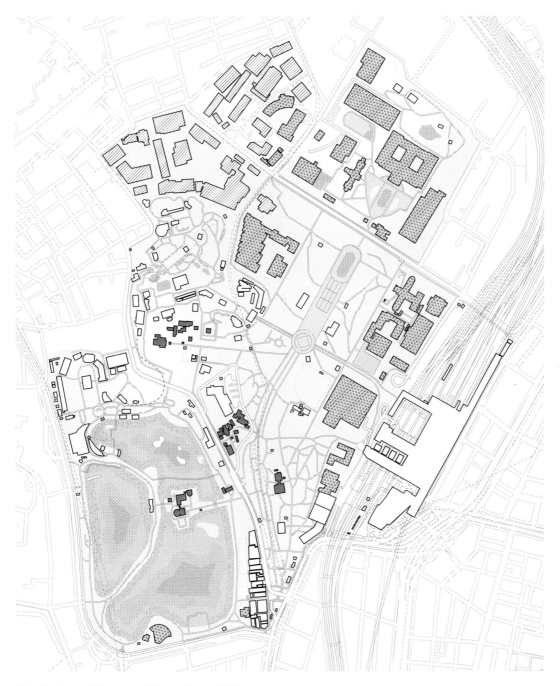

■ Institutional ■ Religous ▨ Educational ☐ Other

The many institutions built in Ueno Park in the last century have created a mixed landscape of buildings and voids that is as much a cultural city as an urban green space

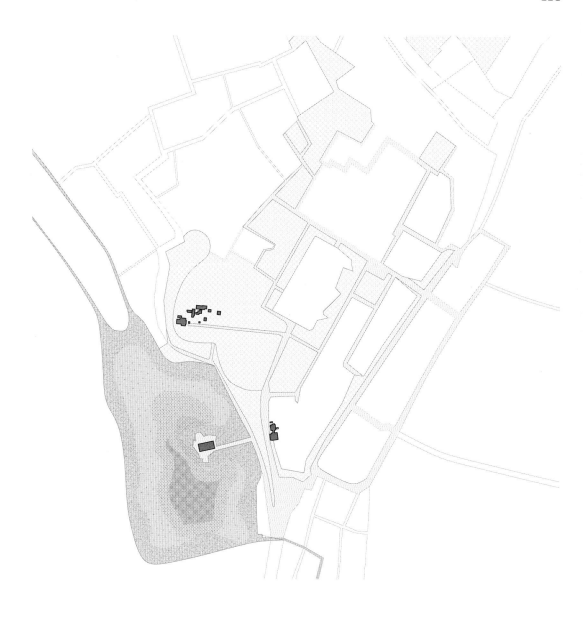

Shinobazu Pond and Benten Temple
Map date: 1867

Shinobazu Pond, a heavily sculpted natural feature of the park, recalls the early history of this area of Tokyo as a center for religious life and recreation. The Benten Temple, which occupies a small island in the pond, was originally constructed in the early seventeenth century. The edge of the pond remains a popular place to stroll and observe people, nature, and the city

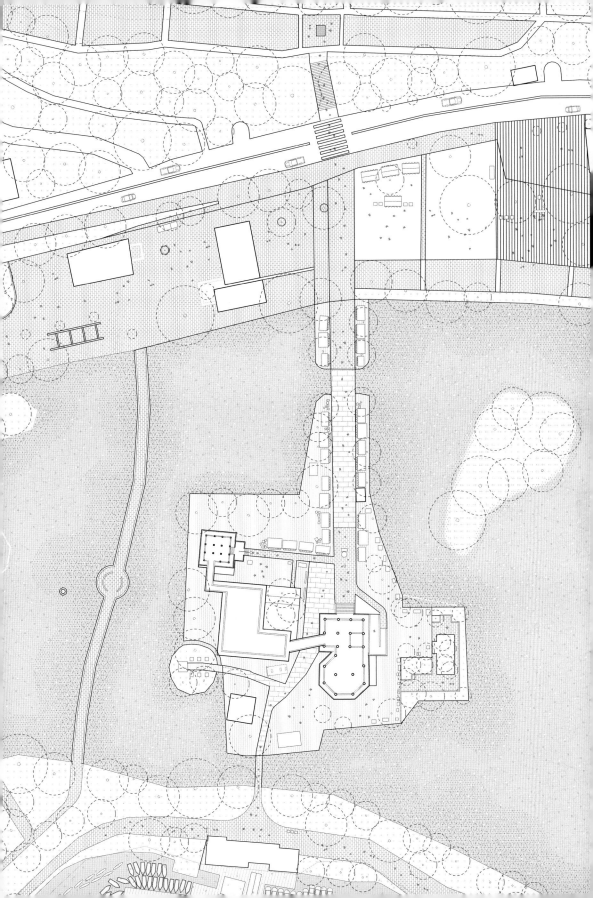

Tokyo National Museum and Grand Fountain
Map date: 1945

The grand, symmetrical composition of the Tokyo National Museum, and the axis that leads to it, were conceived as symbols of Japan's progress and modernization. The current main building of the museum, designed
by architect Jin Watanabe, opened in 1938. The open space in front was used for imperial functions and
remains a popular event venue

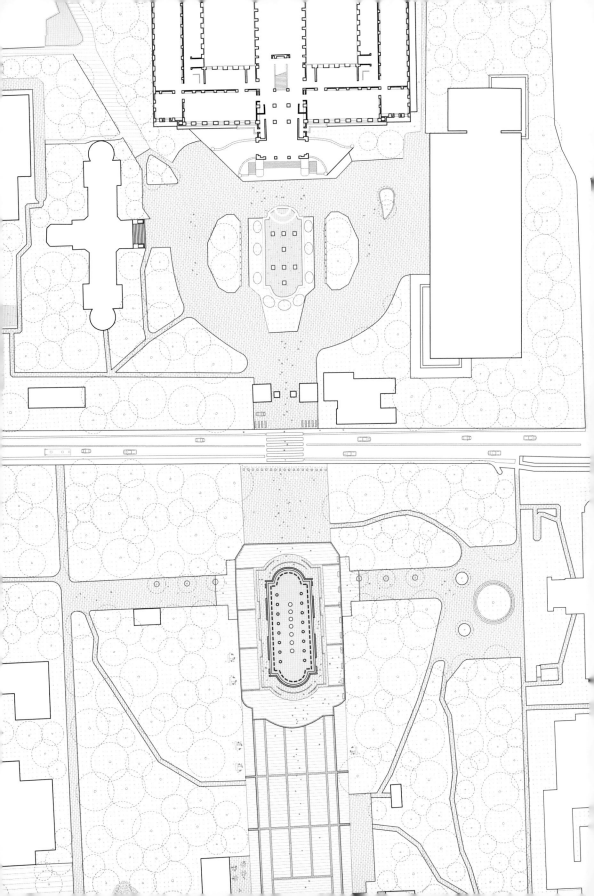

Tokyo Bunka Kaikan and National Museum of Western Art
Map date: 2022

The National Museum of Western Art, Le Corbusier's only building in Japan, was executed by Japanese
architects who had apprenticed in his office in Paris: Kunio Maekawa, Junzo Sakakura, and Takamasa
Yoshizaka. Maekawa also designed the Tokyo Bunka Kaikan, a concert hall located directly to the south.
Together with the west entrance to Ueno Station, these structures frame one of the most active and
modern public spaces in Ueno Park

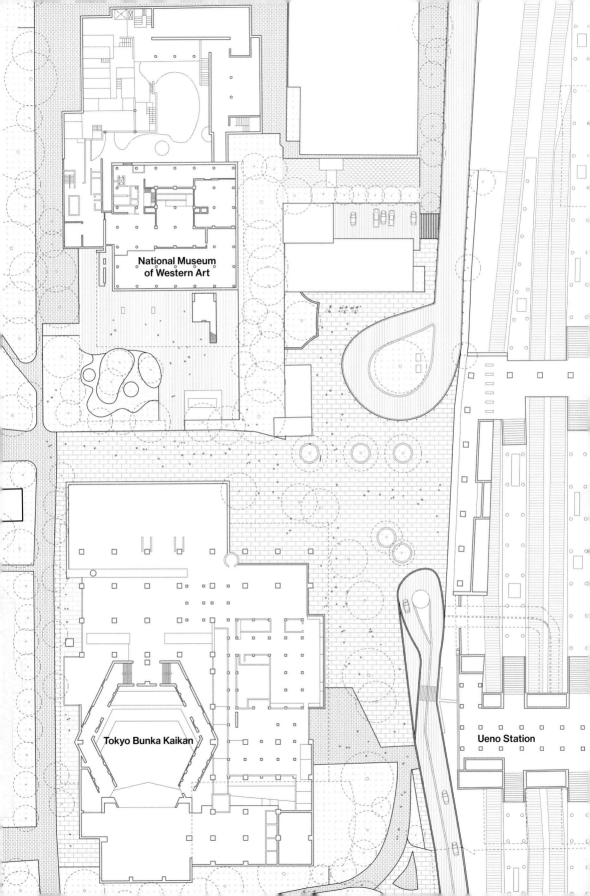

National Museum
of Western Art

Tokyo Bunka Kaikan

Ueno Station

JO NAGASAKA: THE URBAN INTERIOR

● DON O'KEEFE

Jo Nagasaka/Schemata Architects, OKOMEYA, 2015. The open corner of a rice shop in south Tokyo. Photo © Kenta Hasegawa

2 OKOMEYA. The shop is one of several new businesses to open on the once-struggling Miyamae shopping street. Photo © Kenta Hasegawa

Turn a corner in Tokyo and you might find anything. Buildings of every imaginable form and use jostle for position along narrow streets. Elevated concrete expressways snake above unpaved alleys festooned with potted plants. Bicycles, statues, and trash cans burst from the slots between houses.

In contrast to this heterogeneity, development in Tokyo is increasingly polarized between vast high-rise complexes in the urban core and abandoned houses in languishing exurbs. As corporate architecture practices monopolize projects, small firms are locked out of most significant commissions. At the same time, young designers have grown more interested in the social function of urban space since the glossy, object-obsessed peak of the Bubble Era. But how can they act on these ambitions? In a city where every square meter is accounted for, what kind of project, and what approach to its design, can open up space for collective life? Can enterprising architects craft new modes of practice to influence the shape of Tokyo?

These are some of the questions that animate Jo Nagasaka, proprietor of Schemata, a twenty-five-person design firm in Tokyo. Nagasaka built his practice on small, sensitive interior design projects for fashion houses and retailers, but as his office has grown, his interests increasingly lie in the capacity for design to influence the public realm. Strikingly, though, he has not sought larger projects in pursuit of this goal. If anything, the average size of his commissions has decreased since the early days of his practice. (He completed a nine-storey, 1,600 m2 residential building in 2004 and has not returned to this scale since.)

Nagasaka has chosen a different route entirely, one that stresses the agency of the small-scale project in affecting large-scale change, if only indirectly. His work raises the question of how individual architectural acts can influence a community, and how the specific resolution of material details can change the way people inhabit and interpret their environment.

Renovation Aesthetics

The Okomeya rice shop opened on Tokyo's Miyamae shopping street in 2015, filling the vacant ground floor of an early Showa-era townhouse (1926–1945). The modest wooden structure is enclosed by a stucco parapet wall intended to mimic the more solid and modern masonry or concrete construction then used in major commercial buildings in central Tokyo. Nagasaka, who designed the renovation, stripped back everything below the shop's tiled eaves to expose a slender wooden structure. The solid stucco mass above seems to levitate (FIGS. 1, 2).

The corner of the store opens to both the Miyamae shopping street and an adjoining residential alley, allowing interested shoppers to pass through and signboards and products to spill out into the street. Once the metal shutters roll up in the morning, the shop floor is fully open to the air. The space behind the counter is enclosed with butt-jointed plate glass. Without mullions, the

3

4

3   Jo Nagasaka/Schemata Architects, Sayama Flat, 2008. The interior of an apartment, which Nagasaka renovated only by removing elements. Photo © Takumi Ota

4   Jo Nagasaka/Schemata Architects, House in Okusawa, 2009. The renovated exterior of the house retains the original entry sconce. Photo © Takumi Ota

distinction between workspace and the semi-public sphere beyond is minimal. The height of the product displays steps down to the corner, leaving paths of vision and travel through the shop unobstructed.

Like many of Nagasaka's renovations, Okomeya was created as much by removing elements as by adding them. In one 2008 project, Sayama Flat, he renovated a large apartment building only by removing material (FIG. 3). The following year he completed the House in Okusawa, in which gypsum walls and ceilings are peeled back to expose patches of floor joists or rough wooden bracing studs. Sometimes these ad-hoc decisions seem like architectural comedy. In the Okusawa house, Nagasaka scrubbed the facade of all detail, only to leave a single kitschy sconce (FIG. 4). At other times, they recall the language of contemporary art: the assemblage or the ready-made, for instance. In the Sayama Flat, a stripped-down wall shows off bundled pipes and the unseemly backside of a prefabricated bathroom. Precisely because they are less refined, these techniques make both the process of design and the methods of construction more intelligible.

In Okomeya, Nagasaka removed extraneous interior fixtures and case-work to celebrate the remaining artifacts of the building, the worn posts and delicately carved transom frames. These elements are juxtaposed against new display cases made of light plywood, creating an impression somewhere between high design and the DIY aesthetic: precisely the cultural intersection in which Nagasaka operates.

The Ripple Effect

Renovations now occupy the center of Nagasaka's practice, and he believes they have a special communicative potential, an ability to connect with people that new construction lacks. "The good thing about renovations is that they don't look too ambitious," Nagasaka explained. "A neighbor who sees the finished work would think, 'Maybe I could do this with my house.' On the contrary, if you build a perfect new house, you won't feel you can do the same thing three houses down the road. The ripple effect of making a new building is not as strong as renovating one."

At Okomeya, the simplicity of the design and the accessibility of off-the-shelf materials might encourage others to emulate the shop—an example of the "ripple effect" Nagasaka hopes his work will have. "As constrained as renovation is, it can attract people around it," he explained. "It raises the potential of invigorating the place." In fact, the rice shop itself was conceived as part of a revitalization plan for the Miyamae shopping street, which is struggling to survive.

For much of the twentieth century, Miyamae was alive with activity. Emanating from a rail station in southern Tokyo, the narrow road was lined with banks, grocers, restaurants, bars, and other businesses that served the commuters who passed by. But like many other neighborhood main streets in Japan and around the developed world, Miyamae spent much of the 1980s and 90s in decline. Errands that once took local consumers to agglomerations of independently owned stores could now be accomplished in large, one-stop complexes in bedroom communities or attached to rail stations. The more recent onset of online shopping hasn't helped the average Japanese shopping street, or *shotengai,* as they are known.

Miyamae has had some recent successes in combating this decline, one of which is Nagasaka's design for Okomeya. The shop is operated by Owan Inc., a social-media-savvy communications firm whose office is in the same neighborhood. They also run a nearby bakery as part of their revitalization scheme for the area. The rice shop is one of many newer businesses hoping to resuscitate the shopping street, most of which follow the model of Okomeya. These piecemeal renovations are the low-budget passion projects of the young—of people carving out spaces for themselves in the city's forgotten quarters.

Being on the Ground

For Nagasaka, the ground floor is the most important. "On the ground floor all kinds of people come in," he explains. "Relationships with neighbors come into play. I think it's important for projects to have a social relationship with the outside world. When you are on the ground floor, you are inevitably involved with a variety of people."

Like the Okomeya rice shop, Nagasaka's other ground-floor renovation projects complicate the distinction between public, private, and commercial space. Practically, this is often achieved using some combination of operable facades, custom furniture, and diffuse interior layouts. A recent project for coffee chain Blue Bottle in Yokohama was too small to include indoor seating. Instead, modular furniture expands out of the facade during the day, temporarily invading the street edge and encouraging people to gather.

On the east side of Tokyo, Nagasaka renovated an aging bathhouse called Koganeyu as part of another local revitalization effort. Most of the interior is necessarily private, but the front of the bathhouse is oriented to the street by means of an open facade. A large glass transom brings light deep into the space, penetrating back to the baths, while an entry of sliding glass panels exposes a standing bar to the street. A small row of curtains (*noren*) hide the faces of the people drinking, but the bar itself is visible as a kind of advertisement (FIG. 5).

For all their charms, there are also limitations to relying solely on retail projects for the revitalization of the city. What kind of civic life is fostered when the public realm is relegated to places for shopping and dining out? When asked, Nagasaka agrees and recounts his search for ways to expand his practice beyond the confines of commercial projects, however scrappy and community-oriented. "I'm thinking about it a lot. Japan is a country of consumption, where it's hard to find ways to spend time without spending money," Nagasaka says. "What I'm working on now is an interface between the city and people, or architecture and people."

But where does this interface take place? Earlier generations of architects, influenced by the clear dichotomy of public and private space in Modernist planning theory, believed the expansion of open space was the best way to enhance public life in the city. Nagasaka, like many of his contemporaries, is more likely to search for public life along the teeming lanes of a peripheral neighborhood than in the grand parks and plazas of the urban core.

Public Relations

From the earliest days of his practice, the constant in Nagasaka's work has been craft and material experimentation. His engagement with the public role of architecture developed later, after years of collaborating with clients and witnessing the surprisingly far-reaching consequences of modest interventions. Nagasaka's interest in the narrative of projects—his desire to show off the ideas and products of his clients—parallels his interest in calling attention to the isolated fragments of architecture that he preserves in his renovations. "Rather than having a specific idea of what I want to make, my approach to any project is to observe, think about what the person wants to do and the location, make some kind of discovery, and then give shape to it. It's not just people, it's also places. I care a lot about the building or land that was originally there. Even the most trivial things are important to me."

In part because his projects have been successful in capturing public attention, Nagasaka increasingly works with clients whose goals extend beyond having a more attractive shop. For many of them, the operation of a small business is a medium by which some other goal is reached, like the revitalization of aging buildings or districts (the Okomeya rice shop, for instance).

Nagasaka has completed a series of these socially engaged and materially opportunistic projects that operate at the intersection of interior renovation, furniture design, and small business development and promotion. "I want to attract people and make sure that the work I've designed will operate properly. I want to support people from backstage," he explains. "I'm not just designing architecture but also promoting the effect of what we design as PR." This expanded scope of work is now part of Nagasaka's practice, and an asset potential clients cite when seeking his services. From the perspective of these clients, the role of the architect is not necessarily to design a building, or even to renovate one, but to develop a strategy for whatever aspect of their organization deals with physical space.

Invisible Development

Recently, Nagasaka has been engaged in a revitalization project on the island of Jeju in South Korea. Since the architectural phase of the project is still some distance off, Nagasaka explains, "we began by designing furniture. We believe it's necessary to activate the town first." Eventually, this mobile outdoor furniture will populate the space between independently renovated buildings, forming a connective tissue within the town. "I've started to call this kind of project 'invisible development,'" Nagasaka says. "If you just tweak things little by little, the effect of the work will last longer and have a larger impact."

These ideas are visible in Nagasaka's recent work for institutions searching for affordable ways to reorient their relationship to the public, especially since the pandemic. "I was commissioned by the Museum of Contemporary Art Tokyo to create pieces of urban furniture that would attract people to the park in front of the building and make it a museum for everyday use," Nagasaka said. He designed a variety of shelving, seating, and other furniture that can be easily rearranged with a standard floor jack. The lightweight furniture, built from cork and wood, is scattered through the museum and into the park, establishing a continuity of public space. Nagasaka has deployed sets of flexible furniture elsewhere, too, including in a plaza adjoining the heavily trafficked Tokiwa Bridge near Tokyo Station.

In the seaside city of Onomichi, Japan, Nagasaka is renovating a house as the first step in a more ambitious attempt at "invisible development." Some of his staff from Tokyo have relocated there permanently and, Nagasaka hopes, will conduct workshops on the renovation and repurposing of old structures. "There are many towns in Japan that are in decline or even on the brink of collapse. I think architects can be involved with this issue," he explained. "For example, architects could build a platform for new activities, thereby communicating with the townspeople. And if people elsewhere realize that this model can be applied to where they are, I'm sure some of them will try. I would be happy if people understood the activities we initiated in Onomichi as prototypes."

Commercial interiors may remain the bread and butter of Nagasaka's practice, but these forays into neighborhood and town revitalization signal a desire for greater self-determination. This is another way in which Nagasaka's work traces the trajectory of Japanese architectural practice in recent years. In an era of rapid demographic change, other well-known architects have begun to engage with depopulated rural areas. Toyo Ito has been working on the island of Omishima for years, and a host of internationally recognized architects have contributed to the rebirth of Naoshima and other islands as destinations for art and culture. Nagasaka credits some of his interest in this work to figures like Masataka Baba of R-Fudosan, a renovation-focused real-estate firm, and Yoshihiko Oshima of the architecture practice Blue Studio (whose writing appears elsewhere in this volume). For many younger architects, Nagasaka included, the interest in renovation, revitalization, and public communication is a means both for solving social problems and winning back professional agency.

The Urban Interior

Fittingly, Nagasaka's own office, a three-story workshop in central Tokyo, is the most complete synthesis of his interests in a single project. He and his employees carried out the renovation by hand during 2020, taking advantage of free time created by pandemic-related project cancellations. The direct, improvisational method of construction echoes the process used at Sayama Flat, with layers of material peeled back to expose the history of the building's occupation and use.

The finished office retains the raw aesthetic of the original warehouse, a steel-frame structure with a concrete deck, wooden partition walls, and conventional aluminum sash windows. The additions, such as they are, retain the same language; tables and bike racks resemble saw horses, and unfinished wooden shelving is suspended by threaded steel rods. The construction process was well documented and published alongside the finished work online and in magazines, with special attention given to unusual architectural fragments and picturesque assortments of refuse.

The office does more than showcase Nagasaka's aesthetic obsessions. The ground floor hosts an eclectic mix of semi-public spaces: meeting rooms, a commercial kitchen, and a flexible shop floor that is used for model-making and events (FIG. 6). Local regulations permit them to operate as a retail space on occasion, and even to sell food and drinks. "It's a kind of experiment," according to Nagasaka. "Our space is not just an office. It can be an exhibition venue or a space for workshops and other activities to communicate with people who live nearby." All of the employees have their desks on the upper floors except for Nagasaka, who prefers to work on the ground level.

The spatial and material composition of the office suggests a social as well as an aesthetic stance, a piecemeal approach to a patchwork city. "There is a relationship between the concept of 'invisible development' I mentioned earlier, and the interface between furniture and architecture," Nagasaka explains. "Renovation doesn't just change the inside of a building but also the neighboring buildings, and activities across the city." Even a modest project can be both a metaphor for the city and a catalyst for its development.

Nagasaka may have stumbled into the professional space he now occupies, but he has dedicated himself to exploring its potential. His practice is the product of the same conditions that circumscribe many other small offices in

5

6

5   Jo Nagasaka/Schemata Architects, Koganeyu, 2020. The bathhouse Nagasaka designed in east Tokyo includes a bar that opens to the street. Photo © Yurika Kono

6   The new office of Schemata, Nagasaka's 25-person design practice, doubles as a neighborhood event space. Photo © Yuzo Fujii, courtesy of Schemata Architects

Tokyo today. Part of their entrapment can be attributed to an age-old paradox of architectural practice: you can't do a museum until you've done a museum, you can't do a library until you've done a library. But some of these limiting conditions are specific to contemporary Tokyo, where the same handful of firms compete for every new skyscraper that sprouts up from the rubble of a lost neighborhood.

Rather than continue to participate in a game that can seem unwinnable, Nagasaka has attempted to change the rules. Setting aside the architect's native scale, the individual building, what relationship can design establish between the person, the city, the room, and the object? In pursuit of this question, Nagasaka's work makes an important contribution to the tool kit of a new group of architects hoping to affect the city in the only way they now can: small projects with limited means. Working in the expanding gray area between private and public space, Nagasaka offers a glimpse of what it might mean to create a truly urban interior.

ARCHITECTURE AS AN URBAN MIXER

● KAYOKO OTA

1   Coelacanth and Associates, Shibuya Stream, 2018. Interior view. Trajectories of various activities cross in a network of voids. Photo © Hidetaka Horiguchi

Denial or surrender? A contrast in how one encounters reality seems to be dividing the attitudes of architects in Japan, typically between those who started practicing before and after the turn of the century. One camp tries to offer society an alternative model of architecture by refusing urban reality, while the other tries to offer a solution through negotiating with that reality.

The chain of "star architects" from Kenzo Tange to Tadao Ando to Sou Fujimoto established their signatures by invoking catalysts for change in uncontrollable urban conditions. To do so, they needed to have a vision for a desirable urban form. Their visionary premises were exchanged throughout the architectural community and created polemics; not only through built or unbuilt works, but also in magazines, public discussions, and nightly gatherings in bars. All these factors propelled one another in a cycle that lasted from the 1960s to the 90s.

But the younger generation today—those born in the 1980s or later— no longer believes in revolution. In fact, they are willing to engage with social reality and conceive design solutions without the confrontations or visionary scenarios of their predecessors. As a result, the established social criticism of the architectural profession as lacking any consideration of social factors is slowly being overturned. Architects may no longer dazzle as stars. They are no longer maestros or lofty thinkers. Instead, the profession is being re-recognized as one composed of reliable partners who will listen to you, work with you, and come up with a sustainable solution.

In a Sea of Generic Buildings

During the two decades after the bubble burst in 1991, two things facilitated this change in attitude. One was the combined hardships of the postgrowth era, which made it inevitable for Japanese society to redefine its values. The two earthquakes of 1995 and 2011 are often said to have triggered a fundamental shift in attitude within the architectural profession, whose members had previously believed that their essential mission was to construct society—and who saw that belief broken in an instant. However, likely more critical was the change in outlook within Japanese society as it began to shrink and age. The upward vector of growth that was never questioned in the past century was suddenly reversed, forcing professionals to change their premises and objectives around making architecture.

The second cause of this new approach was a neoliberalism that intensified divisions in the construction industry. During the postgrowth period, the country was trying to get out of the long economic stagnation triggered by the bubble burst. In 2001, the government adopted the strategy of dynamically deregulating urban development schemes as a way of rescuing the sunken economy. Funds and capital were concentrated in large-scale development

2

Shibuya Stream. Bird's-eye view at night.
Photo © Daici Ano

projects in strategic areas in Tokyo and other large cities. As a result, the CBDs and downtowns in large cities became an exclusive stage limited to risk-free performances undertaken by major developers, general contractors, and large-scale corporate design firms. Super-high-rise buildings became a typology off limits to challenging ideas; any real experiments were prevented by the amount of capital involved.

Thus, architects with small- or medium-sized practices are practically unable to participate in shaping the future of a large portion of cities, an area increasingly filled with large-scale developments. By and large, architects of the younger generation do not confront this trend. When they began practicing, this territorial divide had already become too large to handle. Instead, younger architects survived by redefining their role. After all, they had no choice but make themselves needed in the territory they were allowed, that of the neighborhood, the urban periphery, and non-urban areas. Having acquired an awareness of social engagement, they no longer needed to make bold design gestures. Instead, they are more concerned with how to make what little space is available more livable and more socially interactive through the techniques of renovation, adaptive reuse, and activating spatial gaps.

This is a rough portrait of the postgrowth generation of architects; however, what's alarming is that on either side of the divide—in the market-driven large-scale developments or in the low-rise neighborhoods—architects have withdrawn from experimentation and architectural innovation.

Rewriting User Behavior

Consequently, it came as a surprise when the medium-sized studio Coelacanth was commissioned to design a super-high-rise building as part of a new large-scale development, Shibuya Stream, in downtown Tokyo. The studio, led by the partners Kazuko Akamatsu and the late Kazuhiro Kojima,[1] had been acclaimed for their educational institutions in regional cities such as schools and libraries, typologies that may be straightforward in appearance but are filled with subtle ideas based on the close observation of users as well as a socially conscious vision. But the scale and the location of the building was totally unexpected, even for a resourceful studio like Coelacanth.

While Shibuya Stream may look like a generic high-rise building, a hidden ingenuity lies within the low-rise (ground to fifth floor) portion that contains various public programs (FIGS. 1, 2). From the sixth floor up, this super-tall slab is occupied by the headquarters of Google Japan and a business hotel. The logic was that by heightening the attractiveness of the low-rise part, the value of the whole building would rise even if (as foreseen by the owner and architects) the low-rise part would never generate as much profit as it should.

I   Kazuhiro Kojima passed away in 2016 before the construction of Shibuya Stream was completed.

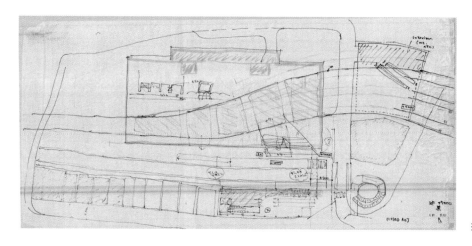

3

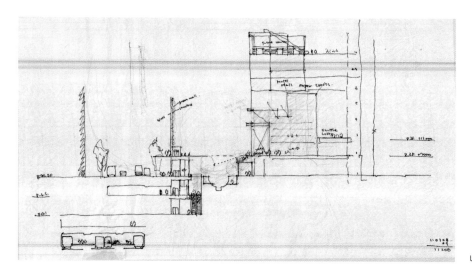

4

3 | Shibuya Stream. Early-stage sketch of the site plan. © Coelacanth and Associates

4 | Shibuya Stream. Early-stage sketch of the section. © Coelacanth and Associates

To this end, the architects made the low-rise part as open as possible for public use as a way of maximizing attractiveness.

The thin and long plot is surrounded on all sides: the nearby major train and subway stations of Shibuya are found both above and below ground, along with a canal, two crossing thoroughfares layered with an elevated highway, and a quiet neighborhood. A web of pedestrian passes connecting eight different lines stretches underground. The architectural challenge included how to effectively make the building relate to this hyper-dense, complex urban infrastructure (FIGS. 3, 4).

In order to achieve this task, the designer "hollowed out" a network of voids within the solid mass of the low-rise part of Shibuya Stream. This network branches out in all directions to connect to neighboring elements as well as different parts of the building on different levels, all within the low-rise part of the building (FIG. 5). The conventional segmentation of a public approach to a tall building—moving from the entrance door to the mall to the exit—was distorted and reorganized with this network of voids.

The trajectory of the user begins with a large opening punched into the foot of the building (FIG. 6). This opening lets you in at any time of the day, since there is no facade or shutter, after which you climb up a large staircase to reach a wide passage that penetrates the long side of the building. As an interior component, this passage is designed to work as the main street of this building, seamlessly connecting with the real streets around the building (FIGS. 7, 8).

After bringing you to the "main street," the void network takes you to a variety of situations. You can climb up further with a staircase or escalator toward the Shibuya station, which is visible at the end of the void channel. Or you can turn left to enter a gently curved street lined with restaurants or go further up an escalator to where a vast, semi-outdoor public lounge unfolds. Or take a right after the big stairs and walk further toward an open deck and an elevated highway. At one point, the void channel branches out vertically to the fifth level, where an escalator carries you to the office lobby or the theater foyer. Activities on the upper levels are visible from the "main street" on the second level.

A lively "outside" dining environment has been created by the main street lined with restaurants; behind this happy result lies a slow process by which the architects had the strict system of managing indoor restaurants and shops deregulated. The new street was carefully planned and crafted to create an informal atmosphere (FIG. 9): the "inner facades" of the upper level of the restaurant street were covered with as-cast concrete and hot-dip galvanized steel instead of typical interior finishes in order to establish a rough, street-like feeling. Although in fact an old, familiar street was lost to the Shibuya Stream development, attempts were made to liberate the interior space from some of the conventions of a high-rise building.

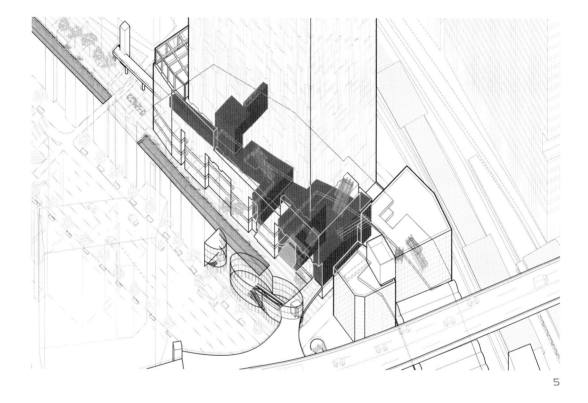

5 | The void network of Shibuya Stream drawn by Wentao Guo for the Japan Research Initiative, Harvard University Graduate School of Design, 2022

The void channel further branches out at several locations between restaurants to reach the outside. Like the large opening at the entrance, the ends of these corridors have no facades. Exposed to the outside, these alley-like corridors add depth to the visitor experience.[2] One can enjoy the view looking down the canal or at a train pulling in the station, or hide from the hustle-bustle and sit on a bench and enjoy the quiet and fresh air (FIG. 10). As Akamatsu describes, "we wanted to cut out and highlight the view of the surrounding situation to refresh the minds of the users. Just an unexpected moment of natural breeze is nice."[3]

Strategy of the Street

The network of voids—or "porosity," in Coelacanth's term—flamboyantly and uninterruptedly penetrates the low-rise part of the building in all directions. In effect, it works as urban infrastructure: it connects the building with the diverse urban elements surrounding it while transforming itself into a new kind of street rather than a mall. So, efforts were needed to blur the boundary of architecture and civil engineering to allow the high-rise building to effectively merge with the existing infrastructure. For the same reason, the architects insisted on clearing the large entrance void of any structural columns or an escalator, all of which were mandatory. As a result of intense collaboration with engineers and urban planners, Coelacanth succeeded in making an exceptionally large open space at the entry, which invites people in, lets them sit anywhere they like, and occasionally, in front of the building, offers them a public program of performances. In effect, the staircase works like a plaza (FIG. 11).

The void channels also mix various movements inside; not only physically, but also through sightlines that ensure visual communication between different parts of the building. Those people heading for private zones (offices, hotel) and those heading for public zones (station, theater, restaurants, pedestrian paths) inevitably cross in space, and together they create bustling urban scenes. As a way of highlighting some of these movements, bright yellow coloring was applied to the escalators and some doors.

Furthermore, the void channels physically communicate the outdoor environment to the indoor spaces: they let in natural light and sound, and even weather. As Kojima and Akamatsu wrote, "We've been exploring how we could compose a situation where you feel as if you were in the woods, bathing in the sound of stepping onto fallen leaves, the light that trickles through the leaves, the soft winds, and the spaces that connect as they come in and out of

---

2   Fumihiko Maki and others made a compelling analysis of the space of *oku* [space deep inside] in a Japanese city, which has had a strong influence on Japanese architects. Fumihiko Maki, et al, *City with a Hidden Past* (Tokyo: Kajima Institute Publishing, 2018).

3   Interview with Kazuko Akamatsu by the author in April 2018.

6 | Shibuya Stream. Large opening with
a wide staircase at the building entrance.
Photo © Hidetaka Horiguchi

7 | Shibuya Stream. Landing on the second
level after the wide staircases. Photo
© Daici Ano

8 | Shibuya Stream. Escalators traverse
the void, which branches off from the
"main street" into another channel.
Photo © Daici Ano

8

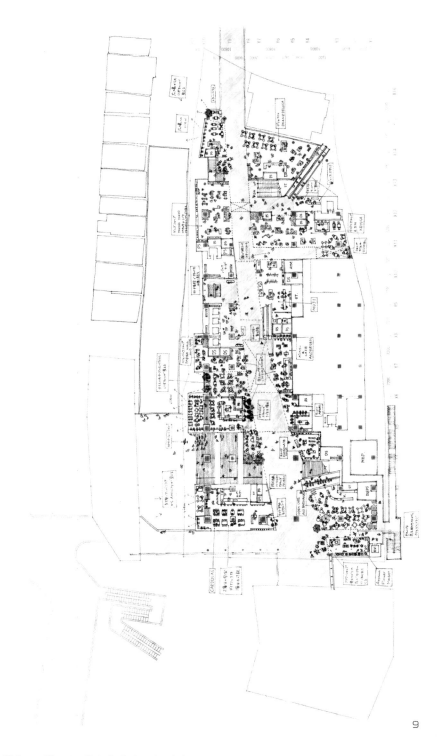

9

9 | Shibuya Stream. Detailed sketch of the
"main street" lined with restaurants,
which was used for obtaining consent from
the restaurant owners. © Coelacanth
and Associates

sight between the grove of trees."[4] The image of woods was also a representation of a concept: "a field of 'small arrows' flowing in diverse directions within a building."[5] In Shibuya Stream, the "small arrows" are navigated in "a fluidity as if walking in the woods."[6]

Coelacanth's concept of stretching a network of void in a building inevitably reminds us of two architectural ideas conceived by OMA: one is the "strategy of the void" in their 1989 proposal for the new national library of France, and the other is the Euralille project, an urban masterplan for a large-scale urban complex located near Lille's existing railway station that would include a new TGV (high-speed) station.[7] Of the latter, Rem Koolhaas wrote: "The station becomes an urban artery. The section was developed to be permeable from many points so that it performs as a connector. … It connects various parts of the new city…"[8] While leaving these "parts" to other architects, OMA as master planner carried out the "permeability" of the project through an unusual operation: "in the infrastructurally most complicated area we decided that through a reverse process of creation we would simply eliminate a part—create a void, a hole—where we could reveal all the surrounding forces. Even though you're deep underground there is daylight; you still have a window to the city and a view of the TGV."[9]

At Shibuya, the void evolved from holes to streets. Instead of punching holes at chosen locations, the architects dug a web of tunnels through a solid mass. These tunnels seamlessly bring the streets inside the building, intensifying its relationship with its surroundings. Also, the void allows the architects to compress or juxtapose different settings, or permits urban phenomena that are common in streets to happen inside a building. Dislodging the common language of a skyscraper, the low-rise part of the building presents a new form of privately owned public space, where the experience of being in a city and sharing it is celebrated.

Master Planning Architecture

The success of this "materializing the void" strategy in Shibuya is owed, in addition to intense teamwork among architects, structural and civil engineers, and urban planners, to the expanded perspective of the socially engaged architects who worked on the project as an urban master planning project rather

4	Kazuhiro Kojima and Kazuko Akamatsu/C+A, *Essence Behind* (Tokyo: Lixil Shuppan, 2016), 75. The authors used the Japanese word *zokibayashi*, meaning manmade wood products like firewood and building materials, maintained as part of a sustainable ecological cycle.
5	Kazuhiro Kojima, *Chiisana yajirushi no mure—Mies moderu wo koete* [Gatherings of Small Arrows: Beyond the Mies Model] (Tokyo: TOTO Shuppan, 2013), 160–162.
6	Kojima, 182.
7	Kojima himself acknowledged influence from the Brazilian architects Oscar Niemeyer and João Vilanova Artigas, whose design for the Faculty of Architecture and Urbanism Building at the University of São Paulo apparently inspired the designing of fluidity through Shibuya Stream. See Kojima, 72–78.
8	Rem Koolhaas, *SMLXL* (Rotterdam: 010 Publishers, 1995), 1186.
9	Koolhaas, 1200.

10

11

10 | Shibuya Stream. "Alleys" in between restaurants that are exposed to the outdoors. Photos © Kayoko Ota

11 | Shibuya Stream, photographed in 2019. The front space and the big staircases are occasionally used as a stage for public events. Photo © Ryohei Tomita, courtesy of The Nippon Foundation

than as a purely architectural one. Shibuya Stream is part of a large-scale urban development project with several other skyscrapers around the Shibuya station that were granted exceptions for height and volume in exchange for accommodating public uses. In the current common Japanese practices for large-scale urban development, which is left in the hands of large corporate firms, the public-usage portion usually consists of a few standard patterns, the most common of which is providing an open space around a building. In the case of Shibuya Stream, the site's limited size meant that the standard pattern couldn't be applied, and the architects took advantage of that situation to fulfill the project's mission to maximize attractiveness to commuters, visitors, and pedestrians.

The exceptional choice of architect was made possible with the recommendation of Hiroshi Naito, the chairperson of the council supervising the design of the entire development around Shibuya station. He wrote, "We made a list of a dozen architects and asked each building organizer to choose the designer from the list. When selected, we told each selected architect that the more unusual the proposal, the better. We wanted to avoid this place to become another patch of dry, profit-based skyscrapers. We wanted to enhance diversity in this new quarter of Shibuya through the unique thinking and expression of designers."[10] In the design system defined by the council, the selected architects are supported by major corporate firms to cope with a scale and complexity that they haven't previously dealt with.

As Naito so insightfully perceived in the Shibuya site, the need to inject new blood into the large-scale development market is critical in order to break the repetition of formula-led developments (which will, after all, shrink the value of built products). To overcome the isolation of a skyscraper and make it more shareable in our increasingly gentrified urban conditions, we need more architects willing to combine daring and ingenuity with an urban perspective, as demonstrated by Coelacanth.

10   Hiroshi Naito, "Diversity in the New Shibuya," *Shinkenchiku* (November 2018): 41.

A NEW PERSPECTIVE FOR URBAN ARCHITECTURE

● ERIKA NAKAGAWA

1

1 | Erika Nakagawa, Hilltop House (project in
progress). Model of existing conditions.
Photo © Yuji Harada

For someone like myself who was born, raised, and lives in Tokyo, it is the archetypal cityscape, one that has had an undeniable impact on my architectural design.

Until I was seventeen, I lived in a condominium apartment near the intersection of two major thoroughfares within walking distance of Shibuya Station, in what might be termed downtown Tokyo. Our household consisted of my parents and myself, an only child—a typical nuclear family—though our home was extremely compact even for three people. I didn't have a room of my own, so when I wanted to have my "own space," I learned to improvise according to the circumstances. To prepare for a high school exam, for example, I would extend my territory into the hallway by setting up a folding table there. If I wanted to expand my turf so I could spread out textbooks and other study materials, I would hang a shelf in vertical space by placing a board over the horizontal beams in the room.

Like weight training, the know-how I built up in this manner later proved useful. As an architect, I came to approach building design by thinking of spaces in terms of elements and areas, not merely rooms. When contemplating the optimum living space for residents of a home, I treat it as something they should be able to compose from various architectural elements on their own, not have it bestowed upon them in the form of preestablished rooms. Living space should be viewed as a three-dimensional entity—a volume—rather than a two-dimensional layout; indeed, I have found that human beings interact with their environment in three dimensions. Lately it occurs to me that these ideas have their origins in the strategies I devised out of desperation during my teenage years.

As I conceive it, this "volume" is a bit different from a typical room defined by a floor, a ceiling, and walls that form a fixed space larger than the humans inhabiting it. Rather, it is a space for daily life created from the aggregation of small elements that are closer in scale to the human body. I like to refer to such spaces, which are defined by the different materials that comprise one's familiar daily space, as "spaces of small elements."

Something else about my childhood also comes to mind. The apartment house my family lived in faced a sloping street, and the building's entrance, which was open to but recessed from the street, was divided into two sections on different levels, a driveway for cars and a staircase for pedestrians. The driveway sloped downward into a parking garage, while the staircase led upward to the apartments, past a landing where the mailboxes and the manager's office were located. I was very fond of this split-level, partially exposed recess, which existed thanks to the slope of the street it faced. Unlike the "spaces of small elements" I mentioned, this recessed volume did not just belong to the building but was connected to the surrounding topography and hence to a larger scale of space than the building alone.

Although our home was extremely cramped, the breezes blowing and sunlight shining into the shared space of the entrance helped to dispel that sense of confinement. I felt as if my home contained not only the apartment we occupied, but the entrance and the street and the hillside too. It was through that cheerful entrance, created by the topography outside our building, that I ventured out into the streets of Tokyo. I experienced the three-dimensional volumes of the split-level entrance and of the slope outside as part of the same continuum, with no boundary between them. That daily experience very naturally imbued in me a sensation of dwelling not just in my apartment, but in the neighborhood at large.

Urban space has two scales—one larger and one smaller than a building—that are seamlessly connected via the flow of people in and out of those buildings. Though architectural structures are always, for expediency's sake, treated as lying within a site's boundaries, their actual volumes never stand alone, but rather exist in a continuum with their surroundings. To my way of thinking as an architect, this continuity lends itself to an undeniably richer experience than the stand-alone model. Just as every stroll through a neighborhood yields a different experience, every building's site is unique. Therefore, the continuity of a building with its surrounding urban space will augment the originality of the building as contemplated by the architect with the originality of the site and the experience associated with it. The result is a truly innovative work of architecture—more unique, certainly, than a building designed in isolation from its surroundings.

Volumes in a Continuum

My objective, which is to create architecture that offers a new experience through its connection to the land it is on, diverges significantly from the aims of conventional architecture, which severs itself from the land and treats experience as an afterthought. This difference necessitates changes in the very process of architectural creation.

To begin with, I build large models that force me to think on a physical level, paying attention to specific details to an unprecedented degree. I take into consideration the everyday experiences and hidden originality of the locale—factors generally ignored in conventional design—and study elements both old and new without discriminating between the two. Instead of ignoring anything smaller orw larger than a building, I attempt to link them and the building together. To do this I utilize the three-dimensional volume of the model rather than rely on plans or perspective views. This approach is indispensable not only to the process of creating a work of architecture, but also of simultaneously elucidating how it can be used and what kind of experience it can impart.

Models help us discover new possibilities for linking architecture with the city and with the land. When building models, my office always treats the entire area that will impact the building as our "site," not merely the lot within the property lines (FIG. 1). Since one cannot build a model that perfectly reproduces an actual neighborhood, we give careful thought to the materials and forms best used to express the essence of that neighborhood in three dimensions.

Constructing a site model in this manner reveals to us the hidden originality of the site, something we would have otherwise overlooked. Over the course of building the model, the essence of the neighborhood that we wish to link with our project gradually comes into view. When we pay close attention to the type, size, arrangement, and density of the materials that create the atmosphere of the neighborhood, it compels us to keep those attributes in mind as they apply to the building we are designing. Before we know it, the design process has begun.

We try to give earnest thought to the self-evident fact that every site is different for every building we design. Then we try to express, in our architecture, the original qualities of the site that intrigue us to the point of enchantment. The result should be architecture that introduces a new experience to the existing volumes to which it is connected—a borderless, seamless experience, so that entering the building feels like a natural extension of a stroll through the neighborhood. I believe that scrutinizing the volumes of a model and applying the sense of physical reality we gain from it to our design is the most rational method of achieving architecture of this sort.

Everything Can Be Architecture

Constructing a site model is a type of urban research. Since our approach consists of analyzing a neighborhood as a three-dimensional aggregation of diverse elements and then creating architecture that forms a continuum with this volume, we directly incorporate this research into our design. That said, the characteristics we identify through our research are nothing special—they are simply things that architects have traditionally ignored.

Close scrutiny of a cityscape's composition reveals not merely the differences among its constituent materials, but also the fact that its charm derives from the accumulated activities of the people who live there, as well as from the accumulation of time itself. Realizing this important truth has persuaded me that it is the everyday, commonplace, familiar things we encounter that inspire the most original architecture.

Words sometimes oversimplify the landscapes and activities that define a place, whereas a detailed three-dimensional model gives unadulterated visual form to the essence of the place. Just as different places in the same city,

2

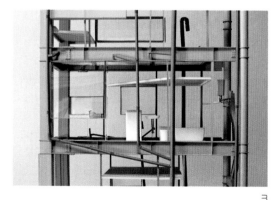

3

4

2 | A typical high-density neighborhood of wooden houses in Tsukishima, Tokyo. Photo © shiki_kimama, courtesy of tsuzuritabi.com

3, 4 | Erika Nakagawa, A Neighborhood in a House. Detail of the structure and piping model. Photo © Yuji Harada

Tokyo, are composed of different materials, the materials in our models vary with the site, as do the manifestations of human activity there.

"A Neighborhood in a House" is an apartment complex of SOHO units, with five floors above ground and one floor below. It occupies a very small site of about 28 square meters but faces a 33-meter-wide thoroughfare, thus occupying an urban-scale setting. However, this scale dramatically reduces to human size just behind the buildings lining the thoroughfare, where one enters a typical high-density neighborhood of wooden houses. What is striking is that nearly all of these houses seem to have been enlarged or altered by their owners using small, hand-installed metal fittings. The exterior of each building reflects a determination to utilize the urban space in three dimensions by finding, within the confines of each small footprint, tiny spaces that would not appear in any floor plan. Not only the fittings, but even the piping reflects this thinking in its defiance of the conventional wisdom that pipes should be as short and straight as possible. The result is a townscape shaped by the skill and ingenuity of the people living there, working from a logic exclusive to their neighborhood (FIG. 2). My sense was that the site itself called for architecture that embraced both the city scale and the human scale, the old and the new—as well as the plans of the architect and the residents' interpretation of them.

We built several models of varying scales in order to examine the volume of the neighborhood from different angles. In the design that resulted from this analysis, we used materials for the building's exterior that diverged from the usual windows and exterior walls. Instead, we covered it with elements typically kept hidden: piping, posts, meters, and potted plants cultivated by individual residents (FIGS. 3, 4). This configuration extended to every floor via a common staircase that formed a residential "alley" in three dimensions (FIG. 5). Our aim was to achieve an interactive affinity with the neighborhood and its unique appeal, a quality to which conventional architecture has paid little heed. In pursuing this objective, I think we created a new type of building facade with a one-of-a-kind originality not seen in self-sufficient, stand-alone structures (FIGS. 6, 7, 8).

"Hilltop House" is a two-story wooden residence. Like "A Neighborhood in a House," it is in a high-density neighborhood of wooden houses, but the atmosphere and materials of the two neighborhoods are considerably different. Perhaps because the entire area used to be leased property, the neighborhood of "Hilltop House" has many blind alleys. It also has a fair number of wooden rental apartment houses typified by common stairways attached to their exteriors and accessed from the alleys. These stairways exude the power of vertical open spaces, serving as indispensable passages amid the crowded lanes and houses of the neighborhood. Meanwhile, the narrow, one-meter gaps between the lots—smaller even than the alleys—are filled with a magical clutter of human activity: goldfish tanks, potted plants, cat food, laundry,

5

6

7

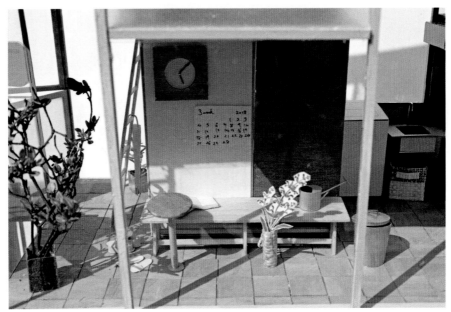

8

9 | Hilltop House. Side view of the model
without roof. Photo © Yuji Harada

tricycles, bug-catching nets. This arrangement, in which neighbors share the spaces left among the leased lots, exemplifies the use of urban voids that belong to no one in particular as common resources that are veritable distillations of a neighborhood's charm. The use of these voids creates the ambience of the neighborhood and enriches, however modestly, the lives of its residents. Inspired by this urban topography of nameless voids, we decided to design a house that would enable residents to find or create spaces indispensable to their daily lives (FIG. 9, 10, 11).

Architecture Predicated on Continuity

We are attempting to replace the underlying premise of architecture as an exclusive entity detached from its surroundings with an inclusive conception of architecture as something connected to all manner of elements. This new premise immediately renders the boundaries of a work of architecture ambiguous, turning it into more of an area than a single structure. Architecture with area-like boundaries—of which "A Neighborhood in a House" and "Hilltop House" are examples—permits an expansion of the territory of day-to-day life (FIG. 12); on occasion, the boundaries themselves may serve as living spaces. The facades of such buildings do not define the building as a self-contained, finished product, but rather function as media that represent the neighborhood at large, open and welcoming even to passersby.

Adopting this view of architecture could well alter our views on the concept of beauty in architecture as well as its relationship to time. Instead of beauty as preconceived by the architect, consider a beauty achieved through the accumulation of time and of human interpretation. This is permanence unlike the sort of permanence anticipated by architects until now. It is the permanence of a garden, an accumulation of richness that simultaneously embraces uncertainty. Instead of trying to preserve a work of architecture in its original state, I want to recognize decay as something that leads to a new phase, and permanence as something born of perpetual incompletion and reinterpretation.

The allure of Tokyo as a city derives from its accumulated strata of uncertainties—the products of topography, earthquakes, fires, war—on a scale that boggles the human imagination. As an architect engaged in the work of adding yet another layer to those many strata, I want to create architecture that does not turn inward, severing itself from its surroundings, but looks outward, extending into and interacting with the rest of the city. In this way I hope to engage with Tokyo's unique brand of urban magic.

10

Erika Nakagawa, Hilltop House. Part of the
model looking at the house and an alley.
Photo © Yuji Harada

11 Erika Nakagawa, A Neighborhood in a House.
Collage of a model photo with sketches.
Courtesy of Erika Nakagawa Office

11

ALTERNATIVE LARGE-SCALE DEVELOPMENTS AND NEIGHBORHOODS

● MOHSEN MOSTAFAVI AND THE STUDIOS AT THE HARVARD GRADUATE SCHOOL OF DESIGN

In the past two years, we conducted two speculative design studios at the Harvard Graduate School of Design, one focusing on alternative forms of large-scale development, the other on future models of neighborhood revitalization. These studios were partly contingent on the reevaluation of the ideas of two important thinkers. The first are the ideas of Japanese philosopher Tetsuro Watsuji, who wrote about the concept of *fudo*. Often translated as climate or environment, *fudo* is closer in meaning to the notion of milieu—with all its social and political implications. The second theme, developed by the Baltic German biologist Jakob von Uexküll, is the concept of *Umwelt*, meaning "the world as experienced by a particular organism." Whether dealing with a large part of the city or a small part of a neighborhood, the design approach not only had to consider the physical form of an architecture but also its role in connection with the social and natural worlds.

Student proposals intermingle with the existing fabric of the Bakurocho-Yokoyamacho neighborhood in Tokyo

Fudo/Umwelt: Devising Transformative Environments in Japan

A diverse range of projects explored the potentials for the site formerly occupied by the Tsukiji fish market. Instead of the typical developer-led mixed-use project, the designs explore ways in which the area can belong to a more diverse cross section of the population. At the same time, the projects provide opportunities for greater connectivity to the Sumida River, to public space, as well as the exploration of a more sectional urban framework for the site.

↑
Buildings access an artificial landscape at various levels. Student: Isabel Chun

➡
A two-level street system with underground services frees the ground plane for pedestrian use. Student: Saul Kim

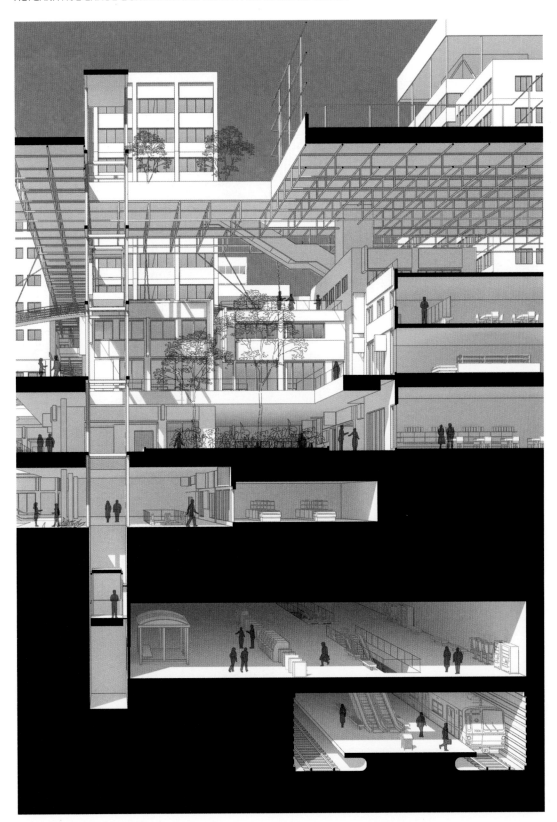

Tokyo: Artifice and the Social World

The Tokyo neighborhood of Bakurocho-Yokoyamacho, a slightly declining garment district, provided the opportunity to create a model for the revitalization of the older parts of the city.

A series of residential, work, cultural, retail, and leisure facilities formed the primary programmatic content of the projects. A key aspect of the approach is its insistence on the need for the simultaneous realization of a multiplicity of building and urban proposals, often at the intersection of social and natural worlds.

 The facade of the dye workshop draws on the techniques of layering, filtering, and opacity used by Japanese textile designers.

 A fabric and dye workshop also contains housing for craftspeople. Student: Hugo Ho

Products arriving by boat or truck are received, processed, and stored on the lower level of this fish market.
Upper levels are used for public functions, including restaurants and a culinary school. Student: Hugo Ho

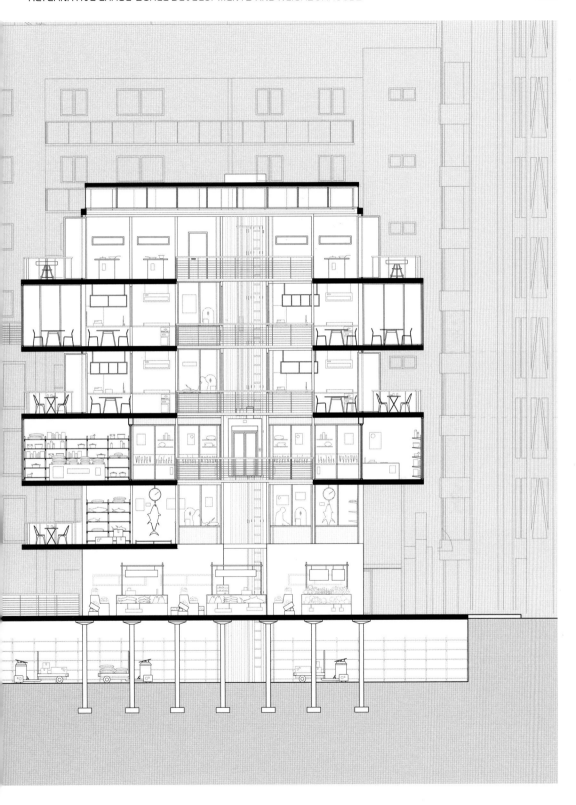

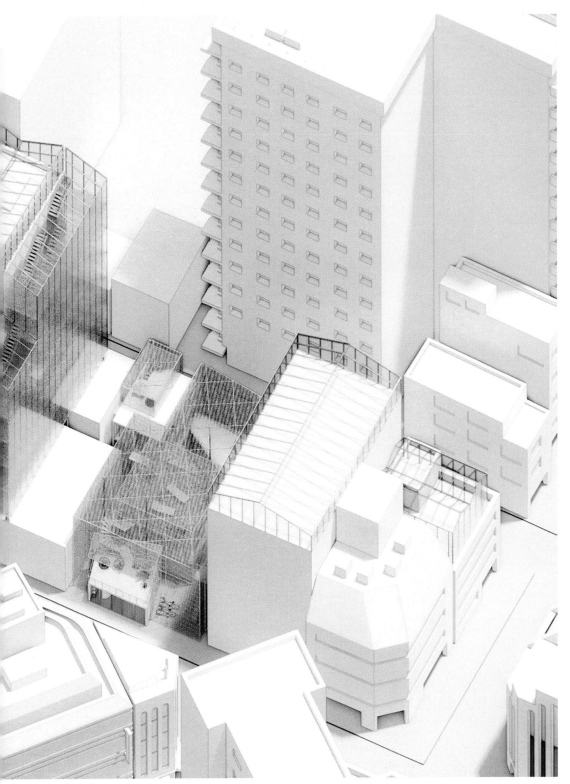

This vertical urban farming project helps residents of Bakurocho-Yokoyamacho reuse neglected rooftops for agriculture and recreation. Student: Andreea Adam

 CODA

PUBLIC SPACE AND THE PUBLIC SPHERE

● CONVERSATION IV WITH HOMI K. BHABHA

● MOHSEN MOSTAFAVI: We are working on a research project focused on Japan and located at the intersection of architecture and urbanization. One of the interesting facts about Japan is the general lack of squares or plazas in the European sense. Demonstrations, for example, take place in other urban spaces such as streets. In this sense, the concept of dissent has an interesting and complex history in Japanese culture, one that until recently had not received much attention. In the past, people used places like the large interiors of Shinjuku, one of the big railway stations for political demonstrations, making speeches, playing music, and singing songs. Given the difference with what we conventionally think of as public space in the West, it's interesting to reconsider the changing status of public space and public sphere in the Japanese context, and how these might differ from Habermas's articulation of the concept of public sphere.

● HOMI K. BHABHA: So, it seems to me that there is something specific happening in Japan and that in itself is fascinating. The Japanese tradition of an interior space of protest seems very intriguing and raises a few issues, such as what signifies the separation—or articulation— between interior and exterior within the politics of everyday life in Japanese culture.

Public space in Habermas's concept of the public sphere has an affinity with the political sociology of the Frankfurt School. As I recall, its genealogy stretches back to the eighteenth-century public spaces in London and other metropolitan centers—coffee houses, cafes, clubs, *piazze*—where writers, politicians, and cultural figures gathered to discuss the issues of their time with a degree of institutional informality accompanied by utter political seriousness.

These public spaces were made possible by a developing urbanity, but they were also enunciative sites that empowered modes of discourse that concurred, dissented, or converged. They were social locations, but they were also discursive *locutions*. Spatially, the coffeehouse was a place of meeting, but discursively it represented a mode of speaking in public as a member of an evolving concept of the public.

In the early eighteenth century, Addison and Steel published the *Spectator Papers* and then the *Tatler* with the aim of dispelling ignorance and developing civil consciousness, as well as the civil practice of interlocution. In the process, coffeehouse public culture contributed to the social architecture of public reform on a daily basis! Chat rooms on the Internet, or the instantaneity of blogging or tweeting, these digital forms of momentary exchange where time is of the essence, make me think back to coffeehouse culture. The dailiness of the public sphere provides a temporality that shapes "imagined communities," as Benedict

Anderson called them, and gives expression and affect to those who occupy public space. Habermas greatly admires the coffeehouse culture of the *Spectator Papers* as an exemplary system of public discourse that enables the circulation of public opinion. This leads to the transformation of the public sphere, to use the title of Habermas's work.

● The articulation of public space is invariably fluid. In Japan, in addition to streets, public parks became sites for public gatherings including demonstrations, similar to places like Speakers' Corner in Hyde Park, London. I imagine the increasing privatization of public space might make it harder today to speak of authentic contemporary interior spaces for gathering. But the point you are making is important. Namely, what are the circumstances that would once again make such spaces truly public, and how might they differ from exterior public spaces?

● Your question is fascinating, and I can only speculate. I wonder whether limits to the truly public, as you put it, relate to restrictions on spaces that are part of the public domain due to surveillance and security. After 9/11, this has intensified in all manner of ways. Limits to the truly public in our time are to do, in my view, with the imperiled status of democracy at present, and the compromised state of the rights of citizenship. I don't want to sound naïve. Citizenship and surveillance have gone hand in hand from the origins of modern democracy. The rise of the public, as we understand it, has always been accompanied by the force of the police. But lately, and especially since 9/11, the dark shadow of surveillance has been the devil's accomplice to the politics of nationalist sovereignty, and it is now difficult to decipher what is shadow and what is substance.

● Habermas's concept is really based on the plaza, and on the already given freedom of people to gather and to acknowledge their own autonomy and agency. Since he developed some of his thoughts on this topic, his position has been criticized, but also developed. Habermas's concept of the public sphere is often compared with Hannah Arendt's conception of citizenship and the public sphere and her articulation of the notions of the space of appearance and the common world. The first places importance on the spaces that enable the enactment of discourse between citizens. These might be called the spaces of freedom and equality. The second is the public or shared world of people and institutions that generally provide the conditions and the context for our activities as citizens.

Is the discourse of public sphere as articulated by Habermas, and even by Arendt, only applicable to societies where there is already a certain capacity for legal participation? And, therefore, when confronting societies where no such participation is possible, what's the definition of the public sphere, if not just simply as subjugated citizens?

●   If the capacity for legal participation is blocked, then what rights do citizens have? In what sense are they citizens except as a meaningless formality? They are, in my view, subjugated citizens. They may also be subaltern citizens who then create groups or movements that resist or transgress political subjugation, and live precariously on the social margins, evading the eye of the law. From a spatial perspective—your interest—the Underground Railroad instituted by African American slaves is a remarkable instance of political agency summoned, against all the odds, in the cause of freedom. These clandestine underground routes were used during the early- to mid-nineteenth century for African Americans who had been enslaved to find their way to free states.

The Ukrainian Maidan Revolution in February 2014 was another instance of trying to retrieve the streets of Kyiv and other cities to articulate an agency of freedom and choice. In these instances, public visibility and the visuality afforded by digital and conventional media articulates a citizenly aspiration at a flashpoint of the destruction of those democratic aims and aspirations.

Something else strikes me which I want to flag, without fully engaging. It is the distinction between public space and public sphere in the context of national territoriality and sovereignty, and urban space as part of the municipal city embedded in the local state. The difference of scale between them is obvious, but the national and municipal also evoke different experiences of public space. In the instances I've mentioned above, there is an overlap. The Maidan 2014 and Tahir Square protests took place on a national scale. This kind of protest has political implications that transcend the city and its urbanity as a gathering space to become a symbolic space of freedom on a national and international scale. But isn't this a doubly articulated symbol of public space? At the aspirational and political level, it addresses the idea of freedom and its legal and institutional violations by the national government that is destructive of public space for the people. However, at the experiential and affective level, the locality of the citizen situated in *this* square, *that* neighborhood, or the *other* park signifies a different scalar relation to spatial belonging and its stakes in the struggle for the protection of public rights, the rights of the people.

●   Related to your comments, as an homage to the work of Ernesto Laclau and Chantal Mouffe, I wrote a piece on the concept of "agonistic urbanism" in

recognition of the spatial and urban dimensions of agonism, as well as to highlight the difference between Habermas's society of consensus vs. the society
of dissensus proposed by Mouffe. But still, the concept of agonistic urbanism
remains contingent on the capacity to participate and for the articulation of
conflictual positions to be permitted.

●   I read your essay with much interest and am in agreement with its
aspirations. I am not qualified to comment on the fascinating architectural, landscape, and design projects to which you effectively tie your
argument. I have a few thoughts to add to this important distinction
that enables, as you put it, "agonism rather than antagonism."

My first thought concerns pluralism as a concept. How, and why,
does pluralism evolve as a liberal way of life? Does religious pluralism,
which we might associate with the liberal value of tolerance, help us to
formulate principles and policies of pluralism that equitably represent
the rights of minorities with respect to race, gender, and sexuality? The
tolerance associated with Western religious pluralism is different from
the demand for recognition and representation associated with minorities. It is too easy to argue that the one is an overdetermined instance
of the other.

To make it even more complicated, plural tolerance, which might
effectively work to keep the peace between Christian sects, up to a point,
might be the justificatory basis for the intolerance shown towards the
religious practices of Jewish, African, or Islamic minorities who belong
to the same plural polis. We might argue that religious fundamentalists
are not pluralists, but that doesn't reduce the fact that we must continually translate between, and within, pluralisms. So, pluralism itself might
be an agonistic ideological apparatus fraught with ambivalences and
ambiguities at a foundational level, rather than a political framework that
can provide spaces for the negotiation of antagonisms. The polarization
that we are living through, as we speak, between majoritarian hegemony
and minoritarian hate-politics on a global scale, might well be the twi-
light of pluralism as we thought we knew it.

My second thought directly responds to your citations from
Chantal. I am with her on her critique of the rationalistic bias of democratic deliberation. I believe that the rationalistic approach leads, in
most cases, to rational-choice policies which serve the dominant classes
and their majoritarian interests.

However, here's my issue. If agonism allows for a dissensual
mode of negotiation, it is because, as Mouffe argues, deliberative
democracy neglects political passion and psychic affect as forces that
shape democratic decision-making. But, in my view, in critiquing

rationalistic deliberation, Mouffe throws out the baby with the bath-water. The democratic subject *is* rational and calculative, but it is a rationality that acknowledges the psychic conflicts and defenses of affective life. The ethical and political existence of the democratic subject—political and phenomenological, effective and affective, indi-vidual and collective—is balanced on a knife-edge of action and decision that is deliberative, but it is not deterministic. It is agential, but it is not rationalistic.

From this perspective, I cannot see why multiplying institutions, discourses, and forms of life would deal with the intersective agonism I've sketched out above. The problem is not about the multiplication of institutions or discourses that might well lead to public spaces that are separate but equal, that evade the democratic aspiration of "equality-in-difference" Etienne Balibar has elaborated for us. The problem is not one of multiplication but of translation that allows us to engage with an agonistic alterity.

●   The state today plays a very significant role, often through a neoliberal agenda, in the formation of the physical spaces or public spaces of the city. Run-ning against that is a revitalization or rediscovery of small-scale neighborhoods, which people in certain instances are trying to help redefine. The concept of the neighborhood is interesting, and it's very much a productive contraposition to the big developments, which could be perceived as exclusionary. In our research, it's been helpful to think about the conception of the public and the idea of sharing Tokyo in ways that are neither limited to the existing neighbor-hood model nor that of the large-scale private development.

In Tokyo, for example, nearly forty years ago, a group of activists began to publish a local magazine to help protect and promote three relatively small neighborhoods as one. They used the name Yanesen, a combination of the letters of the three neighborhoods. Their magazine helped to reinforce a sense of community, which was very important. But are there limits to this type of community?

●   The neighborhood is a fascinating spatial measure of what Raymond Williams once called a "knowable community." Suburban neighbor-hoods are carefully marked out by divisions, security fences, and back-yards, particularly in the States. The growing suburbanization in many parts of the world is a response to what is perceived as the insecurity of urban neighborhoods that increasingly house minorities, migrants, refugees, and people of color. In addition, as progressive urbanists distribute public housing across the city, there is class-and-culture pre-judice against such attempts to establish the just city or equitable urbanism—*not in my neighborhood, you don't!* Here we find antagonistic, not agonistic, urbanism.

Neighborhoods have long histories of persistent poverty, excessive policing, and endemic deprivation. At the same time, they are sites of ethnic belonging and migrant hospitality often misrepresented as "ghetto culture." Neighborhoods are places of refuge despite their disadvantages, or perhaps because of it. They are crucibles of cultural creativity and social transformation in many important ways that may not conform to majoritarian concepts of progress, development, or "social hygiene," a Darwinian concept. The range of transformations that occur in migrant and minority neighborhoods are complex and subtle. The intergenerational time-lag of cultural adaptation and negotiation is considerable, stretching from earlier members who lack social and linguistic skills to later generations who identify with hybrid cultural forms and norms. Such neighborhood scales of transformation do not easily map onto normative frameworks of urban progress. This process is often wrongly read as a resistance to integrate or adapt. And the vicious cycle of stereotypes fires up to feed the embers of racism and prejudice.

Displaced and discriminated populations cultivate their urban life-worlds through rituals of gathering, sharing, exchanging, and affiliating that resist the pressure to keep in step with the pace of progress or change set by the host community. This form of resistance is rooted in the awareness that migrant or minority neighborhoods are often left behind in the redistribution of wealth and power.

The community associated with the neighborhood is most often represented in spatial terms. As you can see, I am more intrigued by its temporal aspects. Coming together as a neighborhood community is as much about spatial togetherness or collectivity—the "we"—as it is shaped by the temporal movement of coming-to-be, or "becoming," a transformative subjectivity and sociality of demographic redefinition and redistribution.

● The notion of hospitality reminds me of Avishai Margalit's *The Decent Society* and how it might be articulated differently from the notions of the "just city."

● Now, Avishai's argument is not only about equality of some kind. Central to Avishai's argument, in my view, is the idea that a decent society is one that does not humiliate. The issue is not simply the risk to life but the risk to living. This is my formulation. I think that the risk to life is more related to the issue of justice, and the risk to living more to the issue of decency.

●   In the context of the city, it is not only the idea that there are legal provisions in place for the delivery of services, but the manner of their delivery, their sense of decency.

●   Absolutely. The delivery of provisions, with a certain notion of dignity. I use the word "dignity" here not in the kind of idealist Enlightenment way, i.e. that we are all born with dignity. There's a difference between being born with dignity and creating it through acts and choices. I am interested in the agential notion of dignity, not in the inherentist notion of dignity. And that is where I think the notion of the decent society emerges as a concept different from that of the just society.

●   It then seems fair to claim that a prerequisite for both a just city and a decent society is the idea of sharing resources, as well a sense of conviviality and humility.

PROSPECTS

● MOHSEN MOSTAFAVI

Tokyo, the world's largest metropolis, is a city of wonder with a vast array of different atmospheres and characteristics. The latest examples of contemporary architecture stand in close proximity to historic districts. Massive buildings made of concrete and glass rise next to modest wooden structures that recall the city's past. Yet much of Tokyo is a city of anonymous buildings realized after the destruction caused by the Allied firebombing of the city during WWII. Many of these buildings are covered with lifeless surfaces of white mosaic tiles—clean and hygienic—making it easy to wash away environmental detritus. But despite the anonymity of much of its architecture, Tokyo manages to sustain a liveliness and a dynamism rarely experienced in other cities of the world. Why is that? Why does Tokyo possess such vibrancy as a capital when it does not boast the same caliber of urban architecture as, say, Rome or Paris?

Perhaps part of the answer lies in the city's capacity to accommodate the contrast between the scales of its architecture, from that found along its main urban arteries to the more intimate and interior scale of smaller back streets and alleyways. This contrast is sustained by Tokyo's planning regulations, which equates the width of the street to the permittable size of buildings.

But the historic distinctions between the scales of main streets vs. back streets is being eroded by the increasing homogeneity of more recent large-scale developments, some of which occupy the equivalent of two or more mega-sized urban blocks. These large urban fragments, at times akin to a city within a city, generate their own logic of formation as well as their own sense of diversity and excitement. But for the participants, the experience of such places is always framed in relation to their awareness of the totality of a development. A nuance like the difference between the experience of a typical street with its anomalies and that of a shopping mall with its adherence to the pure rationality of a system and little or no room for breaking or interpreting the rules. This is essentially one of the major differences produced by the increasing privatization of the public domain.

This book opens the possibility for different ways of recalibrating the relationship between new developments and traditional neighborhoods. Such rethinking requires greater collaboration between the developers, the city, and its inhabitants. *Machizukuri*, the Japanese method of intercommunity dialogue introduced in the 1960s, already provides a formal mechanism for discussions of local projects. But what needs to be nurtured more is the aspirational role of urban governance, both in terms of helping shape future visions and in safeguarding the rights of the city's population. This is also why the notion of "sharing" can be a useful catalyst for imagining how one might construct alternative future communities.

In preparation for such a vision of the city, this book and its contributors provide both an understanding of Tokyo and its formation as well as the role that architecture can and is playing in changing certain patterns and habits of development. Of particular interest is the way in which even small projects can be viewed in terms of their urban contribution.

The framework provided by this book and its exploration of the indispensable connections between social and spatial imaginaries will hopefully be of value to other contexts and locations beyond Tokyo and beyond Japan. Ultimately, our aim has been to reconsider the status of contemporary urban design and to seek alternative ways of describing the relation between architecture and urbanism.

MUSTAFA K. ABADAN
is a design partner at SOM, New York. An award-winning architect, he has designed a wide range of projects that help redefine and enhance urban environments around the world, including the Time Warner Center in New York and Tokyo MidTown.

SHIN AIBA
is a professor of urban planning at Tokyo Metropolitan University. He is actively engaged in planning for regenerating shrinking urban conditions with practical roadmaps. *Heisei toshi keikaku-shi* [History of Urban Planning in the Heisei Era] is one of his acclaimed publications.

HOMI K. BHABHA
is a critical theorist and professor at Harvard University. Specializing in contemporary postcolonial studies, he developed concepts of hybridity, ambivalence, and third space. *Our Neighbours, Ourselves* (2011) is among the many books he has authored.

KENTA HASEGAWA
is a photographer. He earned recognition among architects of the younger generation in Japan, including Jo Nagasaka, Tsubame Architects, and 403architecture[dajiba], for his new approach to everyday urban life and generic spaces like that of the Narita Airport Terminal 3.

KOZO KADOWAKI
is an architect. He is a partner in the firm Associates and teaches building systems design at Meiji University as an associate professor. A critical voice in architecture, he curated the Japan Pavilion exhibition at the 2021 Venice Biennale, focusing on the shareability of buildings.

HIROTO KOBAYASHI
is a professor at Keio University and a principal at Kobayashi Maki Design Workshop, specializing in architecture and urban design. By taking a holistic and researched approach to designing living environments, he engages with revitalizing urban and rural areas in and outside of Japan.

MASAMI KOBAYASHI
is a professor at Meiji University specializing in urban planning and architectural design. He has worked on a number of urban revitalizing initiatives, including for Shimokitazawa, where he has taken actions to protect the neighborhood's identity since 2004.

JOUJI KURUMADO
is an architect and advisor to and former managing executive officer at Takenaka Corporation. Currently, he is writing a doctoral thesis on a system for long-term analysis and evaluation of large-scale development projects at the University of Tsukuba.

SEIJI M. LIPPIT
is professor of Asian languages and cultures at UCLA, where he teaches modern Japanese literature and culture. His writings on literature, modernism, and urban space in twentieth-century Japan include *Topographies of Japanese Modernism* (2002). His current research focuses on the spatial and cultural practices of postwar Tokyo.

MITSUYOSHI MIYAZAKI
is an architect and head of the Hagi Studio. Following the successful HAGISO complex, he expanded a neighborhood regeneration project by creating a network of revitalized houses that extended beyond the original neighborhood of Yanaka in Tokyo.

MAYUMI MORI
is a writer. In 1984, she founded the zine *Yanaka, Nezu, Sendagi*, which immediately raised public attention to the old neighborhoods in Tokyo facing the risk of erasure due to development. She has since authored many books while actively engaged in preserving historical buildings.

MOHSEN MOSTAFAVI

is an architect and educator who served as dean of the Harvard University Graduate School of Design. As a professor of design, he is now leading the Japan Research Initiative, among other programs. His books include *Ethics of the Urban: The City and the Spaces of the Political* (2017).

JO NAGASAKA

is an architect and principal at Schemata Architects. He gained recognition for redefining renovation work as a new genre. Acclaimed for designing successful retail spaces through tactful renovation, he now works extensively on large-scale projects inside and outside Japan.

ERIKA NAKAGAWA

is an architect and head of Erika Nakagawa Office. Her experimental approach to architectural design, whereby large models represent her engagement with user's sights and behaviors in detail play an important role, has made her one of the most promising young architects in Japan.

DON O'KEEFE

is a designer, writer, and research associate at Harvard University. He has contributed to *The Architectural Review*, *The Japan Times*, and other publications. In 2022, while an assistant professor at Keio University, he helped launch the Fumihiko Maki Archive.

YOSHIHIKO OSHIMA

is an architect. As managing director and creative director of Blue Studio, he was responsible for the success of a number of renovation and urban regeneration projects, demonstrating that architecture can alleviate social challenges. He is also helping revitalize communities across Japan through education.

KAYOKO OTA

is an architectural curator and editor. Before joining the Japan Research Initiative at the Harvard University Graduate School of Design, she curated Japan-based projects for the Canadian Centre for Architecture and was commissioner of the Japan Pavilion at the 2014 Venice Biennale.

JORDAN SAND

is a professor of Japanese history at Georgetown University. His research has focused on architecture, urbanism, material culture, and the history of everyday life. His publications include *Tokyo Vernacular: Common Spaces, Local Histories, Found Objects* (2013), as well as articles on a range of topics in the history of the city.

YOSHIHIKO SONE
is an in-house architectural advisor at Mitsui Fudosan, where he has worked
on a number of large-scale developments including Tokyo Midtown and
Coredo Muromachi overseeing the design, technical solutions, and green-
oriented planning. Prior to joining Mitsui Fudosan, he practiced architecture
in Japan and the US for more than 25 years.

TSUBAME ARCHITECTS
is a design practice founded by the architects Takuto Sando, Motoo Chiba,
and Himari Saikawa. By developing an in-house think tank, the firm extended
its role and gained recognition for developing a new approach to participatory
architectural design and urban development.

RIKEN YAMAMOTO
is an architect. The head of Riken Yamamoto & Field Shop, he is also engaged
in education. Currently he is a visiting professor at the Tokyo University
of the Arts. As an author, he advocates for the design of spaces that mediate
between individuals and the state.

SHUN YOSHIE
is an urban planner. As a lecturer at Waseda University, he is exploring "the
geography of desires" in a consumerist society while also working on reorganizing the Waseda campus in such a way as to interact with the neighborhood
and the rest of the city.

We wish to express our cordial appreciation and gratitude to the following people and organizations, each of whom generously supported our research and this publication:

Daici Ano
Tatsuto Asakawa
Benseisha Publishing
Coelacanth and Associates
Kajima Institute Publishing
Mitsuhiro Kanada
Masami Kobayashi (Greenline Shimokitazawa)
Haruka Kuryu
Linda Lombardi
Shino Miura
Mayumi Mori (Yanesen Kenkyukai)
The Nippon Foundation, Diversity in the Arts
Obayashi Corporation
Kae Onoyama
Michihiko Suzuki
Shomei Tanteidan [Lighting Detectives]
Harumi Tago
Takumi Ota Photography
Tokyo Metropolitan Archives
Tokyo Metropolitan Government
Ryohei Tomita
The Urban Renaissance Agency

Special thanks to Takenaka Corporation and its honorary chairman, Mr. Toichi Takenaka, for their generous support of the Japan Research Initiative at the Harvard University Graduate School of Design.

—Mohsen Mostafavi and Kayoko Ota

SHARING TOKYO: ARTIFICE AND THE SOCIAL WORLD

EDITORS
Mohsen Mostafavi
Kayoko Ota

DIRECTOR OF DESIGN RESEARCH
Don O'Keefe

JAPAN RESEARCH INITIATIVE TEAM
Qin Ye Chen
Wentao Guo
Zheng Lei
Ayami Akagawa
Vladimir Gintoff
Yang Lv

TRANSLATION
Alan Gleason

TEXT EDITING
Ophelia John
Elizabeth Kugler

COORDINATION
Marcus Ferolito
Donna Lewis

BOOK DESIGN
Takumi Akin, Folder Studio
Jack Burnside

This publication is part of the Japan Research Initiative at the Harvard University Graduate School of Design.

COLOPHON

PUBLISHED BY
Actar Publishers, New York, Barcelona

All rights reserved
© edition: Actar Publishers
© texts: their authors
© drawings, illustrations and photographs: their authors

DISTRIBUTION
Actar D, Inc. New York, Barcelona.

New York
440 Park Avenue South, 17th Floor
New York, NY 10016, USA
T +1 2129662207
salesnewyork@actar-d.com

Barcelona
Roca i Batlle 2
08023 Barcelona, Spain
T +34 933 282 183
eurosales@actar-d.com

INDEXING
English ISBN: 978-1-63840-060-8
Library of Congress Control Number: 2022944893

PRINTING AND BINDING
Arlequin & Pierrot, Barcelona

Printed in Europe

PUBLICATION DATE
September 2022